WAGE ACCOUNTING IN DEIR EL-MEDINA

WAGE ACCOUNTING IN DEIR EL-MEDINA

Richard Mandeville

Abercromby

Press

ISBN: 978 0 9930920 0 8

A CIP catalogue record of this book is available from the British Library

First published in the United Kingdom in 2014

Cover Illustration
Recording the annual harvest, TT 17 of Nebamun
(adapted by Benedict G. Davies from T. Säve-Söderbergh, *Four Eighteenth Dynasty Tombs*, Oxford, 1957, pl. XXII)

Published by:
Abercromby Press
12a Elm Park Road
Wallasey
United Kingdom, CH45 5JH.

CONTENTS

List of Abbreviations viii
List of Illustrations ix
Preface xi
Introduction xiii

CHAPTER 1 ACCOUNTING METHODOLOGIES IN THE RAMESSIDE PERIOD 1
1.1 Accountants and accounting in Ramesside Egypt 1
1.2 The meaning of *diw* and *dni* 3
1.3 Fractions and mathematics 4
1.4 Volumes used in ration accounting 6

CHAPTER 2 SOURCE MATERIAL AND METHODOLOGY 7
2.1 Documentary evidence from Deir el-Medina 7
2.1.1 Ostraca 7
2.1.2 Papyri 9
2.2 The "Journal of the Necropolis" 11
2.3 Methodology and problems encountered 12
2.3.1 Selection of the material 13
2.3.2 Dating the material 15
2.3.3 Data presentation and analysis 17
2.3.4 Accounting and recording 18

CHAPTER 3 VOCABULARY AND TERMINOLOGY 20
3.1 Headings and expressions used within documents 21
3.1.1 *dit diw*, "giving/distribution of rations" 21
3.1.2 *pꜣ dit diw*, "the giving/distribution of rations" 24
3.1.3 *rdyt*, "what was given (as rations)" 24

3.1.4	*ỉw*, “delivered”	26
3.1.5	Other formulae	27
3.2	Accounting terminology	28
3.2.1	*wꜥ nb*	29
3.2.2	*wp st*	29
3.2.3	*ỉr.n* and *dmḏ*	33
3.2.4	*wḏꜣt* (*ḏꜣt*)	37
3.2.5	*ẖry-ḥꜣt*	42
3.2.6	*ꜥḥꜥ*	43
3.2.7	*wḥm*	44
3.3	Conclusion	47
Chapter 4	**Chronology of the delivery dates**	49
4.1	Day, month and season of delivery	57
4.2	Rations, festivals and the daily calendar	66
4.3	Papyri from the late Ramesside period	70
4.4	Days of delivery: a comparison	72
4.5	Basic ration payment variances: arrears or advance	74
4.6	Conclusion	80
Chapter 5	**Recipients and quantities**	83
5.1	The source material	84
5.2	Ration amounts and mathematics	85
5.3	The workmen: hierarchy and rations	86
5.4	Recipients of rations	89
5.4.1	Individual groups of recipients	91
5.4.2	Total amount of rations delivered	93
5.5	The class and order of the workmen in the recording	99
5.6	Late Ramesside papyri	103
5.7	Changes during the Ramesside period	106
5.8	Conclusion	109
Chapter 6	**Recording procedures in the ration accounting**	111
6.1	Examination of the writing	112
6.1.1	Original source documents examined	112
6.1.2	Examination of high resolution black and white photographs	115
6.1.3	Examination of digital images	121
6.2	How did the scribes prepare their documents?	123
6.3	Closing the books and ending the period	124
6.4	Emmer and barley: recorded separately or together?	127
6.5	Other procedures not implemented	129
6.6	Conclusion	131

CHAPTER 7 RECORDING ERRORS 133
7.1 Errors in the totals 134
7.2 Addition errors 135
7.3 Omission of words 137
7.4 Omission of individuals 138
7.5 The frequency of errors 138
7.6 The acceptance of errors and validity of the document 140
7.7 Conclusion 141

CHAPTER 8 THE SUPPLY OF RATIONS 143
8.1 Original source of the rations 144
8.2 Provider institutions for grain 146
8.3 Accountability within the supply chain 148
8.4 P. Turin 1895+2006 (Turin Taxation Papyrus) 149
8.5 Conclusion 152

CHAPTER 9 A MODEL FOR RATION DELIVERY AND DISTRIBUTION SYSTEMS 154
9.1 The evidence for silos 154
9.2 Part 1: From field to village enclosure 158
9.3 Part 2: From village enclosure to the workmen's houses 159
9.4 Conclusion 162

CHAPTER 10 CONCLUSION 163

APPENDIX 1 DAILY CALENDAR SHOWING RATIONS AND ANNUAL FESTIVALS 169
APPENDIX 2 DOCUMENTS DETAILING CATEGORIES OF RATION PAYMENT RECIPIENTS 179

Bibliography 187
Source References 194
Index of Sources 199

ABBREVIATIONS

ArOr	*Archiv Orientální*, Prague
Ashmol.	Ashmolean Museum, Oxford
BiOr	*Biblioteca Orientalis*, Leiden
BM	British Museum, London
BMSAES	*British Museum Studies in Ancient Egypt and Sudan*, London
CdE	*Chronique d'Égypte*, Brussels
DeM	Deir el-Medina
GM	*Göttinger Miszellen. Beiträge zur ägyptologischen Diskussion*, Göttingen
IFAO	Institut Français d'Archéologie Orientale, Cairo
JARCE	*Journal of the American Research Center in Egypt*
JEA	*Journal of Egyptian Archaeology*
JESHO	*Journal of the Economic and Social History of the Orient*, Leiden
K*RI*	Kitchen, *Ramesside Inscriptions: Historical and Bibliographical* I–VIII, Oxford, 1969–90
MDAIK	*Mitteilungen des Deutschen Archäologischen Instituts Abteilung Kairo*, Cairo
OrAnt	*Oriens Antiquus*, Rome
O.	Ostracon
P.	Papyrus
SAK	*Studien zur Altägyptischen Kultur*, Hamburg
UCL	University College London
ZÄS	*Zeitschrift für ägyptische Sprache und Altertumskunde*, Leipzig & Berlin
ZDMG	*Zeitschrift der Deutschen Morgenländischen Gesellschaft*, Leipzig & Wiesbaden

ILLUSTRATIONS

TABLES

Table 1.	Documents recording the delivery of basic ration wage (*diw*)	51
Table 2.	Documents recording the delivery of additional ration wage (*dni*)	54
Table 3.	Papyri from Ramesses IX–Ramesses XI	55
Table 4.	Basic rations: days of delivery of basic rations	58
Table 5.	19th–mid 20th Dynasty: days of delivery of basic rations	60
Table 6.	Additional rations: days of delivery of additional rations	61
Table 7.	Basic rations: month and season of delivery of basic rations	64
Table 8.	Number of examples recording delivery of rations compared with festival dates	67
Table 9.	Late Ramesside papyri: days of delivery of rations (*diw* and *dni*)	70
Table 10.	Late Ramesside papyri: month and season of delivery of rations (*diw* and *dni*)	71
Table 11.	Days of delivery of rations: Ramesses II–Ramesses V (*diw*) and Ramesses IX–Ramesses XI	72
Table 12.	Basic rations: documents recording variances between the issue date of the document and the period to which the delivery relates	75
Table 13.	Additional rations: ostraca recording variances between the issue date of the document and the period to which the delivery relates	76
Table 14.	Period variances of basic and additional rations	78
Table 15.	Late 19th and mid 20th Dynasty: number and percentages of examples recording different individual groups as receiving rations	91
Table 16.	Frequencies of total rations (*diw* and *dni*) as a percentage of a complete delivery	93

Table 17. Late 19th and mid 20th Dynasty: mean distribution of rations per delivery 97
Table 18. Workmen categories: number of documents by period 100
Table 19. Workmen categories: percentage of documents by period 107
Table 20. Number of documents containing named individuals receiving rations 109
Table 21. Documents with and without errors 139

FIGURES

Fig. 1. A comparison of *diw* between the two periods from the 19th to mid 20th Dynasty and solely the mid 20th Dynasty 59
Fig. 2. Days of delivery of *diw* and *dni* from the 19th to mid 20th Dynasty 62
Fig. 3. Days of delivery of rations: Ramesses II–Ramesses V (*diw*) and Ramesses IX–Ramesses XI 73
Fig. 4. Percentages of texts recording different groups of workmen as receiving rations 92
Fig. 5. Total rations distributed as a percentage of a complete delivery 94
Fig. 6. Categories of workmen: percentages by period 108
Fig. 7. Location of silos in Deir el-Medina 157

PREFACE

The primary purpose behind studying procedures of accounting in an ancient society is to collate and expand on areas of existing knowledge, and research other previously untouched areas in order to provide a better understanding of the recording, and where possible, physical procedures of wage accounting. This can then fill in gaps in the knowledge base in the internal administrative system of Deir el-Medina, and to a lesser extent, the logistics of transport and storage of the ration grain prior to it being received by the village workmen. The subject has been kept narrow to allow a concise study of ration accounting and associated procedures, in turn allowing scholars to delve deeper into comparisons of accounting techniques used for grain rations with those used for other consumables brought to the village such as wood, fish and temple supplies. Similarly, there is the high potential to examine wage accounting procedures during other time periods within ancient Egyptian society, or other locations throughout the ancient world such as Greece, Rome and Mesopotamia.

The material within has been derived mostly from primary sources, that is the ancient documents themselves, which take the form of transcriptions published into a more readily available format. Reliance has been placed on my own translations of this material and where possible my own interpretations in addition to existing work by scholars such as Jaroslav Černý and Jac Janssen. These have been used, incorporated and added to, with the inclusion of areas of research which have for the most part remained unexplored, resulting in, it is hoped, a research project which contains enough new material to justify the time spent on the research, as well as highlighting areas where the definitive answer can not be given, thus fostering future studies within the wider area of accounting, and wage accounting in particular.

It has not been deemed necessary to include a brief synopsis of either the New Kingdom or the Ramesside period, or even the village of Deir el Medina itself, since there is a considerable amount of existing publications containing background details, both within the general literature and the more specialised works on the village. Instead, the focus will be entirely on accounting for rations; however there is the need to discuss the preliminaries such as dating, what exactly an accountant was, how numbers and weights were used, and most importantly, problems encountered in the methodology of selecting the primary data. There are instances where there is more than one delivery on a single document, or where one delivery covers more than one period, lost or damaged dates, recipients of rations and amounts, and many areas where the evidence is lacking and has to be supplemented by suggestions.

There are many terms used in the textual record, many of which denote localities or concepts relating predominantly to Deir el-Medina and the immediate vicinity, and out of these, only two which are crucial to understanding the village and its organisation, need to be briefly explained at this point. Firstly, *pꜣ ḫr* is used to denote the Tomb; not the eternal resting place for any given pharaoh, but the central administrative unit at Deir el-Medina the workmen were part of. Secondly, the *ḫtm* (*n pꜣ ḫr*) is taken to mean the administrative centre of the Tomb, often referred to as the Enclosure, probably a building which acted as an interface between the village and the outside world, and where rations were handed out to the workmen.

During the course of researching the material for my doctorate I would like to acknowledge the contributions of my supervisors, Professors Mark Collier and Christopher Eyre, for their time and valuable comments and the opportunity to discuss a wide variety of ideas. Since both are familiar with the village in different ways, it has allowed me to incorporate the recording, economic and reality aspects into my research, as well as highlighting the areas for which evidence is severely lacking. Similarly, I am indebted to the valuable comments and suggestions made by Dr Ben Haring and Dr Robert Demarée of the University of Leiden, whose works stimulated my own interest in this fascinating community. I would also like to express my gratitude to Dr Roland Enmarch (one of my examiners), and to Dr Benedict Davies for editing and typesetting my manuscript. It is fortunate that the majority of ration documents can be found in published material, but there are several records which are as yet unpublished. Access to these is available from Černý's Notebooks currently housed in the Griffith Institute in Oxford; I wish to thank the staff at the Griffith Institute for speedily supplying me with each transcription requested, in electronic format. Only on one occasion have I had to work from the hieratic, this being the relevant sections of P. Turin 2002. I would also like to thank Helen Whitehouse at the Ashmolean Museum in Oxford for allowing me special access to the Ashmolean Museum ostraca during a period of major refurbishment to the museum's Egyptian galleries. Thanks are also given to Kamila Zychaluk of the Statistics Department at the University of Liverpool, who gave me valuable advice and clarifications on the statistical testing methods used in the present study, as well as refreshing my own memory on this particular subject. Finally, none of this would have been possible without the Arts and Humanities Research Council, to whom I am extremely grateful for funding my research.

INTRODUCTION

Wages have always played a major role in civilisations, but even so it is important to differentiate between the concept of wages both today and in the ancient world. In modern western society, a wage is a fixed and regular payment for work, in other words, a financial payment for labour. Ancient Egypt in the New Kingdom was a society without coinage or money, where workers were paid in kind. This was a payment which was not strictly a payment, but subsistence for living. This wage consisted of emmer wheat (*bdt* or *bty*) and barley (*it* or *it m it*), which were the main ingredients in the two staples of the ancient Egyptian diet, bread and beer. Despite the importance of wages in local and regional economies, much work remains to be done on the subject, primarily due to a lack of surviving evidence, but also perhaps due to the subject being perceived as mundane and trivial compared with issues on religion, donkey texts and personal letters. However, there is enough datable material surviving at Deir el-Medina to allow an in-depth and detailed study on a select group of individuals at one place in a relatively specific point in time: the workmen's village at Deir el-Medina in Thebes during the Ramesside period. There are enough gaps in our knowledge of the mechanics of wage accounting to allow additions and occasionally reviews of existing work, but also to research new avenues in order to supplement and add to what is already known, which in turn will allow scholars in the future to compare and contrast other aspects of the administration, and also form a solid basis for research in the event of further textual material turning up that may add to the existing corpus.

There can be some confusion over exactly what is meant by wages, and for the purposes of the present study it is necessary to elaborate on this. In its narrowest sense, wages consisted of grain rations, but there were also other commodities that the workmen received on at least a semi-regular basis. Janssen's assertion that wages were known as *ḥtri*[1] may be correct in so far that this term covered most of the commodities supplied to the workmen by the state, including wood, fish, vegetables, cakes, breads, confectionaries, and so on. However, it may be more correct to treat the term *ḥtri* as something encompassing not only these essential supplies but also more infrequently

1 Janssen also correctly adds that its usual meaning is more concerned with taxation and levies (1975a: 457).

delivered items. These were not actually "wages" in the strictest sense since grain rations were not classed as *ḥtri*. In order to alleviate any confusion between the terms "rations" and "wages", only the grain element will be examined using the broad terminology of "rations"

The texts utilise two terms, *diw* and *dni*, to indicate rations, and since delivery patterns varied so greatly in relation to the amounts delivered and the timing of delivery, closer examination of the documents and the patterns of delivery indicates that these terms had more specific definitions. The meanings of *diw* for the first payment of a given month and *dni* for any subsequent payments are those adhered to in the current literature[2], but a closer investigation will be carried out in §1.4 to check their validity. Due to the high degree of variability in the designations of workmen included in any given distribution list, and to a lesser degree, the amounts paid to some of these classes, it is very difficult to ascertain full ration schedules for all individuals[3]. Ration lists are available with names and amounts[4], but one or more *dni* payment was not necessarily part of the same wage as the preceding *diw* payment. The amounts were sometimes the same irrelevant of what the rations were classed as, but occasionally there was no label apart from the grain type. There are examples where the standard payment was not that which was recorded[5], and the manner of recording in terms of the format of the document, and the way the wage values were written, was not always consistent; therefore it will become apparent that the documentation is not uniform in nature, and it does have its problems[6] such as criteria for initial selection, dating and how the texts fitted in with reality.

Grain rations were an important component of the mechanics of the economy of Deir el-Medina. This was not only because the workmen needed food to live and any surplus could be used as barter, but by examining the amounts delivered, the vocabulary used, the formats of the documents and the dates recorded, it will hopefully be possible to glean information concerning the accounting system, if it may be called as such, and discern any differences between those distinct time periods for which we have the greatest amount of material.

The present study uses a corpus approach, where as many texts as possible are utilised, since in many studies of material from Deir el-Medina, a more selective approach has been taken primarily to show that phenomena occurred, but not necessarily if it was in fact the norm. The corpus (discussed in §2.1) includes a number of fragmentary ostraca which contribute to the overall

2 The notion that *diw* and *ḥtri* are so similar they can both be termed as "salaries" as implied by Valbelle (1985: 152) is incorrect since the latter does not include rations. *ḥtri* includes regular commodities such as wood and fish delivered by the *smdt*, as well as more infrequently delivered items such as cakes and dates.

3 Janssen (1997: 13). The rations of each category of individual will be discussed in Chapter 4 along with the frequency of each class of recipient and the total delivery amounts.

4 Some examples with a more substantial list of recipients are: O. Cairo 25608, O. DeM 376 and O. DeM 377. A selection of documents shows lists where the list is limited to perhaps the foreman, scribe and a given number of "men" being recorded, and examples of this include O. Ashmol. 184, O. Cairo 25592, O. DeM 329 and O. DeM 375.

5 Examples include O. Cairo 25689, O. DeM 377 and O. BM EA 50726. Many parts of a given month's rations are either lost or were not recorded; even when there are complete records, adding the basic and additional rations together does not always give the same results in total.

6 This important point is discussed in depth in §2.3.

analyses, those texts which have tended to be left aside as insignificant and largely ignored, so that the number of documents drawn upon is higher than that in previous studies on the subject. Although some work has been carried out on the subject of rations, this is for the most part either limited to the amounts paid, or else the issue of rations has been briefly incorporated into a more substantial publication; there are still many gaps remaining which this study will attempt to fill. A thorough examination of the whole corpus recording rations can open up several avenues of possible questioning, including the delivery dates, format and writing of the ration documents, the frequencies of the inclusion of given workmen in the delivery lists and the total amounts distributed at one time.

One key relationship is that between the texts and the dates, particularly the day but also the month and season, so it is essential to bear in mind the proportion of texts within the whole corpus which are dated, and take into account both the date of the text and the month which the deliveries relate to. This in turn can facilitate statistical breakdown to provide an analysis on a number of issues and an attempt to answer related questions, such as what proportion of deliveries could be classed as late, did the season have any effect on delivery patterns, was a record kept every time a delivery was made, and were the deliveries recorded those actually made. The results may ultimately provide some evidence for a description or account of the organisation of operations at Deir el-Medina, including what the scribes did or did not do when things did not work out as planned. Despite many documents lacking a date or recording only a month or day, these should not be discarded as useless; on the contrary, since many of these can be dated fairly accurately with reference to names of datable personnel and can prove a strong asset in other matters such as terminology and wage amounts. In short, this study will bring together a comprehensive corpus of available material through which it may be possible to isolate key delivery periods and engage the reasons behind this.

Vocabulary, terminology and the format of the documents are important factors in studies dealing with both a linguistic component and the recording and ultimate uses of the documents. In common with documentation from other spheres, ration records have standard headings which are not restricted to ration contexts, but also terms specific to accounting, which might open the possibility of one further avenue of research to explore other spheres for similarities and differences, including other non-ration commodities. Therefore attention will be given to the words used, their context and their relationship between each other, and pinpointing their exact meanings and any obvious changes in usage over the course of the Ramesside period. As a result, this will hopefully allow future studies to compare meanings and vocabulary used, and importantly this includes notable absences of specific words within wage accounting and other aspects of social life.

Examination and analysis of the recipients of the rations, including both the number and class of workmen, and the amounts recorded, are looked at with the aim of ascertaining how complete the ration lists were, and answering the question of what a complete ration list looked like. Since there is no indication of what a complete ration list consisted of, assumptions have to be made depending on the size of the workforce at a given point in time, with the objective of calculating both the average delivery and the average number of recipients. Documentation from three distinct time periods is examined primarily due to the survival of the evidence, which is predominantly towards the end of the 19th Dynasty, the years spanning the last part of the reign of Ramesses III and first half of his successor Ramesses IV, and the last three reigns of the 20th Dynasty. Having these periods between which there are definite gaps in the evidence allows a comparison over the course of the Ramesside period and also ensures that results can be produced even if the sample size is not great.

It will become apparent throughout that only so much is known about the physical procedure by which rations were given out and recorded, so part of the aim is to attempt to speculate and use the material to suggest some possibilities and eliminate others. This is true both with the distribution of grain to the workmen, the methods by which grain was brought to the village as well as the way scribes recorded such details and, to a lesser degree, who was accountable for each component of the process. One aspect of this is to examine the writing of ostraca for which physical access is possible, and ask the question whether or not the scribes prepared their records, at least in part, in advance. This may help to determine scribal procedures, how they recorded rations payments and perhaps where this was done.

When dealing with a subject which forms a pivotal role in modern society, care must be taken not to impose our modern conceptions onto the ancient data. The role of the ancient Egyptian "accountant" is not the same as modern equivalents, and importantly, the notions of accounting and accounting conventions are completely different. Having said that, recording procedures which we would take for granted in accounting today are examined with the aim of highlighting notable recording techniques as well as notable absences; the most obvious absentee being double entry bookkeeping. With this in mind, a comprehensive analysis is performed on the various types of numerical errors, looking at both their frequency and magnitude, thereby ascertaining the degree of freedom allowed by scribes and the effectiveness of ration records where errors existed. The main issue here concerns the errors—did they really matter and did they affect the accuracy and requirements of the ration lists?

The subject of ration accounting is important for a number of reasons. There are enough gaps in the existing literature to warrant a long and detailed study, but some of the areas where there is some doubt, and those where results have previously not been conclusive, can also be re-examined and enhanced. Prime examples include terminology, scribal errors in the amounts, variances and delays in ration payments, and the analysis of total rations and recipients in the ration lists. After examining in detail a lengthy list of accounting issues, one of the primary objectives is to provide a model of ration distribution which details how rations could have been transported and delivered, recorded, and accounted for at various stages of supply, from the field to the homes of the workmen. Many suggestions have to be made and incorporated into the model, and although the evidence forthcoming is extremely variable within these links, there is still enough surviving evidence to provide such a model, all of which can be added to in the event of further finds coming to light. In short, the overall aim of the present study is to provide a full, detailed and as complete as possible analysis of ration payments in one study, which other scholars can use and add to in the future.

Since the primary excavations at Deir el-Medina by Ernesto Schiaparelli (1905–1909)[7] and

7 Schiaparelli (1927).

Bernard Bruyère (1922–1951)[8], a number of studies centred on administrative matters, including specific aspects of grain rations and many related topics, have been published. In the intervening years the Berlin Museum, under the direction of Georg Möller, worked there during the 1911 and 1913 seasons[9], before the concession was awarded to the French at the end of the First World War. The village itself is the subject of a wide range of studies covering religion, archaeology, literature, economics, administration and social life to name but a few, and as a result, the interest in the village is intense enough so as to foster academic work for many years to come. In order to provide a detailed overview of previous work on the subject, the primary publications with a significant component on grain and rations are highlighted and reviewed in the following paragraphs.

The first scholar to investigate matters concerning the administration at Deir el-Medina was Černý in his work "Prices and Wages in Egypt in the Ramesside Period"[10], published in 1954. Most of this article is focused upon the exchange rates of gold, silver and copper, a selection of tradable commodities and their measurements (*khar*, *oipe* and *hin*). The final few pages concern rations paid to the workmen, but apart from a very brief outline of the organisation of the crew, this section wholly concentrates on the amounts given to each class, with the evidence consisting of twenty-five documents coming from the sources as follows: eleven from the Ostraca Deir el-Medina (O. DeM) series, four from the Ashmolean (including those belonging to Gardiner), three from the Cairo collection, plus one each from the Petrie (now UCL), Strasbourg, Munich and British Museum collections along with three papyri. The study tends to be more in a simple narrative style on a narrow range of issues, concentrating primarily on the ration each class of workman received, but it only briefly discusses emmer and barley and their recording in red and black respectively. As a result, the sources used by Černý in a rations context are limited and can be seen to be a subset of the wider corpus used in the present study. However, his work undoubtedly serves as a base point for discussions and testing both material not initially considered and the data obtained subsequently against the results provided by Černý.

The next significant published work containing ration data was Helck's substantial tome *Materialen zur Wirtschaftsgeschichte des Neuen Reiches*, written in several parts during the 1960s. The fourth part contains a section where the author has taken a selection of ostraca and papyri and discussed, relatively briefly, a range of issues such as grain transport, prices and grain deliveries[11]. Although now largely superseded, at the time the study provided valuable information on aspects of ration distribution and included topics such as vocabulary, the colours of the ink used in the writing, as well as concentrating heavily upon dating matters. Since a number of issues are covered in little detail, much of this section has followed on from Černý's *Prices and Wages* and provides more recent scholars with a good foundation of evidence and ideas upon which to build.

Twenty years after his initial study on prices and wages, Černý's *A Community of Workmen at Thebes in the Ramesside Period* was posthumously published[12]. It deals extensively with the individual groups of workmen such as foremen, scribes, doorkeepers and the like, as well as investigating

8 Bruyère (1924–1953).

9 Published by Anthes (1943) from Möller's excavation notes.

10 Černý (1954).

11 Helck (1964b: 580-603).

12 First published in 1973, and reprinted as the third edition as Černý (2004).

the evidence for the *ḫr*, or the Tomb establishment. An extensive amount of textual evidence was used; despite most of the study being of use for reference and background purposes, there are small sections which mention rations, albeit very briefly. It is of importance to subsequent and current research on the administration of Deir el-Medina; many scholars have published their own work following on and directly influenced by Černý, and it remains to this day the most comprehensive study on the workmen themselves, with the possible exception of Davies' *Who's Who at Deir el-Medina*[13].

Following on directly from Černý's initial study, Janssen collated a large amount of textual evidence in order to produce his invaluable work *Commodity Prices from the Ramessid Period*, published in 1975, and split into three broad parts. The first is concerned with the sources and dating, a format which the present study incorporates and updates. The second part forms the crux of the book, where Janssen examines approximately 1,250 prices covering a considerable selection of commodities, including foods, basketry, furniture, animals, tools and a multitude of other items. The last section is concerned with economics and exchange, and part of this is about rations[14], including the grain rations as well as other, more irregular, payments of consumables which were not in the strictest sense wages, but which were provided by the state in addition to grain rations. This section uses Černý's study as a benchmark and greatly expands on it, and includes some mention of the days of ration delivery based on ostraca mainly from the Journal of the Necropolis, as well as expanding the overall database by adding other consumables such as vegetables, fish and wood. Yearly totals of additional commodities are estimated by factoring surviving records and providing the results in tabular form, and comparing over a period of about ten years, thus giving us a sense of recording reliability and a rough idea of what quantities were provided. The present study takes some of these themes and provides further in-depth analysis on this subject, expanding the rations data set and taking individual time periods for which the evidence is more abundant. Janssen concludes that payments were irregular, small, and were therefore relatively unimportant[15], notions that will be shown in this study to be not wholly accurate.

Dominique Valbelle's 1985 publication, *Les Ouvriers de la Tombe,* incorporates many aspects of previous works, but starts with an introduction concentrating on the 18th Dynasty, a period often omitted in Deir el-Medina studies on the basis of a lack of evidence[16]. The book is split into five parts; the first collates and details the texts, which is particularly useful since individual papyri are handled separately, rather than being included solely within the main discussion. The second part moves onto the subject of the Tomb as an institutional setting and the workmen themselves, and includes only a short section on rations; in common with other studies the subject of rations is treated as marginal. The third part provides historical details on the village in chronological order; the fourth part discusses life and death within the village, and the final section details social morality, justice and religion. Whereas much of the study contains a lot of valuable material and complements other publications well, for such a key component of village life and functionality,

13 Davies (1999). This is an invaluable study concentrating on the workmen and genealogy, which men lived during which time, and their relationships with other workmen.

14 Janssen (1975: 455-493).

15 Janssen (1975a: 471).

16 Valbelle (1985).

there is unfortunately scant information on rations.

Two more recent essays by Janssen consist of the first two chapters in a series of short studies published as *Village Varia*[17], and only at this point does the subject of rations seem to be granted more prominence. The first of these provides background information about the nature of payments, such as differentiating *ḥtri* (wood, fish and luxuries such as cakes and dates) and *mkw* (irregular deliveries of goods such as meat, natron and oil)[18], and briefly mentioning the sources of grain supply. This chapter is brief and facilitates the possibility of considerable expansion, which the present study aims to achieve by examining the physicality, recording and accountability throughout the complete supply chain of grain from field to village. The second chapter expands in detail on Černý's initial study but does not deviate from that specific topic, despite the increased number of texts examined and detailed discussion contained within, but even so it provides a framework to allow further testing of the ration amounts and to check for any changes over time, and is an essential inclusion for any study on ration payments and distribution.

There are many gaps in our knowledge of matters concerning scribal technique and processes, but much use has been made in the present study to Donker van Heel and Haring's recent publication *Writing in a Workmen's Village*[19], which is split into two broad parts. The first is centred on duplication of the material and, in particular, the use of drafts and multiple documents written by individual scribes, while the second moves into the sphere of language, discussing document classification and headings. As the authors rightfully acknowledge in their introduction, many features of the daily activities of the scribes are missing. Some aspects of their investigation are followed in the present study both as a continuation of existing work and as an extension. Individual scribes wrote multiple documents and the same information was recorded on more than one document[20], but an attempt to explore and verify the methodology of how the writing was written has not been made until now, even within the limitations of the material available for physical viewing. The language element is expanded to include phrases and vocabulary used not just as headings but still confined to a ration context and more importantly, a comprehensive selection of accounting terminology is examined and analysed, thus filling in one current gap in our knowledge. This approach can be applied to different spheres such as legal documents or personal letters.

The Deir el-Medina Database[21] is an online resource which has been complied in recent years by scholars at Leiden University, and no serious project on Deir el-Medina can fail to make use of it. This extensive resource catalogues documents covering every facet of village society and provides information such as the document's size, a rough or exact date where possible, provenance, how the item was acquired and a brief summary of the contents, and includes a search

17 Janssen (1997). Provisions in general are discussed in Chapter 1 "The Sources of the Workmen's Provisions" (pp. 1-11), and ration payments in Chapter 2 "Rations and Ranks" (pp. 13-35).

18 Janssen (1997: 1-2).

19 Donker van Heel & Haring (2003).

20 Donker van Heel (2003: 39). The evidence presented is not solely restricted to rations, for example the records of Qenherkhepeshef and many of the texts from the Journal of the Necropolis.

21 The Deir el-Medina Database can be found at http://www.leidenuniv.nl/nino/dmd/dmd.html, and as of August 2014 consists of over 4,600 ostraca, papyri and weights.

engine which can sort by a number of variables. The ability to select documents by keyword is especially valuable and time-saving as there is a large number of sources recording a given word, be it a commodity, technical term, class of workman to name but three. As an example, if "grain" is entered, this generates a long list of documents which enables the user to examine each one in turn, and similarly, a search can be performed on the transliteration *it* (grain), *bdt/bty* (emmer) or the required grain type, and a list of documents will be shown. The importance and usefulness of this resource can not be understated and continuous use has been made throughout.

The present study takes not only smaller texts on an individual level, but incorporates a wider range of documents from a larger number of collections with a more expansive spread of issues which need addressing, in effect creating a wider research agenda significantly different from previous work. Ration payments are marginal to most of the key literary resources; this allows the present study to take this important subject by examining a multitude of aspects relating to rations and ration accounting both in a physical sense and what was recorded. These domains can be expanded upon, where there are gaps in our knowledge they can be highlighted and shortfalls can be filled in. Areas where previous work has been carried out still form part of the present study; although it is necessary to restrict the evidence to rations, this can allow direct comparisons with other spheres. Furthermore, there are a number of aspects which are new and previously have been either discussed very briefly in the existing literature or are completely absent. It is hoped that the present research has expanded greatly on existing works, creating a valuable and accessible study that will foster future investigations of the community's administration, economics and social life.

CHAPTER 1

ACCOUNTING METHODOLOGIES IN THE RAMESSIDE PERIOD

§1.1 Accountants and Accounting in Ramesside Egypt

While dealing with a modern discipline in an ancient setting, there is a strong temptation to approach it from the same viewpoint we would if we were studying the modern equivalent, and impose modern terminology and concepts onto ancient society, while making assumptions which are prevalent and taken for granted in the modern subject. This is especially true in social settings and the scholar researching ancient practices in fields such as law and accounting has to be wary of the differences. There are concepts for which there is no exact Egyptian equivalent, taxation being perhaps the main example. The individuals and processes involved, the guidelines set by the central administration, the conceptual framework and even more technical matters such as terminology and vocabulary must not be assumed to mean the same as in business today.

In response to this, two issues have to be addressed here. The first is what exactly an "accountant" in ancient Egypt was, and the second is more a matter of terminology in as much as whether "accountancy" *per se* existed, and if so what could be classed as accounting. Modern accounting encompasses a large number of tasks, but is appropriately summed up as being concerned with recording, classifying and summarising data and communicating1 it to both independent entities, such as banks and tax inspectors, and to those within the business whose own decisions will be influenced by what they are told.

The ancient Egyptian "accountant" had no computers to use to check his figures, no money existed since society was at this time economically based on barter and reciprocal exchange. Double entry bookkeeping, upon which modern accounting is based, did not exist until the Middle Ages, and this method had its origins in Italy in the fourteenth century[2], or perhaps even

1 Wood & Sangster (1967: 4).

2 de Roover (1956: 133), in the belief that by AD 1300 merchants used equity and expense accounts, and double-entry existed in all but a formal rule of finance. Accounting as a discipline developed heavily in Italy in the second half of the fourteenth century and the techniques became more widespread via international trade. An early English example is the ledger of Thomas Howell, a London merchant, which dates from between 1519 and 1527. It is likely that double entry bookkeeping did exist in ancient Egypt, albeit

earlier[3]. Given this background, it would not be entirely incorrect to say there was no such thing as an accountant in ancient Egypt. Several years ago, Mahmoud Ezzamel wrote a paper on the emergence of the accountant[4] and this highlights their relationship to the formal institutions in ancient Egypt while emphasizing that accounting was central to the efficient running of society. The first half of this paper concentrates on the scribe and his profession, including the importance of numeracy in the scribal repertoire[5], which suggests that the accountant was simply a scribe who got involved with numbers and economics. Scribes were well versed in numbers as well as words so they could record economic transactions such as donkey hiring, which was a major part of the working economy at Deir el-Medina, as well as stock taking, the recording of commodities brought in to the village, taxation, personal inventory lists, the rations for the workmen as well as more specific records such as the bakery accounts from the time of Seti I[6]. Accountants were not a separate class of personnel in their own right as they are today; rather they were scribes who performed specific functions.

Accounting in the western world is formally guided by conventions and practices set by the regulating bodies, but this was certainly not the case in ancient Egypt, where rules were enforced by central and provincial officials on behalf of Pharaoh[7]. Undoubtedly, rules were occasionally broken by enterprising individuals, but there is little proof of this happening in the textual record—probably intentionally so—and no evidence as to what happened to the culprits. In contrast to today, where every set of figures, accounts and financial reports have to be checked and scrutinised by an independent body, such auditing did not exist in ancient Egypt, where the words, actions and conduct of the individuals representing the state were accepted without the need for further checks. In brief, each institution such as a temple or a granary had at least one scribe who was responsible for the recording of economic matters, and the overseers of these institutions reported back to the vizier. Balance sheets and profit and loss accounts did not exist and strictly speaking there was no concept of assets and liabilities, although "credit" did exist in as much as people held items on behalf of others[8]. Accounts and lists were drawn up on the basis of expenses and income for the general purpose of the parties involved rather than for the state, unless state property was involved.

Accounting and recording can be split into two levels of general activity. On a public level, accounting was concerned with the inflow of commodities and provisions such as that recorded on the Turin Taxation Papyrus (see §8.4), the transport and storage of state owned property and

not in name, since the Wilbour Papyrus does exhibit some of its features.

3 Gordon (1956: 202) assumes the emergence of double-entry bookkeeping to be prior to 1300.

4 Ezzamel (1994).

5 Ibid., 232-4.

6 Ezzamel (2007: 193-195).

7 The best example of evidence supporting the implementation of regulations is a text known as *The Duties of the Vizier*, found in a number of Theban tombs, most notably that of Rekhmire. The vizier was Pharaoh's deputy and also head of the civil administration. See van den Boorn (1988: 310-317), for a summary of the activities of the vizier.

8 The existence of an open credit system has been proposed by Janssen (1994: 129), based on the term *nty m-di* to indicate the absence of a middleman in economic transactions or short term loans in a society without money.

summaries detailing income, taxation, maintenance and provisions for feasts, and ideally making sure that state property did not go missing and was accounted for. These records indicate that the state, primarily by means of the temples, provided the economy with the framework for the redistributive mechanism which ensured the movements of commodities in and out of official entities such as the stores, workshops and granaries. On a private level, accounting was more concerned with recording barter transactions between individuals, items given to craftsmen in payment for services rendered and inventory lists. All these are abundant in the textual record at Deir el-Medina and show that there was a thriving, albeit small-scale, private market within the village for commodities used in both household consumption and as provisions for deceased relatives in their tombs[9].

§1.2 The meaning of *diw* and *dni*

It is all too easy to accept that *diw* represents the first ration delivery or distribution in a given period and that *dni* denotes those over and above this initial delivery. Thus their meanings must be examined in more detail with reference to specific examples. There are over a hundred and twenty examples[10] which indicate a record of *diw*, and thirty-three for *dni*, which instantly suggests the increased importance of the former over the latter in the recording procedure. In modern western society, wages are paid in a lump sum at a set time, but in Ramesside Egypt this was the exception rather than the rule. Significant events were recorded in the Journal[11], such as a visit by the vizier, the death of a pharaoh, the movement of royal tomb furnishings and also the delivery or arrival of rations. A glance at the complete dated ration corpus listed in Tables 1, 2 and 3 (see below pp. 51-56) reveals that almost every Journal document which records a ration delivery records the delivery of *diw* as opposed to *dni*,[12] while highlighting the relative importance of *diw* in terms of document type rather than frequency of recording. It is safe to assume that the most important delivery was the first and that if there was any shortfall in what a workman would expect as his rations, then there would be extra payments to make up the monthly quota. *Diw* must therefore indicate the first payment of rations made in any one period.

The meaning of *dni* is more problematic. One possible meaning is that of arrears, that is, if the previous period had no delivery. Here we are hindered by the confusion over the due date of the rations. Unfortunately, and not surprisingly, many documents are incomplete records, where either the amount is less or there are fewer individuals on the distribution list. There is another word which is used in commodity records—transliterated *wḏ3t* or *ḏ3t*—which relates to arrears, balances and remainders in the commodity records so the meaning of *dni* as arrears is incorrect. The first scholar to propose a meaning of "Nachlieferung"[13] or "subsequent rations" was Helck,

9 Janssen (1975) includes a wide variety of products, commodities and consumables covering a variety of contexts and functions. A range of economic matters are dealt with by Eyre (2010), including markets and the urban economy. For private sector craft work at Deir el Medina, see Cooney (2007).

10 The difference between the numbers of texts and examples used is discussed in §2.3.1.

11 The meaning and composition of the "Journal" is examined in §2.2.

12 The only exceptions are O. DeM 427, which records *diw* and *dni*, and O. UC 39626 vs., which records an emmer ration payment list of *dni* for II *3ḫt*.

13 Helck (1962: 585), but with no justification or explanation.

but perhaps the best way of approaching, and checking, this is to examine the order of recording, that is, which term came first in an individual document. There are examples where deliveries of both types of rations were recorded, but only two documents contain the month of delivery. O. Ashmol. 111 rt. records two sets of distribution, both of ½ *khar* to a group of individuals; lines 2 and 3 specify *diw* and lines 4-6 record *dni*, both on the same day, IV *šmw* 9. O. DeM 179 rt. is a distribution list starting with *dni*, with lines 4-5 recording diw deliveries. However, the former relates to III *ꜣḫt* and the latter to IV *ꜣḫt*, so in both cases the *diw* preceded the *dni* within a given month. Despite the lack of *dni* in the Journal records, these two examples should suffice to show with confidence that *dni* related to any additional ration allocation after the first, whilst noting that it is impossible to match up a *dni* payment with a corresponding *diw* delivery with any degree of certainty.

§1.3 Fractions and mathematics

The reading of numbers needs no explanation, but things get slightly more complicated when fractions are used. Fractions were written in two ways. The most common method of recording fractions used by the Egyptians was carried out by using *r* to denote a 'part'[14]. The number written below this was equivalent to the denominator in English, so the sign represented "the fifth part" (out of five), or ⅕. Since the numerator was one, with the exception of ⅔, fractions were denoted by a set of additions, for example ⅗ would be written as ½ + ⅒. The second method was used for measurements of grain and land, so it would follow naturally that almost all the ration records used this method, the corn measure[15], which was based on the eye of Horus 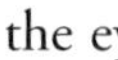. In the ration documentation, the Horus eye fractions are those of the *oipe*, and not of the *khar*; care must be made to differentiate the dot for *oipe* with the circle for ¼ *oipe*. The corn measure adapted the following notation:

½		1/16	
¼		1/32	
⅛		1/64	

Perhaps the most appropriate way to examine the writing of fractions in ration lists is to highlight a short but appropriate example of a ration delivery note, O. DeM 379, in hieroglyphic form with an accompanying transliteration and translation. This reads as follows:

ꜣbd 4 prt sw 25   IV Peret, Day 25

14 Gardiner (1957: 196).
15 Gardiner (1957: 197).

dit diw n ꜣbd 4 prt	Distribution of rations for IV Peret

wnmy ẖꜣr 46½ (ipt) 1/16	Right: 46½ *khar* 1/16 *oipe*

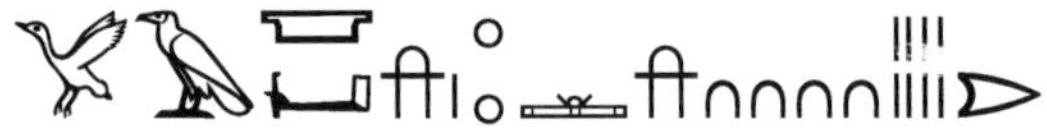

pꜣ iry-ꜥꜣ ẖꜣr 1½ dmḏ ẖꜣr 48 (ipt) 1/16	The doorkeeper 1½ *khar*. Total 48 *khar* 1/16 *oipe*

dmḏ ẖꜣr 63¾ dmḏ ẖꜣr 110¾	Total 63¾ *khar*. Total 110¾ *khar*.

Although many examples record straightforward ration payments, O. DeM 379 demonstrates the additive nature of fractions by recording separate amounts and using simple addition to create the fractions. Therefore, in line 3, the amount is written as $46\frac{2}{4}$ *khar* + 1/16 *oipe* equalling $46\frac{33}{64}$ *khar*. This example also shows the incomplete nature of records as it is not known where the total in line 5 of 63¾ *khar* came from; perhaps from the Left side with the breakdown being recorded on another ostracon which has subsequently been lost. There is also an error in the addition since $48\frac{1}{64}$ *khar* and 63¾ *khar* do not add up to 110¾ *khar* but $111\frac{49}{64}$. This in itself highlights another potential problem which will be discussed shortly, namely the uncertainty of whether measures of 1/16 *oipe* (1/64 *khar*) were actually given out. Since scribes recorded grain by noting the number of sacks, whether full or partially full, it was only necessary to use the simplest numerical notation as presented on O. DeM 379, so these more complicated representations were unnecessary for the recording procedure and were therefore not used in the ration records.

It was easy to hand out and record half and quarter measures, but there does not seem any obvious reason why smaller measures such as 1/16 *oipe* would have been distributed apart from being used as a balancing item. An analysis of errors within the rations lists will show that mistakes in the multiplication were very rarely made, so the scribes were competent in both multiplication and division, which were in essence addition by adding a number of equal portions. The mathematics in the above example suggest that such a measure may have been arbitrary, but taking 1/64 *khar* as 1.2 litres, if the classical measurement of the *khar* as discussed in §1.6 is accepted, would indicate otherwise, and that this measure was in reality fairly insignificant. These uncertainties are demonstrated in one short ostracon, but were all too common in the administration.

One speculative possibility is that somebody received a small amount which was not physically measured, so 1/16 *oipe* was the assigned value to account for it in the records, and the recording of anything smaller may have resulted in a cluttered record. Similarly, it is difficult to ascertain how the scribes accounted for any shortfall, it is quite plausible that this 1/16 *oipe* measure would have sufficed. The measurements recorded on O. DeM 841, an ostracon recording *diw* rations for the epagomenal days, are even more precise, again being in fractions of *oipe*[16], and therefore so specific that it can hardly be imagined that the grain was ever accurately measured. Far more likely is that the amounts were calculated pro-rata and thus recorded.

§1.4 Volumes used in ration accounting

The standard unit of measurement of grain during the New Kingdom was the *khar* (*ḫ3r*), which can be loosely translated as "sack" but will remain untranslated throughout the study. In addition, the smaller measure, the *oipe* (*ipt*) equalled ¼ *khar*, and the latter notation will be used throughout this study. The *hin* was usually used to measure oil and fat, but in one example, O. Ashmol. 262, the measure is used alongside the *khar* to signify an amount of rations[17]. O. DeM 841 is enlightening in terms of measurements since rations given to the foreman and the scribe are recorded in *oipe* and the even smaller measure, the *ro* which was written in much the same way as *r* "part" above but with a second *r*. Thus the measure on O. DeM 841, 2, is written  and translates as 5 *ro* ⅓. This equates to 1/5⅓ *khar*, or ⅔ *oipe*.

In short,

1 *khar* = 4 *oipe* = 76.88 litres
1 *oipe* = 40 *hin* = 19.22 litres
1 *hin* = 8 *ro* = 0.48 litres
1 *ro* = 0.06 litres
1 *ro* = ⅛ *hin* = 1/320 *oipe* = 1/1280 *khar*

The widely accepted classical measurement of weight was 1 *khar*, which equalled 76.88 litres[18]. The main problem, and it appears insurmountable, in trying to weigh grain is the differences in weights between crops. Not only does one grain of emmer have a different weight to one grain of barley, we have no idea of the weight of grains of the ancient Egyptian crop varieties. One *khar* equates to one sack, which is an arbitrary value, but how large a sack was is not obvious and therefore doubts are raised over whether a *khar* was in fact a measure a man could carry. Similarly, unless either the size of the sack or the number of grains within were different, one sack of emmer would not weigh the same as one sack of barley, so applying a specific numerical value in litres or kilograms to a *khar* seems inappropriate. All this seems to suggest that the *khar* was a unit of volume and not a unit of weight and forms the basis for the classical measure; alternatively it is possible that the term was applied to a single donkey-load. Until a viable proposition is accepted, there seems little alternative to accepting the classical measure.

16 O. DeM 841 is examined in more detail by Grandet (2003: 19-20). Janssen (1991: 93-95) and Spalinger (1991) discuss the mathematics behind the calculations in O. Ashmol. 262 and O. DeM 841 (formerly O. IFAO 1406).

17 A brief discussion of the *khar* during the Old and Middle Kingdoms is made by Helck (1974: 136-137) followed by notes on the *khar*, *hin* and *heqat* during the New Kingdom.

18 On the basis of differing measurements of the *oipe* in the Middle Kingdom context of the Heqanakht Papyri, this measure was not the same throughout Egyptian history. For a short discussion on the *oipe* and its relationship with the *heqat* measurement, see Allen (2002: 143-145).

CHAPTER 2

SOURCE MATERIAL AND METHODOLOGY

The textual evidence relating to the administration from Deir el-Medina is extensive, with the vast majority of the administrative and economic material being of two types: ostraca and papyri. There are literary texts, including student exercises, and non-literary texts[1], both of which were scribed in Late Egyptian, the written language of the 19th and 20th Dynasties. Non-literary texts in particular reveal a great deal about daily life within the village, and include the records of deliveries, prices and transactions of commodities, and it is to this group that ration texts belong, thus forming the basis for the examination of accounting practices and procedures.

One major problem when attempting to interpret much of the material is context. Many ostraca and papyri were acquired by collectors in the nineteenth century, and apart from the Grand Puits finds and the library of Qenherkhepeshef, only a small number of the texts have been recorded in their context[2], so there is often no indication of their original find spots. This has led to an absence of information which might otherwise have been gained such as the dating of some undated documents and the assembling of ancient archives. Even the ostraca found at the Grand Puits had accumulated over many years, probably as a result of periodic clearances, and no stratigraphic context was recorded.

§2.1 Documentary evidence from Deir el-Medina

§2.1.1 Ostraca

At Deir el-Medina and its surroundings, the geology of the limestone is such that it splits naturally into layers, enabling the easy and cheap gathering of stone suitable for writing. This type of ostraca is very rarely found outside the Theban area, although it is impossible to know how widely

1 The term "non-literary" is used throughout as referring to style and content, not to any linguistic feature of Late Egyptian. This is discussed by Černý & Groll (1993: LIV-LV).

2 Originally stated as none having been found by McDowell (1999: 26), as several of the papyri from the Qenherkhepeshef library were stolen before they were recorded so even this find was not complete. However, several of the Berlin and Cairo ostraca as well as recent finds by the Basel Expedition (Dorn (2011)) in and around the "huts" near KV18 contradict this.

they were used elsewhere at this time[3]. The size of the flakes of stone varies considerably; most are slightly larger than the human hand, making them easier to write on while being held, as well as being portable and easy to store. However, the question as to whether administrative records were retained is a matter of some debate. Thousands of ostraca were found in what is now known as the Grand Puits, or "Great Pit", to the north of the main entrance to the village. This enormous crater was the result of several attempts to dig a well to find water during Ramesside times and perhaps later in the Ptolemaic era[4], and was subsequently used as a refuse pit in antiquity.

The finds of ostraca in their entirety did not form a single archive, and neither did they all come from the same place. However, at both the Grand Puits and the Kom Sud[5] large numbers of ostraca were found, strongly indicating that archives were kept, a statement further supported by the texts exhibiting the same handwriting, subject matter and find date[6]. There are groups of ostraca which can be assigned broad provenance and have briefly been summarised by Eyre[7], as follows. The Valley of the Kings ostraca (such as many of the Cairo collection) deal with the tomb building work during the 19th and 20th dynasties; and those from the Valley of the Queens (such as many of the Turin collection) date to the early 20th Dynasty and cover much the same thing. Furthermore, the ostraca can be split into two very broad groups based on find locations and material; those found in and very close to the village itself tend to be pottery while those found in locations such as the Valley of the Kings tend to be stone. Not including the occasional single text, the earliest surviving ostraca date from the mid 18th Dynasty and record details of work at the temple of Deir el-Bahri, where they were found[8]. The use of ostraca became less frequent towards the end of the 20th Dynasty, perhaps as a result of the move from the village to Medinet Habu during the early years of Ramesses XI when the immediate availability of limestone was more limited, but even so the bulk of the currently known finds are some thirty years prior to this. Having said this, around a hundred ostraca, consisting mainly of name lists, are currently being studied by Robert Demarée; these may shed some light on the final phase of Deir el-Medina and the transition into the 21st Dynasty.

When examining primary material, upon which so much of this study is based, there is one perhaps obvious, but often overlooked, problem with many of the ostraca. They were written in hieratic, and like many people's handwriting today, ancient writing is often unclear and variable in quality. The signs are often difficult to identify and transcribe, and much of the writing has faded over time while lying in the sun for three thousand years as well as being in museum storage. Papyri were more official documents but the ostraca were written for daily activities, as in a community where everybody knew everybody else, what was recorded was what was needed for the village inhabitants to understand, and they were not written for archaeologists thousands of

3 Eyre (1987a: 168).

4 Bruyère (1953: 26).

5 Donker van Heel (2003: 14). The series of ostraca O. DeM 32-47, found at the Kom Sud, were written by the same scribe and deposited together; his analysis is presented on pp. 72-76.

6 Donker van Heel (2003: 15). Additional sets of texts are also mentioned which may be further evidence for the presence of archives.

7 Eyre (1987b: 25).

8 This material is largely unpublished, but is currently being studied by Malte Römer at Berlin.

years later. The condition of the ostracon can be an issue; some are well preserved but since pottery can break and limestone easily chips, others are damaged, resulting in key parts of the writing being lost.

§2.1.2 Papyri

The vast majority of papyri from the Theban area now in museum collections were acquired by wealthy patrons from the antiquities market during the nineteenth century, so there is no indication of their original find location. A number of papyri have been found in Deir el-Medina, but all those which were found in situ came from one source—the library of the mid 19th Dynasty scribe Qenherkhepeshef and his descendents[9]. Texts on papyrus were also both literary and non-literary; many of the papyri in the British Museum were found in the vicinity of Medinet Habu, but may have been written in Deir el-Medina prior to the migration of the workforce to the temple. Most of these relate to administrative matters and tomb robberies and some were very lengthy in their content even if much key information has been lost due to folding and damage to the edges.

There are several possible reasons for the increased use of papyrus over ostraca as a medium of recording towards the end of the 20th Dynasty. It is clear that in general the ostraca predate the papyri at Deir el-Medina[10], and the imbalance of the relative presence of the two media has fostered the debate as to whether ostraca were used as drafts for papyri[11]. It has been suggested[12] that drafting did take place in Deir el-Medina, although primarily the environment in which this took place seems to have been what may be loosely termed as "judicial". Information may have been written on an ostracon for temporary storage, to be copied up onto papyrus and stored in the official archives, if they existed, sometimes with extra details added to the final papyrus[13]. Perhaps the less skilled scribes wrote on ostraca or in haste. This last statement and the propensity for the use of drafts were suggested by Černý[14], on the basis of the large number of corrections found on ostraca compared with those on papyri. The opposite is equally possible, where the parts of the master copy on papyrus were copied into relevant sections of smaller ostraca when required for specific administrative tasks. The suggestion that the administration of lower ranked members of society may have used ostraca[15] and papyrus was used by the educated elite is possible, but there

9 The contents of the archive and their history are discussed at length by Pestman (1982).

10 There are many examples of papyri from the early to mid 20th Dynasty. For example, a search of the Deir el-Medina Database using "Ramesses III" as a dating criterion, but without any contextual restrictions, brings up a result of eleven papyri, though this does not include those broadly dated to the "early 20th Dynasty".

11 Donker van Heel deals with the duplication of information in a wide range of situations, including examples of drafts (2003: 1-38).

12 Allam (1968: 121-128) and reinforced by Donker van Heel (2003: 18) based on judicial examples while bearing in mind that this practice was not necessarily carried over into administrative texts. The only evidence for *possible* drafting in ration accounting is the distribution of rations recorded on O. Ashmol. 184 and O. DeM 376, which will be examined in due course.

13 Černý (1973: 226). That papyri did have additional information covering a wide range of subjects is evident from the ration papyri alone in Table 3.

14 Černý (1931: 212-213).

15 Allam (1968: 128). Although unlikely, the possibility of the use of writing boards (Eyre 1980: 10)

is nothing to indicate that this was the case, as we would expect both media types to be present if they were being used in parallel.

The possible use of drafting and archiving needs to be expanded upon at this point. The variation in the quality of handwriting may be seen as evidence to strengthen this, but as is the case today, even a single individual's handwriting can change depending on the requirements, time and physical location. Copying of texts existed throughout the Old and Middle Kingdoms and continued during the New Kingdom[16], and the same seems to hold with drafting. A good example is the 5th Dynasty Abusir Papyri, which records a series of monthly temple income accounts and lists. These were almost certainly produced from other documents and notes, which indicates that accounting techniques were evident during the Old Kingdom[17]. There still arises the question of where they were stored; there was either one central storage area or several places where individual scribes kept their own documents, which may well have been away from the village at their private houses, though the evidence is inconclusive.

Doubt is shed on the media distinction since there are examples of letters on both ostraca and papyrus which were given to the vizier[18], despite there being no evidence that summary records or accounts were also sent. The scribes of the village were suitably qualified and competent to perform the administration on behalf of the vizier, and sent details as and when necessary. An indication that this was done is indicated by P. Abbot 6.23 which states that officials of the Tomb travelled north to where the vizier was, with their memoranda (*sḫ3w*)[19]. It is possible that some ostraca were kept while others were discarded and reused, so overall, ostraca as objects undoubtedly performed a different number of roles within the community.

The expense involved in acquiring the raw material would have been an issue, but there is no evidence to suggest that papyrus was too expensive to use. The labour involved in preparation resulted in a significant cost of papyrus, perhaps the equivalent of several days' ration payments of a workman for a roll[20]. Although there are many examples of papyri being cut up and reused, or used as a palimpsest where writing has been washed away and replaced[21], the reason was not one of expense but whether it was readily available, especially given that the village was relatively isolated and goods were delivered at irregular intervals[22]. Availability was a major issue, if something was easy to get hold of and it was suitable, it would have been used, as ostraca were at Deir el-Medina.

can not be discounted. They were cheap, easily cleaned and, therefore, the records would not have survived.

16 Donker van Heel (2003: 6) provides some examples of both ostraca and papyri, but not from a ration payment administrative context.

17 As an example, this is indicated by two accounts lists which have been replicated by Kemp (1989:114-5, 118-9), a daily income for the temple for one month and an inventory list.

18 For examples, see Donker van Heel (2003: 31-32).

19 For a detailed discussion of the use of *sḫ3w* "memorandum", see Haring (2003: 108-110).

20 A general statement put forward by Bagnall (1995: 13) but without reference to any place or time period.

21 Examples of the reuse of papyrus include P. Turin 1888+2085 rt., P. Turin 1898+1926+1937+2094 rt. IV/V and P. Turin 1906+1939+2047 rt. IV and vs. Ostraca were also reused, such as O. Cairo CG 25512 and O. Turin 57072.

22 Eyre (1980: 44-45).

The general consensus is that the inhabitants abandoned Deir el-Medina in around Year 8 of Ramesses XI, but there is no direct evidence to back this up.[23] All that can safely be stated is that the move took place some time during the reigns of the last three kings of the 20th Dynasty and that it was probably a gradual process. It is not known how many of the workmen moved to the temple at Medinet Habu, only that it became the administrative centre for the Necropolis. After the move, the scribes had better access to a papyrus supply at the administration centre of the temple, which was undoubtedly one reason for the increase in its usage. In contrast, it was less convenient to obtain limestone flakes to use as ostraca. With the temple already in use, any storage facilities could be used for matters involving the workmen in addition to the existing material with little change in methodology required on the part of the scribes. The reason behind the increased use of papyrus owed more to the convenience of supply and it suitability than to economic cost of production or the rate of literacy[24].

§2.2 The "Journal of the Necropolis"

Most of the texts which record deliveries, rations, trade, disputes, watch duty and contact with outside the village come from Deir el-Medina itself. Within this group is the "Journal of the Necropolis", an important series of texts for aiding in determining the presence, or otherwise, of any patterns in the delivery of rations. What is usually meant by the term "Journal of the Necropolis[25]" is a large group of ostraca dating from Year 24 of Ramesses III through to the early part of the reign of his successor, Ramesses IV (Year 3), and includes the group O. DeM 32-47 from the Kom Sud. There was certainly material outside this time period written on both ostracon and papyrus which were part of the Journal. Documents such as P. Greg from between Years 5 and 7 of Siptah, P. Turin 1884+2067+2071+2105 and P. Turin 2013+2050+2061, dating to Ramesses IX towards the end of the occupation of the village, were also part of a journal, and show that it was kept for periods outside the core period for which the majority of the evidence survives. The number of Journal texts that have been lost, or remain undiscovered, can only be imagined. Despite this, it is not known whether or not there was a continuous series of documents or a single set of records written throughout the life of the community of workmen, though the Journal should be viewed as a variety of records of activity, events, absences and commodity distribution that were of interest to the community.

It is often overlooked that the component of the Journal dating from Ramesses III to Ramesses IV related almost invariably to the Right side of the workmen[26]. So for this side, it recorded the name of the watchman on duty, the daily distribution of provisions recorded by the scribes at the

23 A brief discussion of issues such as the date, place, and possible reasons behind the move, are discussed by Häggman (2002: 319-325).

24 Estimated by Baines & Eyre (1983: 86) at between 5% and 7.5% of the village population, or five times the national rate, with the increased literacy rate being a reflection of the large amount of contact with writing.

25 Hereafter referred to simply as the "Journal", although "Journal texts would be better, since the idea of a single comprehensive daybook can be dismissed.

26 The same watch duty system already existed earlier, at the end of the 19th Dynasty, see Collier (1996). Although most of the evidence is for the Right side, there are a few ostraca which seem to prove that the same system also functioned for the Left side.

Enclosure[27] at Deir el-Medina as well as special events such as the death of Ramesses III and visits by the vizier. These ostraca are the most precisely dated of the texts as there is often a year recorded in addition to the month and day. Crucially, the name of the workman who was on watch duty was recorded after the date in the majority of cases, and it is this information which can often enable us to allocate an ostracon to a date even when one is not fully recorded. This same workman was responsible for deliveries at the Enclosure. Helck[28] was able to draw up a duty roster or "Turnus List" which followed a strict rotation, only changing upon retirement or death of a workman, a move to the other side of the gang or, as at the accession of Ramesses IV, an increase in the workforce. From this it is even possible to chart the career progression of some individuals.

It has been estimated that throughout the entire period of the Journal, 96 months, around 100 ostraca were written, of which forty-one are known to have survived[29]. If, as is almost certainly the case, it related to one side only, then the percentage of the whole journal which has survived is likely to be about 20%. The records for the other side are either undiscovered, so there may well be a further large scale deposit yet to be found, or else they have been irretrievably lost.

It is interesting to note what does not appear in the Journal records. Apart from rations, which were sometimes recorded as being delivered by a given individual and other times as a mere notification that they were delivered, there is no record of other grain deliveries in the form of emmer and barley. Other products delivered include firewood, fish, vegetables and pottery, but there is little evidence for gypsum or pigments, which were key components in the preparation of tombs. The commodities in the Journal were non-daily but regularly delivered items which were individually small and portable, not valuable and perhaps not of great importance. This may explain the relatively few Journal ostraca which include ration deliveries; a subject which will be returned to in due course. As a result, the implications of the Journal ostraca are more indirect; they can be examined for any pattern in ration deliveries and any absences can be noted, in which case there must have been a record which was either lost or written separately on a different ostracon. Therefore it is unlikely that the Journal will directly aid the investigation of accounting procedures, but could provide a framework in terms of time and instances of deliveries to which other material can be added.

§2.3 Methodology and problems encountered

The approach taken is to collect the primary sources, tabulate them into three relevant groups based initially on date, from which further tables can be drawn up, and present the results in the form of a discussion which includes not only the recording, which is seen today, but also aspects of reality relating to the physical procedure of ration delivery. By including this, and by not restricting the study to only the final product of the accounting and recording procedures, it not only alleviates the sometimes abstract nature of recording figures and accounting, but more

27 For an ongoing discussion on the *ḫtm n pꜣ ḫr*, see Ventura (1987); McDowell (1990: 93-105); Burkard (2006); Koh (2006); and Eyre (2009).

28 Helck (1955: 27-38), and subsequently added to. The result is the Turnus Lists included on the Deir el-Medina Database.

29 Janssen (1992: 85). This may be a slightly optimistic figure based on a shorter time period as opposed to the 104-month period proposed below.

importantly, it provides reasons for such recording, how and why certain procedures took place and the physical reality of the process where possible. There are many areas where the evidence is not forthcoming, so some suggestions will be made; these are stated with the discussions taking a more logical, but also more speculative course.

This approach seems to fit well with most of the current research on Deir el-Medina, which for the most part is less concerned with the archaeology and more about social life and reality. The structure of the project was chosen because it follows concepts through from start to finish, and also because it will indicate areas where the evidence is not available or has not survived, so future work can use the framework to produce more definitive results should more material be found. With a subject like accounting, even if most modern concepts were not yet developed by the end of the second millennium BC, the ancient data can be explored to search for any realistic equivalents. Examples of this are the writing up of delivery records at least in part before the event itself, the closing off of the books at the end of a month, evidence for external checking and stock movement. Looking for the presence, or otherwise, of such practices in a Ramesside setting can not only allow a direct comparison with modern techniques—although the value of such a comparison would be limited—but one avenue of future research could be to trace the development of accounting systems through time incorporating other civilisations such as Mesopotamia, Classical Greece and Rome.

§2.3.1 Selection of the material

To create a corpus of documents, the selection of the material was initiated by inserting "grain", "rations", "wages" and the transliteration equivalents into the Deir el-Medina Database. A substantial list of results was extracted which was narrowed down to 165 documents once the context of each was examined. This was done by directly translating the relevant part of the text or examining the context, thereby providing a comprehensive list of examples which could be explicitly listed, and which would allow sorting and analysis in a manner appropriate to the requirements of the study. Naturally, there were a small number of examples which did not show up this way and these came to light usually as a result of background reading, such as those recording the delivery of grain, or texts without any obvious connection via the database to wages or rations. These were examined wherever possible, and added to the corpus if it became obvious that rations were being detailed. However, in the majority of these, the grain is not for the workmen but used as offerings for mortuary cults or used during festivals, even if the possibility of redistribution is strong.

Not all texts exhibit clearly the features and details which would be expected, leading to the problem of ambiguity. Some texts which are clearly ration texts, but not labelled as such, record individuals receiving specified amounts, while a moderate number[30] record the delivery of rations as a very short entry in a single line, but this was not an indication that rations were delivered to the village from outside. The lack of any supplementary details is down to a lesser degree of importance and the need to provide additional details as part of the Journal. Occasionally it is

30 O. Berlin 12631 rt. 11 (and rt. 17 for previous months); O. Berlin 12633 vs. 3 and rt. 3; O. DeM 32 rt. 12; O. DeM 38, 10; O. DeM 42 vs. 8; O. DeM 43 vs. 9; O. DeM 44 rt. 19; O. DeM 45 rt. 19; O. DeM 156 rt. 6; O. DeM 159, 6; O. DeM 162 rt. 8 (date lost); O. DeM 288, 3; O. DeM 427 vs. 9; O. Turin 57043 rt. 9; O. Turin 57072 rt. 1-2; O. UC 39648, 7.

not clear if the records indicated this or a distribution to the workmen[31]. In these cases the latter is assumed, while a handful of others are lists of individual lines consisting merely of a day and amount[32] and no indication of any location or recipients.

Sometimes a delivery was recorded as being by a named or titled individual[33], and sometimes to a specific location[34]. Such records were common in, but not exclusive to, ostraca from the Journal. However, although most of the texts in the Journal are dated, they are not accounts or delivery schedules and they do not record any amounts. Therefore, one could argue that they lack the necessary details to include them in any statistical analysis. This highlights a second potential problem in the interpretation of ration lists: the difference between bringing rations in from the granaries of Thebes to the village and the handing out of grain to the workmen. At first glance, the short Journal entries appear to be instances where rations were brought to the village from outside, but the use of *dit diw*, "distribution of rations", indicates that this was not the case. Only on O. DeM 153 vs. 9, O. Strasbourg H117, 1, O. Turin 57429, 11 and probably on O. DeM 712, is it indicated, by the use of *šsp* "received" and *iw* "delivered", that rations had been brought from the supplies in Thebes. Therefore, although the terms "distribution" and "delivery" are used interchangeably, where the delivery is from Thebes this will be clearly stated.

Despite this, since much of the analysis will be based on the proportion of the time period for which we have records, the pool of documents will include texts which are distribution schedules or accounts and also those which are mere statements of delivery. During the 104 months from Year 25 IV *šmw* to Year 2 III *prt*, even allowing for the years 29 and 30 for which we have very few Journal entries (but several non-Journal lists), they survive for 34 months or 33% of this time period for the one side of the crew; and half this for the workforce as a whole. When attempting to ascertain the presence or absence of any patterns in ration deliveries, examination of the Journal is necessary (see Appendix 1), together with additional material which can be dated and included with the Journal texts.

In order to facilitate detailed statistical analysis, it is important to be clear about what is meant by an "example", given that not all texts have the same number of records. This leads us to the third potential problem, which is the difference between the number of texts examined and the number of examples within the texts. To highlight this, there are two areas of ambiguity with any possible selection; firstly multiple dates within the same text, and secondly deliveries of *diw* and *dni* on the same date or in the same document. In addition, *diw* and *dni* are not always implicitly recorded, so we have to assume that any non-labelled text and amounts relate to *diw* unless the numerical values clearly imply *dni*, and these will be highlighted in the analysis. There are two

31 O. Ashmol. 11 vs. 3; O. Ashmol. 274, 5-8 (ends of lines are lost); O. Cairo 25280, 1-2; O. Cairo 25533, vs. 9-10; O. Strasbourg H117, 3.

32 O. DeM 712; O. DeM 838; O. DeM 844.

33 O. Ashmol. 107, 2 (Hori); O. Ashmol. 200, 2 (Min[...]); O. Ashmol. 274, 5 (water-carrier Ash[...]); O. Cairo 25280, 1-2 (scribe Amenemipet); O. DeM 34 rt. 11 (water-carrier Panebdemi); O. DeM 577 rt. 7 (Bakenwerner) and vs. 1 (Seti); O. Turin 57429, 11-12 (Pia, two successive months, although no commodity is shown as being delivered); O. UC 39661, 2 (scribe Hori).

34 O. Ashmol. 200 rt. 4 (placed "on the shore"); O. DeM 840, 3 (*ḫtm n pꜣ ḫr*); O. Michaelides 73, 3 (*pꜣ ḫtm*).

distinct dates of ration distribution recorded on five documents[35] which provide a total of ten examples for the analysis and not only five, since selecting lines to be discarded from the analysis would render it useless. The accounting techniques used for individual deliveries and distribution of *diw* and *dni* can differ; the amounts recorded being one example, therefore the importance of separating them can not be understated. As a result, a further eleven texts[36] record separate distribution of both *diw* and *dni* and this separation will provide an additional eleven examples. It is irrelevant whether there were records of *diw* and *dni* on the same day or not, the analysis would count them as two distinct examples. Given these potential problems and solutions, statistical analysis must be performed on the number of examples, and not the number of texts.

§2.3.2 Dating the material

In any study on administration over a period of time, it does not come as a surprise that the dating of the documents is paramount to the whole study. Dates have been assigned over the years by scholars such as Kitchen, Helck and Collier and are summarised on the Deir el-Medina Database for each document, which was noted with its date and the dates the rations related to, including the day, season and year wherever possible. Despite having this information readily accessible, there are still a number of problems with dating which will be explained in the following paragraphs, so each provided date was verified prior to inclusion. The material selected was split further into documents dated before Ramesses IX[37] and those after, with the latter group consisting entirely of papyri. The earlier group was split into two, depending if the delivery consisted of basic or additional rations. The result is the lists shown in Tables 1, 2 and 3, which are presented in such a way that the required information relating to variances in delivery period can easily be extracted.

There are also occasions where the date of recording is doubtful, but an educated reading can be surmised, perhaps one which would not be regarded as significant to the results. The exact day may not be stated[38], may be omitted completely[39], or occasionally there may be an error in the writing itself[40]. Occasionally dates are recorded within the body of the text, but the condition of the ostracon, usually as a result of part of the sherd being broken and lost, has rendered it impossible to ascertain the date of the ration delivery[41]. This last group of ostraca has not been included in the analysis which follows. The dates of the period covered rarely mention anything other than the month or months the rations relate to.

The dating of texts and therefore their placement in chronological order is problematic, since apart from the Journal texts, few record complete dates with regnal year and month. Furthermore, since the format of the texts and palaeography are limited, the examination of names is still

35 O. Cairo 25685; O. DeM 153; O. DeM 381; O. DeM 621; O. Munich ÄS 397.

36 O. Ashmol. 111; O. Cairo 25685; O. DeM 179; O. DeM 184; O. DeM 252; O. DeM 374; O. DeM 382; O. DeM 737; O. DeM 845; O. DeM 849; and O. Strasbourg H110.

37 It will become clear that the period between the end of the reign of Ramesses IV and the start of that of Ramesses IX is one where there are no texts which can be dated with any degree of certainty, so the time split for the material is a natural one for the purposes of the present study.

38 On O. DeM 345, the date recorded could be any day between 10 and 19 inclusive.

39 O. Cairo 25608.

40 O. DeM 184, 1, where Černý has indicated a probable error in the month.

41 O. DeM 162 rt.; O. Turin 57043; O. UC 39648.

probably the best dating criteria[42]. The Journal texts record names and complete dates during a relatively short period, and even when regnal years 1 and 2 are shown, the presence of the names makes it clear the reign is that of Ramesses IV. Thus a framework can be made from these texts, to which other texts without full dates can be added. A large proportion of the available material relates to the period from Year 25 of Ramesses III through to Year 4 of Ramesses IV, after which relatively few individuals can be attested with complete confidence[43]. Even within the Journal, there are periods for which we have very few Journal texts, for example during Years 29[44] and 30 of Ramesses III. Caution must be made with texts dated to "Year 4" for example, where there is a strong temptation to rigidly assign a text to a specific king, usually Ramesses IV, V or VI[45] where, in reality, there is no certainty of correct allocation. Often, the best we can do is to provide only a rough date, in which case the ostraca would be grouped aside from the securely dated documents. As a result, the wider dating range of texts, such as "Mid 20th Dynasty" or "Late Ramesses III –Ramesses VI" allows for a greater margin of error while using any information which relies on dating and we run the risk of arriving at incorrect conclusions.

Appendix 1 incorporates a reconstruction, as far as is possible, of the Journal of the Necropolis covering the period from Year 25 of Ramesses III to Year 2 of Ramesses IV. The methodology is effectively the same as that employed by Janssen[46], with some additions, although there are a couple of dates where this study differs from his. Janssen's original dating of O. DeM 160[47] has been corrected on the Deir el-Medina Database and is included, being assigned to months I and II *šmw* of Year 1 of Ramesses IV, based on the duty rota. O. DeM 169 has been dated to Year 25 I *šmw*, since it joins with O. Berlin 12633, as opposed to Year 28 II *šmw*, for which we have no records, but the duty rota is the same for both periods. A broken line indicates a lost or damaged part of the text, while a text in brackets signifies that the text was not part of the Journal, but can be dated correctly. Therefore it can be seen how valuable the Journal is with its associated duty rota, and where a low regnal year can be assigned specifically to Ramesses IV, and thus enabling other texts to be fitted into the correct place.

42 Strongly implied by Eyre (1987b: 27). A detailed study on the known names of the inhabitants of the village has been provided by Davies (1999), including lineage of several families so there is some degree of certainty as to the identification of certain individuals who worked at a given time.

43 Eyre, *ibid.*, 28, also states that this date is used as a criterion for ante quem dating.

44 II *prt* 10 in Year 29 is the start of the workmen's strike, which is covered by P. Turin 1880. This may explain the absence of journals as the scribes' attention may have been elsewhere. However, for a community which was so thorough in its record keeping, this is unlikely to have been a major reason.

45 A criticism levelled by Eyre (1987b: 27) at Gutgesell's dating methodology. In addition, some of the dates assigned by Helck (2002) are incorrect, such as O. DeM 654 (p. 275) where no month or year are recorded, and O. Gardiner AG 102 (pp. 284-5). O. Turin 57043 (p. 268) has been dated by Helck to Year 25 despite the complete absence of both a year and names.

46 Years 31 Ramesses III to 2 Ramesses IV, see Janssen (1975: 467-468).

47 Janssen (1975: 466). Originally placed in III – IV Peret.

§2.3.3 Data presentation and analysis

Prior to presenting the data, it is necessary to understand the terminology used in ration accounting. Chapter 3 takes the approach initiated by Haring[48] in discussing vocabulary and terminology, and divides it into two parts. The first and shorter section expands Haring's work by including words and phrases which are not restricted solely to document headings. Of considerably more importance is the second part, which focuses on vocabulary used within an accounting context. A wide range of words is examined, and a comprehensive number of detailed examples is provided and tested in an attempt to provide specific meanings to the vocabulary. In addition, the reasons behind their use are engaged, including the position within the text itself and possible formatting functions, together with any possible complementary usages.

Data is presented and analysed in two significant chapters, which concentrate on the frequency distributions of two distinct aspects of ration deliveries. The first of these, Chapter 4, explores and examines in detail the days and months of ration payments. Concentrating specifically on the dates allows the analysis of the data which can be done in two ways, either statistically or visually. By having a number of tables, it is possible to extract certain data to answer specific questions based primarily not only on the days, but also the decades and months of delivery. The same data is provided in visual form as scatter diagrams, which are particularly useful in showing visual trends over the course of the month between the different data sets, indicating any preferences for ration deliveries during specific work days or weekends, comparing data from different periods, and trying to explain any differences or similarities in delivery patterns. A number of tables and associated scatter diagrams are drawn up for a number of different criteria, for example whether the ration was *diw* or *dni*, or whether the date of the ration payment took place in the 19th Dynasty, from early to the middle of the 20th Dynasty, or the late 20th Dynasty. A statistical test can then be carried out on selected data sets aimed at inter-population relationships and variances between the date of a document and the actual dates of delivery. Finally, the variances are examined to determine the extent and degree of arrears in rations paid and any evidence for advances.

The Journal of the Necropolis supplies a large component of the evidence drawn upon to enable the production of a daily calendar covering a period of several years, and this is provided as Appendix 1. Each full date when a delivery was recorded is noted on the calendar, highlighting the high degree of days for which no delivery was recorded as well as trying to emphasize the presence or absence of any patterns of delivery. With the aid of existing literature[49], the calendar also shows the known festivals held at Deir el-Medina, allowing investigation into any possible connection between festival dates and ration payments as well as providing a framework for future additions in the knowledge base.

For the purposes of allocating material to specific time groupings, Haring's divisions into four groups[50] have been adhered to throughout, thus providing a direct link to existing publications without the need to confuse matters by supplying additional dating variables. There is no indication in the textual record exactly what a complete ration list was in terms of the amounts paid to the workmen; in addition this is new territory previously unexplored. Therefore, the detailed

48 Haring (2003b:124 ff.).

49 Sadek (1964); Vleeming (1982); Sadek (1988); Wikgren (2005); and Jauhiainen (2009).

50 Haring (2003b: 136-139). This split is also used in the discussion of vocabulary and terminology.

investigation of the content of the ration lists is one area where assumptions have to be made. These assumptions are dependent upon the size of the workforce during each of the three periods being examined[51].

This leads on to the second significant area of data management, which relates to the investigation of who received the rations specified and the amounts paid. Both aspects are discussed in Chapter 5 with the aid of tables and associated scatter diagrams. After the preliminary exercise of checking that the rations attributable to the workmen are correct by examining a large selection of documents from all the relevant periods, the chapter adopts two avenues of questioning, both of which need the creation of a benchmark to work with. Only with such arbitrary creations is it then possible to take the existing material and provide accurate results.

The first line of approach looks into the average number of categories of workmen recorded as receiving rations on any given document for the 19th and mid 20th Dynasties, taking O. DeM 376 and O. Cairo 25608 as complete records for these two periods respectively. These two examples have the longest list within the entire corpus, since both have eight classes of recipient, namely the foreman, scribe, doorkeeper, the generic "men" and so forth. A statistical test is performed on the data to check for any significant differences in the recording of ration recipients during the two periods, and the results are presented on a scatter diagram, with possible reasons for any differences being discussed. The second exercise is performed in a similar manner, but requires the creation of what would be considered to be a complete ration list, if every member of one side of the workforce received his complete monthly ration. This total ration amount is created for both periods; the first covering the period when ostraca were predominantly used, and the second is represented by the later Ramesside papyri. The documents are looked at individually, and the total rations recorded on each document, whether explicitly stated as a total or calculated as a series of additions, are converted into a value equal to the percentage of the assumed "complete ration text". The results are shown as a bar chart, and the reasons for intra-period differences are discussed.

§2.3.4 Accounting and recording

Examining the scribal preparation of the documents in detail brings into question aspects of reality, for example whether the scribes prepared their documents in advance and whether they carried out their recording at the same time the workmen were paid. Chapter 6 engages these topics, starting with an investigation of a selection of ostraca, where the hieratic writing itself is closely scrutinised to gain insights into how they were written, the frequency of pen dips, and the possibility that scribes wrote the body of their material prior to being present at the time of payment. Not only do the procedures at the end of the month undoubtedly differ from those adopted today, but they also differ depending upon what commodity is being accounted for, as some consumables such as wood and fish were quota-based while grain was not. Evidence from both papyri and ostraca are examined to disclose the manner in which emmer and barley were recorded, whether the tendency was to record them separately or together within the documents. The chapter finishes with a look at a selection of accounting procedures which are absent from the ration records, and also discusses themes such as accounting concepts, stock valuation and

51 Haring's Groups I and II are treated together due to the lack of material available for either period.

taxation, and exploring the possibility that the ancient Egyptians had any kind of equivalent procedures in the payment process.

The content of the documents is the focus of Chapter 7, with the emphasis placed on the amounts, addition and multiplication used. Janssen's brief section[52] is expanded upon by using a larger body of material encompassing the whole of the Ramesside period, but taking a different approach by checking the material for numerical irregularities without assuming that these are all errors. The documents are examined and all the "errors" in the ration material are collated and arranged into a number of categories as to the type of difference contained; possible errors in the totals and the addition; and omission of words and individuals. Based on the sample size available, an estimate is made as to the proportion of documents containing "errors", which leads onto the final discussions on whether the differences are errors or deliberate mathematical approximations of reality, and the magnitude of the differences and whether they mattered in the context of an ancient non-monetary society.

Chapter 8 combines two issues for which a number of suggestions have to be made, these being the recording and physicality of the supply of rations. Due largely to a shortage of available evidence, the source of the grain is an often neglected aspect of the distribution system, so consequently the chain of supply is included partly for completeness in the entire delivery procedure, and partly because of its direct relevance to rations. The chapter shifts towards the physical procedure of ration distribution, examining the supply chain of grain from the field to the village. The only evidence at the initial stage of the supply process for grain specifically stated to be for rations is contained within the Turin Taxation Papyrus, so a brief discussion of the relevant portions of this lengthy document is included to provide insights into the recording and accountability of the transport procedure, as well as indicating some of the source locations for ration grain. Although a relatively short section, it is important to explore the complete transportation and recording process where the evidence allows; although the locations of the granaries in Thebes are not known, the names of many of them are preserved in the documentary evidence.

The final part of the study pieces together all the evidence and proposes a theoretical model of ration delivery and distribution, in terms of the physical procedure, recording, and accountability within each stage of the process. This is done by taking the evidence we have and suggesting necessary notions where there are obvious gaps in the material, based on perceived reality, logical possibilities and also the occasional comparison from elsewhere. Three broad stages have been identified: the first traces the grain from the field to the granaries of Thebes, the second follows it from there to the village enclosure, and the final stage is from the enclosure to the homes of the workmen. A complete picture of the entire procedure has not been attempted, so there is plenty of scope for adjustments and additions to the model should further material become available.

52 Janssen (2005: 151).

CHAPTER 3

VOCABULARY & TERMINOLOGY

In order to get a good idea of the terminology used within ration documents prior to any in-depth data analysis, a thorough investigation of words and phrases which the scribes used as standard expressions will be carried out, in addition to looking for other idioms more rarely used. Documents will be split up into specified periods of time within the Ramesside period and the use of vocabulary will be compared, and where possible, any significant changes between the periods will be examined along with the reasons behind the use or absence of, individual words. Work has been done specifically on document headings on a broad range of content[1], but not on similar vocabulary used within the body of documents, and little has been done on terminology used within an accounting context. Although restricted to ration accounting, there is considerable scope to expand the discussion into accounting for other commodities as well as other fields of study within the village[2].

The format and content of documents varies according to the type of text, be it from the Journal of the Necropolis, a delivery note or a more lengthy account of distribution, and also the genre of the text. Since detailed lexicographical research would form a lengthy study in its own right, the analysis which follows is context bound, and will only include ration texts. The purpose is not to include every example from every kind of text, but to define these terms within these confined parameters and focus on key words within the rations subset. Haring has produced a detailed analysis on the headings of many different types of document, including those of ration distribution[3], but the study concentrates solely on the initial headings. He has two criteria for text selection: the formula must occur either in the first lines of a text, or after a date at the beginning of the text[4]. In contrast, the present study incorporates texts where such formulae are not neces-

1 Haring (2003a), Haring (2003b: 124-181).

2 A significant number of phrases and words has been catalogued with reference to a brief selection of quoted texts by Helck (1974: 127-132). These relate to many genres of document; only a very small selection of these can be applied to ration texts.

3 Haring (2003b: 136-139).

4 Haring (2003b: 124).

sarily on the first line. Since many ration texts have multiple sections, the formulae are examined in order to analyse a broader range of uses, making it is likely that different terminology is used at different stages within a document. Furthermore, additional accounting terminology will be examined in detail to ascertain its precise meaning from as many surviving examples as possible.

The content of the document and whether or not other formulae are used in the body of the text may indicate differences in scribal techniques depending on the type of document and its date. The documentation of Deir el-Medina during the Ramesside period was not constant in style, but shows significant differences. So in order to make any time comparisons possible, as in the previous chapter, Haring's division of the dates of the texts into distinct groups is utilised and noted again as a memory aid[5].

1st half Dynasty 19	Ramesses I – Year 38 Ramesses II	*c.*1295–1239 BC	Group I
2nd half Dynasty 19	Year 38 Ramesses II – Tausret	*c.*1239–1186 BC	Group II
1st half Dynasty 20	Setnakht – Ramesses VIII	*c.*1186–1127 BC	Group III
2nd half Dynasty 20	Ramesses IX – Ramesses XI	*c.*1127–1070 BC	Group IV

§3.1 Headings and expressions used within documents

§3.1.1 *dit diw*, "giving/distribution of rations"

dit diw n 3bd x[6]	O. Ashmol. 184, 1	Group II
	O. DeM 45, rt. 19	Group III
dit diw n3 rmṯ p3 ḫr[7]	P. Turin 2015, 1	Group IV
dit r diw n 3bd x[8]	O. DeM 621, rt. 1	Group II
date + *dit diw n 3bd x*[9]	O. DeM 611, 2	Group II
	O. DeM 852, rt. 1	Group I
dit diw n 3bd ḫ m-drt NN	O. Ashmol. 107, 1	Group III

5 Haring (2003b: 126). In addition, note 4 gives a breakdown of all presently known texts, in percentages, attributed to each period, with the majority of the dated texts being from the late 19th Dynasty or the early 20th. 42% are undated.

6 Also O. Ashmol. 262, 2 (undated); O. Berlin 10661, 3; Group III); O. Berlin 12631, rt. 15 (Group III); O. Berlin 12631, vs.7 (a small damaged part may also read *p3 dit diw*; Group III); O. Berlin 14210, 1 (Group III); O. BM EA 50739, 1 (Group II); O. Cairo 25685, rt. 5 (undated); O. Cairo 25809, rt. 1-2 (Group II); O. Cairo 25809, vs. 1 (Group II); O. DeM 42, vs. 8 (Group III); O. DeM 252, 1 (Group III); O. DeM 384, II:1 (Group III); O. DeM 427, vs. 12 (preceded by day; Group III); O. DeM 638, rt. a.1 (undated); O. DeM 734, 1 (undated); O. Munich ÄS 397, 1-2 (Group III); P. Turin 2013 + 2050 + 2061, rt. I:x + 7 (Group IV). Sometimes this is preceded by the present passive element *iw.tw* such as O. DeM 38, 10 (Group III) and O. DeM 156, rt. 6 (Group III).

7 Also line 6 of the same text.

8 The initial part of *dit* is broken, so this may be part of a participle *rdyt* or less likely *inyt*. Also rt. 6.

9 Also O. Cairo 25698, 1 (Group III); O. DeM 276, 2 (not *n 3bd* but both sides; Group III); O. DeM 345, rt. 5 (Group III); O. DeM 379, 2 (Group III); O. DeM 737, 1 (undated); O. DeM 852, vs. 1 (Group II).

date + *dit diw n 3bd ḫ m-drt NN*[10]	O. DeM 153, rt. 3-4	Group III
	O. DeM 381 rt.1	Group III
dit diw n (date) *in* NN	P. Turin 2013+2050+2061, rt. 2:6	Group IV

Despite there being several minor variations in the composition, this is the most frequently used formula in the Deir el-Medina ration texts, with the most basic form being used on ostraca from the second half of the 19th Dynasty through to at least the reign of Ramesses IV and beyond. Not restricted to ostraca, the common use of the formula is demonstrated by the numerous examples in the papyri, of which only a small number have been noted. Used both at the start of a document and also included further down, almost invariably was this formula followed by a list of ration recipients. Ironically, most of the documents where a month/day precedes the formula can only be assigned an approximate date. A simple statement, its most basic form was used to write Journal entries as a notification that some rations were delivered on a given day. Sometimes this was done *m-drt* (lit. "through the hand of") an individual who was often a scribe. However, in these cases it was likely to have been under the supervision of the scribe, who would not have carried out the physical tasks, and it was actually delivered by other personnel such as a water-carrier who was a member of the *smdt n bnr*, the support staff[11].

If, and it must be stressed that there is no proof to substantiate this, the Journal documents were kept as official records in the *ḫtm n p3 ḫr*, (the Enclosure of the Tomb[12]), and the rations were paid by the state from state supplies, it was important that the proper administrative procedure was carried out, including the names of those who either brought or supervised the delivery of rations. Unlike commodities such as wood, for which each woodcutter had a monthly quota[13] and thus the recording of deliveries and names was necessary, the identity of the individual delivering rations was not important. For these reasons the length of Journal entries was kept to a minimum, with the scribe using his name perhaps to demonstrate that he was in charge.

The shorter versions of the formula were not restricted to Journals, but did tend to be used as headings in the first couple of lines or halfway down the text in cases where deliveries were made and distributed to members of both sides, or related to two different months, such as O. DeM 345. On O. DeM 381 recto the formula is used as a header *m-drt* an individual whose name is lost (*p3…?*), but on the verso there is no heading and the delivery is *m-drt* Eferikh (probably the water-carrier). On each side is a detailed distribution account to members of the crew, including the captains, so perhaps it was only necessary to state "distribution of rations" once, despite the verso being dated two months later than the recto.

10 Also O. DeM 159, 6 (Group III); O. UC 39661, 1 (relates to *dni*; Group III); and possibly O. DeM 381, rt. 1 (*n 3bd* may be lost in the lacuna; Group III).

11 Several studies have gone into detail on the support staff (*smdt*) and their activities, including Janssen (1997: 1-8) and Häggman (2002: 94-106). Deliveries were probably written out by the smdt scribes and Hori was in essence in charge of them; there is little evidence to identify these scribes individually.

12 The location of this entity is still unknown and has facilitated much debate. See Ventura (1987); McDowell (1990: 93-105); Burkard (2006); Koh (2006); and Eyre (2009).

13 Janssen (2003: 18).

hrw pn + dit diw in NN[14]	O. Cairo 25280, 1	Group III?
date + *hrw pn dit diw n ꜣbd ḫ m it m it*[15]	O. DeM 611, 2	Group I
date + *hrw pn dit diw n ꜣbd ḫ n smḥy*[16]	O. DeM 638a, 1	Undated
date + *hrw pn dit diw n ꜣbd ḫ ḥr pꜣ ḫtm*	O. Michaelides 73, 2	Group III
date + *dit diw dit n in-mw*	O. Ashmol. 274, 5	Undated
date + *dit diw m-drt NN*	O. Berlin 12631, rt. 11	Group III
date + *dit diw dit in sš*	O. DeM 10034, 1	Group III
date + *dit diw dit n tꜣy=i mwt m-drt NN*	O. Ashmol. 274, 6	Undated
date + *dit diw n ꜣbd ḫ ḥr pꜣ ḫtm n pꜣ ḫr*	O. DeM 386, 1-2	Group III
date + *dit diw n ꜣbd ḫ ḫtm n pꜣ ḫr*	O. DeM 840, 1-2	Undated
date + *dit diw n wnmy*[17]	O. DeM 10032, 2	Group III
dit <diw n> wnmy n ꜣbd ḫ pꜣ ḫtm n pꜣ ḫr	O. DeM 848, 1	Undated
tp n dit diw n pꜣ 43 rmṯ-ist	O. DeM 180. vs. 1	Group III
tp n dit diw nꜣ rmṯ pꜣ ḫr	P. Turin 2015, 9	Group IV
dit diw[18]	O. DeM 427, vs. 9	Group III
hrw pn iw=tw dit diw n tꜣ ist	O. UC 39648, 7	Group III

Some variations of the basic formula are recorded, with various components being included or omitted, such as *hrw pn* (this day), the month of delivery, the side of the crew which received the delivery, and who the delivery was made by. These longer forms were not part of Journal records, but were used as headings for ration distribution accounts. O. Ashmol. 274 is unusual in format, being more like a Journal, but it only records a handful of entries over a period of several months. Many are undated, but it appears that they were used at least during the late 19th and early 20th Dynasties. Those recording the *ḫtm* are short, and unfortunately can not reveal any further reason as to their composition, since it would have been the logical assumption that the *ḫtm* was the first drop off point for ration deliveries and any distribution to individual workmen would have come from there. Explaining the simple "giving of rations" as recorded on O. DeM 427, vs. 9, and O. IFAO 265, vs. 2, is not as easy as may be expected. We may expect this in Journals. The apparent lack of importance of rations in the latter document, which was not a journal, may be due to the writer being a novice scribe, a lack of space on the ostracon, or perhaps there were more pressing matters within the community at that time.

14 Also P. Turin 2097+2105, vs. 8, where the rations are distributed not by (*in*) an individual but "from the granary"; since P. Turin 2062, vs. 4 is damaged before and after this component, the exact terminology is lost.

15 Also P. Turin 2013+2050+2061, rt. x+4 (Group IV).

16 P. Turin 2081+2095, rt. 7 Col II (Group IV) records the recipients in standard list form.

17 Also O. Ashmol. 21, 1 (*n smḥy*; undated); O. IFAO 300, 5 (*n tꜣ ist*); and P. Turin 2097+2105, vs. 10 (*n tꜣ iswt*; Group IV).

18 O. IFAO 265, vs. 2 (Group III). Line 1 and the start of line 2 relate to other commodities. P. Turin 2097+2105, vs. 12 (Group IV) reads *dit diw pꜣ* after a date but the rest of the line, which probably relates to one or more individuals, is lost. No date precedes *dit diw nꜣ rmṯ pꜣ ḫr* on P. Turin 1898+1926+1937+2094, rt. 2:13 (Group IV).

§3.1.2 *pꜣ dit diw*, "THE GIVING/DISTRIBUTION OF RATIONS"

pꜣ dit diw tꜣ ist	O. Berlin 12633, rt. 3	Group III
pꜣ dit diw n ꜣbd[19]	O. Cairo 25608, rt. 2	Group III
pꜣ dit diw n ꜣbd m-drt NN	O. DeM 376, 1	Group I[20]
pꜣ dit diw m-drt NN	O. DeM 32, rt. 12	Group III
	O. DeM 34, rt. 11	Group III
pꜣ dit diw n ꜣbd <...> *in NN*	O. DeM 371, rt. 1	Undated

The only difference between this and Formula 1 is the inclusion of the definite article *pꜣ* at the start, so in reality it is a variant of the previous formula, which perhaps does little to prove anything other that there were many minor variations which existed throughout the Ramesside period. There are a small number of examples dating mainly from the time of Ramesses III, but O. DeM 376, which has been dated to Siptah, indicates the possible use of the formula at the end of the 19th Dynasty. By this time, the use of *pꜣ* was commonplace in written Late Egyptian, but even so, it is not clear how late the formula was used, but according to Helck, not after Year 28 of Ramesses III[21]. Like the first formula, the use of *m-drt* was prevalent in Journal records, and for the same reasons. There would have been longer versions like that recorded on the recto of O. DeM 371, a short note of delivery to a scribe and perhaps a number of workmen, but in this example the long heading accounts for half of the recto.

§3.1.3 *rdyt*, "WHAT WAS GIVEN (AS RATIONS)"

date + *rdyt r diw n ꜣbd x*[22]	O. DeM 621, rt. 6	Group II
rdyt r diw n pꜣ ꜥꜣ-n-ist	O. DeM 839, 1	Undated
rdyt r diw n nꜣ smdt m-drt pꜣ sš <*n*> *pꜣ ẖr*	P. Turin 2062, vs. 11	Group IV
pꜣ diw n pꜣ <...> *rdyt n=f*	O. Ashmol. 200, 7	Group I
rdyt n tꜣ šnwt	O. DeM 177, 4	Group II
rdyt n in-mw	O. Ashmol. 274, 3	Undated
date + *rdyt n tꜣ ḥmt*	O. DeM 707, 2	Group III

19 Also O. DeM 376, 11 (Group II?); O. DeM 377, rt. 3 (Group III); and O. DeM 382, 3-4 (Group III).

20 O. DeM 376 was found at the Grand Puits in 1949 with several other ration accounts from the 20th Dynasty, thus there is some doubt as to its date. The names recorded occur together in O. Strasbourg H110 from the 19th Dynasty, but almost certainly men with the same names lived together in the time of Ramesses III. See Donker van Heel (2003: 23-25).

21 Helck (1964b: 585).

22 O. Ashmol. 108, 4 (Undated); O. DeM 177, 1 (omits *r diw*; Group II); O. DeM 177, 9 (Group II); O. DeM 179, rt. 4 (Group II); O. DeM 184, rt. 1, 2 and 4 (Group III); O. DeM 184, vs. 3 (Group III); O. DeM 621, rt. 1 (Group II); O. DeM 739, 1 (undated); O. DeM 837, 3-4 (date as header; Group II). The date is not usually written before the formula. O. DeM 839, 2 (Group II) uses *wḥm* to introduce the formula to the same person as in line 1. Since the latter part of O. DeM 10039, rt. 1, is lost, the exact formula is unknown.

rdyt=f šsp m-drt NN	O. Michaelides 65, rt. 1	Group II
date + *rdyt r dni n prt*	O. Cairo JE 72455, rt. 1	Undated

The records which include *rdyt r diw* as part of their construction have many minor differentials in form, but generally the past passive participle *rdyt* tends to be followed by one or both of the associated months and the people, or occasionally the crew itself[23], to whom the rations were given. Many of the texts are dated to the 19th Dynasty, which would suggest that this formula may have been standard at the time[24], although this would assume that the small number of documents available is representative of the administration as a whole. There seems to be a slight tendency for the documents to be written as a list of names in continuous lines, but several are lists with each line covering a named individual. Of interest is the later example P. Turin 2062, vs. 11, which seems to record the rations being delivered to the *smdt m-drt*, (by) the scribe of the Tomb – an odd situation since we would expect the reverse.

The main difference is that in several instances the headings are incomplete compared with the *dit diw* variants. The word for rations is often omitted and the heading, where it is included on the recto, could be omitted completely on the verso, such as on O. DeM 179. The phrase *rdyt* is sometimes repeated in the text, and not always as part of the same phrase. This may imply that there was a lower degree of importance with its use in non-Journal texts. Rather than being unimportant, what was far more likely is that the officials knew what was being dealt with, and as is so often the case, that there was no need for extra detail.

O. Michaelides 65 rt. is simply headed *rdyt=f šsp m-drt NN*, "What he gave. Received through the hand of NN", followed by a short list of individuals, although there is no clarity whether *diw* or *dni* were actually delivered. Considerable amounts of detail are recorded on several occasions, such as O. DeM 179, rt. 4, which has a lengthy entry recording the side as well as the scribe through whose agency the delivery came. Similarly, O. DeM 621, rt. 6, records deliveries for both sides for the same month, using the full notation *rit wnmy* and *rit smḥw* for the two sides of the workforce, although the month is not explicitly stated in line 6. O. Ashmol. 108 rt. has a mixture of phrases used[25], with each phrase applying to a single line entry ending with a numerical value. Similarly, at least three different expressions are recorded on the verso of P. Turin 2097+2105, all after a date recorded in red ink[26].

23 Examples are O. DeM 707, 2 (Group III); O. Strasbourg H110, rt. 6 (Group II). Also on O. DeM 374, 7 (Group I or II), though this relates to dni.

24 Haring (2003b: 136). This is not to say that the formula was not used later, for example O. DeM 707, 2.

25 Rt. 1, *ꜥḥꜥ*; rt. 2, *diw n ꜣbd* without *rdyt*; rt. 3, *wḥm*; rt. 4, *wp=sn rdyt n=f r diw ꜣbd*.

26 Vs. 6, *hrw pn dit diw m tꜣ šnwt*; vs. 8, *hrw n šsp diw in iswt*; vs. 10, *dit diw n tꜣ iswt*. The beginnings of the first five lines are lost; from the remaining text of these lines it appears that there were three previous deliveries recorded, but apart from the possibility of *šsp* in line 2, the formulae are unknown.

§3.1.4 *iw*, "DELIVERED"

iw + date	O. Ashmol. 111, vs. 1	Group II
	O. Strasbourg H117, 1	Group III
date + *iw bty*	O. DeM 712, 2	Undated
iw m + date *m-drt* NN	O. Turin 57429, 11	Group I?

Of all the terminologies, *iw* is perhaps the most interesting since it has two distinct and yet perhaps interchangeable meanings. Context is important, as the differentiation between the physical process of *iw* "delivered" and the accounting process *iw* "entered" is a fine one. In a rations context, a very small number of documents use a variant of this formula instead of the more common examples detailed above. The earlier text O. Ashmol. 111 starts with *iw* as a heading and follows with the date and a broken line of text relating to a balance. The contrast between these lines and those following suggests that they were amounts brought from the external granaries as opposed to distributions to the workmen, which the later lines undoubtedly record. The damaged part of the first line of the verso hinders our interpretation somewhat; it is possible that this may be notification of the entry of a balance of an unclear commodity, which Kitchen transcribes as *bnri* "dates". O. Strasbourg H117 uses *iw* after the date as an introduction to the list of assorted temple commodities, including rations which were delivered from outside, and ending with totals and a balance. O. Turin 57429 shows a tendency to use the formula *iw m* + date *m-drt* an individual; despite the middle part of the ostracon being a delivery list of some kind of grain in the format one would expect from ration deliveries, the exact grain type is not recorded. O. DeM 712 is a delivery schedule of emmer with each line recording a single delivery, using the words *iw* on six occasions and *šsp* "received" on one occasion, to denote the smallest payment of ¼ *khar*.

This feels like a very informal and quick way of recording a delivery, so apart from a personal preference, why the scribe chose to record with this formula rather than the more detailed alternatives is not entirely clear. However, each of these texts may indicate that the commodities were deliveries from outside the village, those brought into Deir el-Medina on a donkey train, so the precise sense between what was a "delivery" and a "distribution" can be captured with this in mind. The more frequent use of *iw* in connection with other commodities such as fish and wood, which are known to have been delivered from outside, appears to confirm this[27]. Perhaps when emmer (*bty* or *bdt*) was delivered for some reason unclear to us, iw was the word of choice, but this is speculation. A possible, though not certain, explanation may be that the hieratic sign would stand out upon reading and that the sign may have been used as shorthand, but even so it does not explain why this phrase was preferred in certain instances. However, a mere four examples within a rations context are nowhere near enough to prove anything except that this form did exist in the scribal repertoire.

27 This is highlighted by Haring (2003b: 127) as being very common throughout the 19th and 20th Dynasties, perhaps also as a form of the shorter *m-drt NN*, but rarely used in the recording of rations. Valbelle (1976: 108) discusses some of the non-ration uses, and has suggested that *iw*, when used with *m-drt*, is an abbreviation of "to come", while *iw m-ʿ=f* shows an accomplishment (*ibid.*, 109).

§3.1.5 Other Formulae

date + *ỉnyt ỉn NN r pꜣ ẖtm*	O. DeM 380, 2	Group III

There are other phrases used in the ration texts for which we have but one or two examples. *ỉnyt* "what is brought" is used as a heading on O. DeM 380[28], and despite there being no record of rations (only "grain" in line 3), the commodity was brought by the scribe Hori to the Enclosure. Some of the amounts which follow are small, which may indicate *dnỉ*, but the list of recipients is in the standard format: the foreman, the scribe and a group of men. It was likely that rations were not always labelled as such, and many generic "grain" deliveries were in fact rations. Even so, the thought of the scribe bringing 26¼ *khar* of grain specifically to the Enclosure seems absurd, unless it was a transfer from one of the grain silos from the cemetery north west of the village.

date + *ỉw=w šsp dỉw n ꜣbd x*	O. DeM 153, vs. 9	Group III
date + *šsp bty*	O. DeM 712, 5	Undated
date + *hrw n šsp dỉw ỉn ỉswt*	P. Turin 2097+2105, vs. 8	Group IV

The Journal ostracon O. DeM 153 uses *ỉw=w šsp*, "they received", which puts the importance not on rations being delivered but on the fact that the workmen obtained them. Why this should have been written in isolation three years after the strikes of Year 29 is not clear, with the document being a record primarily of wood, fish and bread deliveries. However, a possible suggestion is that the scribe wrote the phrase through habit. Perhaps this was one scribe's method of expressing delivery[29], but since there are examples within Groups III and IV, this seems unlikely. We can only guess why the scribe of O. DeM 712 used *šsp* once in isolation instead of *ỉw*, used six times when recording emmer deliveries, since ¼ *khar* stated with other amounts of between ½ and 2¼ *khar* is not unusual. The use of *šsp* in one, possibly two, deliveries recorded on P. Turin 2097+2105 shows the continued, if rare, use of the term in rations texts[30] towards the end of the Ramesside period.

nkt ỉryt n dỉw n ꜣbd x	O. DeM 312, 1	Group II

28 This formula is used in delivery accounts for standard commodities such as grain and bread, and often a date is lacking, implying either that such a document was part of a larger group, some of which would have been dated, or it was meant to be read on the day of receipt only, similar to a delivery memo. See Haring (2003b: 128). O. Berlin 14264, rt. 1, starts with *ỉnyt m-ḏrt NN*, followed by a list of recipients.

29 Helck (1964b: 585). Eyre (1980: 172) suggests that *šsp* refers to something delivered and accounted for properly resulting in a complete transaction. This is quite possible, but surely there were more than a small handful of complete transaction in the documentary record.

30 *šsp* was not confined to ration texts. One of the many examples is P. Turin 1960+2071 (Group IV), which records both sides receiving lamp wicks (rt. 2:4 and 2:6). Faggots are received on P. Turin 1884+2067+2071+2105, rt. 2:5, and *ḥtri* on P. Turin 2004+2007+2057+2106, rt. 2:1. Valbelle (1976: 103) shows that in the Turin Taxation Papyrus, *šsp* is regularly used with several variations such as an associated date and the use of *m-drt*, and concludes that *šsp* could be replaced by rdi (*ibid.*, 107).

Unfortunately the beginning of each line is lost on O. DeM 312, a document unusual in its content, which should possibly not be included in the present study. The use of *iryt*, "which was done/made", may suggest that this is not a heading, but a statement relating to an action concerning rations and not about the actual ration delivery; its uniqueness in this context suggests this is likely.

Grammatically, *iw=w šsp* is of a narrative style with complete sentences, and together with the occasional different phrases in §3.1.5, this suggests a significant oral component within the village society despite the high literacy rate in Deir el-Medina[31]. This is augmented by the examination of the recipients of rations in the delivery lists, who were recorded in more or less the same order; maybe it became standard that the wording was read out and recorded by the scribe at the same time, but it does seem apparent that there was an order of workmen which was fixed in the mind of the scribe.

§3.2 Accounting terminology

Examining the material concerning rations and also other commodities throws up many vocabulary issues. Those dealt with above are mostly straightforward, but the precise meaning of certain words within the body of the documents can only be stated with confidence upon detailed investigation from as many examples as possible within a rations context, and these warrant an in-depth investigation, hence the full inclusion of relevant passages of text. In other words, the vocabulary can be tested against the data, with the most reasonable rendering being accepted. Some phrases used in the accounting procedure are rendered the same as would be expected, but others are more ambiguous and rely on the context of the word or phrase. Although primarily restricted to the Deir el-Medina ration texts, reference is made to words used in a series of grain accounts believed to have been complied in a state granary during the reign of Thutmose III[32].

An "account" is not to be taken as a narrative of how or why a process occurred, but more in context with *ḥsbw* "account", which in the majority of texts from Deir el-Medina relate to a list of items drawn up, perhaps for temple inspections, property divisions and other similar matters[33]. Neither this word, nor the word *snn*, usually translated as "list" or "account", is found in the ration corpus although the latter is more common in texts recording the delivery of bread and other temple consumables as in O. DeM 29. The layout of accounts in a very general sense varies considerably according to what is being recorded and its associated need, but this section will be confined solely to rations.

Accounting jargon varies in complexity; some words and phrases have a standard translation, in which case it is a pointless exercise looking in depth at every single text. In these situations, one example is enough to determine the meaning, but in other situations a more comprehensive

31 Since Deir el-Medina was a specialist community set up by the state for state activities, the high degree of contact with the central administration at Thebes serves as the basis for the assumption of there being a high literacy level. Baines and Eyre (1983: 90) estimate the literate percentage in Deir el-Medina to be 5%-7.5%, possibly five times as much as that of Egypt as a whole.

32 These grain accounts form P. Louvre E3226 and are analysed by Megally (1977).

33 Discussed by Haring (2003b: 104-105); usually the sense is in written accounts rather than calculations.

analysis is required, with several examples provided in order to identify exact translations as well as to facilitate comparisons over time.

§3.2.1 *wꜥ nb*

A widely used component of almost every delivery list, wa nb needs little analysis except an example to clearly state its exact meaning for completeness. O. Cairo 25592 is a short, but complete, delivery list and reads as follows:

1 *rnpt sp 29 ꜣbd 3 ꜣḫt sw 2 dni*	Year 29, III Akhet 2. Additional rations:
2 *pꜣ ꜥꜣ n ỉst ẖꜣr 4*	The foreman, 4 *khar*,
3 *pꜣ sš ẖꜣr 2*	The scribe, 2 *khar*,
4 *s 7 wꜥ nb ẖꜣr 1¾ ỉr.n ẖꜣr 12¼*	7 men, each 1¾ *khar*, making 12¼ *khar*,
5 *s 10 wꜥ nb ẖꜣr 2½ ỉr.n ẖꜣr 25*	10 men, each 2½ *khar*, making 25 *khar*,
6 *sꜣw ẖꜣr 1¼*	Guardian, 1¼ *khar*,
7 *ḥmyt ẖꜣr ¾ dmḏ ẖꜣr* [...]	Women servants, ¾ *khar*. Total [...] *khar*.

The literal meaning of *wꜥ nb* is "every one" and its use in delivery lists is standard as in O. Cairo 25592, always followed by an amount and a total which is effectively the same as a straightforward multiplication. An acceptable alternative rendering is *s nb* "every man", although this assumes the man sign is not written, essentially the meaning is no different. Even though it is occasionally used with a different subject such as *mnḥw* in O. DeM 376, 6, the meaning remains the same, easily translated as "each", and its use is constant throughout the Ramesside period.

§3.2.2 *wp st*

The phrase *wp st* (less frequently written *wp sn*) appears in a number of ration lists[34] and possible meanings of this phrase have been stated as "specify it, introducing a list of items"[35], "namely"[36], "detailed account"[37] and "specify it" meaning details of whatever is being recorded[38]. The relevant parts of the texts are reproduced here and examined to ascertain the exact rendering based on the context of the writings.

O. Ashmol. 108 rt. (undated)

4 *wp sn rdyt n=f r dỉw n ꜣbd 3 šmw ẖꜣr 91¼*	Details of them. What was given to him on account of rations of III Shemu, 91¼ *khar*.
5 *rdyt n=f m ps ẖꜣr 13*	What was given to him as cooking (or suste-

34 O. Ashmol. 48, 7 (Group III); O. Ashmol. 111, rt. 1 and vs. 1 (uses the plural *wp sn*; Group II); O. Berlin 14264, rt. 2 and vs. 3 (Group III); O. DeM 181, 3 (undated); O. DeM 188, 1 (Group I/II); O. DeM 189, I:1 (Group I/II); O. DeM 380, 3 (Group III); O. DeM 852, vs. 7 (Group I/II); O. DeM 10036, 3 (undated); O. Turin 57429, I:2 and I:6 (Group I); P. Turin 1906+1939+2047, 3:8 (Group IV); P. Turin 2013+2050+2061, rt. 1:4, x+5 and 2:2 (Group IV); P. Turin 2081+2095, rt. II:1 and 13 (Group IV).

35 Gardiner (1957: 560).

36 Lesko (2002: 97).

37 Helck (1974: 128), but not within a rations context.

38 Faulkner (1962: 59). Haring (2003b: 116) suggests an imperative.

	nance), 13 *khar*.
6 *rdyt n=f r 3bd 3 šmw ḫ3r 9½*	What was given to him on account of III Shemu, 9½ *khar*.
7 *dmḏ it ḫ3r 113¾*	Total grain, 113¾ *khar*.

Lines 1-3 contains text relating to several deliveries of rations, but *wp sn* is only used relating to the second delivery. Here it seems to indicate how the delivery was split up. This shows clearly what is meant here, but also that there were inconsistencies in the methods of writing on the part of the scribes.

O. Ashmol. 111 rt. (Group II)

1 (Date) *wḥm diw wp sn*	(Date). Repetition of rations. Details of them"
2-3 (List of names)	
4 (*dni* for one month followed by a list of names, without *wp sn*)	

Here, the heading is clearly stated, followed by *wp sn* and a list of recipients, where "them" may refer to the rations or the recipients, but as in the previous example, there is also a list where the terminology is not used. Perhaps the importance of any specifically stated details concerning *dni* was low, but this example also shows differences in scribal recording.

O. DeM 181 (Group III)

2 *s 61 wˁ nb ḫ3r 1¼ ir.n ḫ3r 75½*	61 men, each 1¼ *khar*, making 75½ *khar*.
3 *it m it 29½ wp st p3 3 ḥwtyw wˁ nb*	Barley, 29½. Details of it: The 3 captains, each.
4 *ḫ3r 1 ir.n ḫ3r 3 s 53 wˁ nb*	1 *khar*, making 3 *khar*; 53 men, each
ḫ3r ½ ir.n ḫ3r 26½	½ *khar*, making 26½ *khar*.

After the opening line, which is lost, O. DeM 181 records the use of *wp st*, which appears to be in the middle of a list of recipients, but when the totals (the error in the total in line 2, which should be 76¼ *khar*, is irrelevant at this point) are added, it preceded the second list. The start of the first list is lost so there is no way of knowing whether this list was introduced by *wp st* or not.

O. DeM 380 (Group III)

1 *rnpt sp 2 3bd 4 šmw sw 27*	Regnal year 2, Month 4 of Shemu, Day 27.
2 *inyt in sš ḥri r p3 ḫtm*	What was brought by the scribe Hori to the *ḫtm*.
3 *it ḫ3r 26¼ wp st*	Grain, 26¼ *khar*. Details of it:
4 *p3 ˁ3 n ist ḫ3r ½*	The foreman, ½ *khar*.
5 *p3 sš ḫ3r ½*	The scribe, ½ *khar*.
6 *s 30 wˁ nb ḫ3r ¾ ir.n ḫ3r 22½*	30 men, each ¾ *khar*, making 22½ *khar*.
7 *s 1 ir.n ḫ3r 1*	1 man, making 1 *khar*.

O. DeM 380 contains the most complete example of a text containing *wp st* and lines 1-7 show this well, taking into account the probable inclusion of a further 2¼ *khar* at the end of the list, which had been lost. It is neatly formatted, and the meaning of *wp st* is clear.

O. Turin 57429, I (Group I)

1 *[...] ẖꜣr*	[...] *khar*
2 *[...] ẖꜣr 1½ ,3 dmḏ ẖꜣr 4½ wp st*	[...] 1½, 3 *khar* Total 4½ *khar*. Details of it.
3 *[...] ẖꜣr 1, 1½*	[...] 1, 1½ *khar*.
4 *inyt m wꜣy ẖꜣr ½ 1*	What was brought from a distance, ½, 1 *khar*.
5 *sš Rꜥ-ms ẖꜣr ½*	Scribe Ramose, ½ *khar*.
6 *ꜥḥꜥ ẖꜣr 48¼, 21¼ dmḏ 69½ wp st*	Amount: 48¼, 21¼ *khar*. Total 69½. Details of it:
7 *ꜥꜣ n ist s 4 wꜥ nb ẖꜣr 1½ ¾ ir.n ẖꜣr 6, 3*	4 foremen, each 1½, ¾ *khar*, making 6, 3 *khar*.
8 *rmṯ ist s 48 wꜥ nb ẖꜣr ¾ ⅜ ir.n 36, 18*	48 workmen, each ¾ ⅜ *khar*, making 36, 18.
9 *st 4 wꜥ nb ẖꜣr 1, ½ ir.n 4, 2 dmḏ 69*	4 women, each 1, ½ *khar*, making 4, 2. Total 69.

To the left of each of the top three lines is written what looks like a memorandum recording that the rations were "delivered on" (*iw m*) a stated date. Although the total in line 9 is out on both counts by ¼ *khar*, the meaning of *wp st* is clear, as is its position within the text. O. Turin 57429, I:6, records amounts of emmer and barley, totals them up into one single *dmḏ* (total, see §8.4 below) and then uses *wp st* followed by a list, split into emmer and barley, and finally a total as a single undifferentiated amount.

Two other examples of ostraca show *wp st* at the start of the list. The start of O. DeM 188 reads ... *rit ẖꜣr 59¼ wp st gs=f ẖꜣr 29⅝*, "... side, 59¼ *khar*, Details of it, its half 29⅝ *khar*." A lengthy list follows, which can unfortunately not be checked for its accuracy as both sides of the ostracon are lost. The second example indicates that *wp st* probably did not have a meaning which was fixed. O. DeM 189 is a list of names with accompanying amounts in two distinct columns, which is similar to modern accounting methods. The first line of the first column reads *ḥꜣt-iꜣ ẖꜣr 5½ wp st*, "Hatia 5½ *khar*. Details of it." O. DeM 189 suggests that there was no strict meaning and it may have served a dual function; as a statement and as a formatting tool. Lines 2 to 5 record names and amounts, and a total is also stated in line 5 as 5½ *khar*. A new list starts on line 6, with Bakenkhons receiving 5½ *khar*, but no additional terminology. Translating it as "details of it" is not correct here, since there is no "it" to which the phrase relates. Just as letters contained non-translatable elements of formatting, perhaps accounts did also, but this isolated example does not serve to prove whether this was the case or not.

Only on two occasions does the phrase *wp st* follow a related list of recipients, and one of these, O. Ashmol. 48, has errors in lines 5 and 6 which are either an incorrect number of men or an error in the multiplication.

O. Ashmol. 48 vs. (delivery of *dni*; undated)

4 *wnmy pꜣ ꜥꜣ n ist ẖꜣr 2*	Right. The foreman 2 *khar*
5 *s 16 wꜥ nb ẖꜣr ½ ir.n ẖꜣr 8*	16 men, each ½ *khar*, making 8 *khar*
6 *s 8 wꜥ nb ẖꜣr ¼ ir.n ẖꜣr 3*	8 men, each ¼ *khar*, making 3 *khar*
7 *smḥy ẖꜣr 13¾ wp st*	Left. 13¾ *khar*. (That is) its details (or specification)

O. DeM 852 vs. is a lengthy list of names and amounts with some text lost from the ends of the lines of the second column, the final line of which reads: 2 *khar*. Details of it. Hay ¼ *khar*, Khaemwaset... (the rest is lost, as are line 7 and any subsequent lines). The final two examples are uncertain in meaning and are included for completeness, in addition to highlighting one of the problems which exist in dealing with administrative texts. O. Ashmol. 111, vs. 1, has two equally possible renderings which prompt different interpretations of the process performed in reality.

O. Ashmol. 111 vs. (Group II)

1 *iw* (Date) *m tꜣ ḏꜣt ... imn-nḫt it ḫꜣr ½ wp sn*

(a) Delivered. (Date) From the balance ... Amennakht, grain ½ *khar*. Details of them."

(b) Entered. (Date) As the balance ..."

The verso is badly damaged, but a delivery list follows, so the sense is lost as to which list the "details" relate. On O. DeM 10036, most of lines 1 and 2 are lost, along with the left part of the remainder of the text. In line 3 *wp st* follows an amount of grain but it is difficult to get the sense of the text until line 4, where a date is followed by a list.

P. Turin 2081+2095, rt. Col. II (Group III)

1 *in mw n pꜣ ḫr wp st wnmy ḫꜣr 7½ smḥy* [...]

Water-carrier of the Tomb. Details of it. Right, 7½ *khar*. Left [...]

2 *hrw pn smḥy s 31 wꜥ nb ḫꜣr ¼ ir.n ḫꜣr 7½* [...]

This day. Left, 31 men, each ¼ *khar*, making 7½ *khar* [...]

3-12 (Distribution lists of *diw* and *dni*; no use of *wp st*)

13 *rnpt sp 2 ꜣbd 3 ꜣḫt sw 2 dni n ꜣbd 2 ꜣḫt m-drt wsr-ḥꜣt-nḫt n nꜣ ḥmwt bdt wp st* [...]

Year 2, II Akhet 2 Day 2. Additional rations for II Ahket through the hand of User-hatnakht for the women servants, emmer. Details of it [...]

14 (A short distribution list is followed by a total (line 15))

Even allowing for the ends of the lines being lost, the inclusion of *wp st* in line 1 appears superfluous. Line 3 starts with a new distribution record, so it is possible that its meaning may be wider, to state clearly that the rations are for both sides and how they are being divided. The potential to record more information on papyrus was great, so perhaps more likely here is that the phrase served as a means of formatting the page, drawing attention to the series of deliveries. This would not explain the instance in line 13, where it is included after the word *bdt* "emmer", which is not used elsewhere in the document. It is likely that *wp st* was written to highlight the uniqueness of this particular delivery.

P. Turin 2013+2050+2061 is a lengthy, and fragmentary, document dealing with a series of deliveries at least in part from fishing boats. Not counting the lost parts, it is used on three occasions, again for emmer, consisting of several components: a statement of where it was from + *bdt* + a total + *wp st* + "distribution of rations for a particular month" followed by a list of recipients. It is a clear way of specifying exactly what the rations were, but even so the phrase does not really add anything to the existing details except indicating the rations were emmer as opposed to the standard combination of both barley and emmer. Emmer alone is also the subject of *wp st* on P. Turin 1906+1939+2047, rt. 3:12 but is omitted in rt. 4:6. In contrast, it is inserted into rt. 3:8 in between two delivery lists with no prior heading except *wp st* to split them, implying a slightly different meaning, and one which was not consistently adhered to by the scribes.

Out of the twelve documents that use the phrase *wp st* for ration deliveries, five date from the reigns of either Ramesses II or Siptah. Even though there are examples of its use in papyri, the context and meaning of *wp st* is often lost due to damage of much of the surrounding writing. Despite this being a very small sample, it may be that the phrase was more commonly used at the start of the Ramesside period and became less popular over time, and by the end of the 20th Dynasty its meaning may have changed slightly. A further implication may relate to the use of *wp st* in a wider context, where it may act as a sub-section division; in which case this may explain why in some examples there is usually no terminology for sub-totals (see below) since the previous specification suffices. The reason for writing *wp st* on some occasions and not on others may be due to scribal preference, but it does not explain its inconsistent use within the same document as some of the later papyri examples show.

§3.2.3 *ir.n* AND *dmḏ*

These two words, commonly used in ration delivery texts, are treated together since they often occur in the same sentence, but there are many other instances where only one of the two words, usually *dmḏ*, is present. Examples of all possibilities will be presented from Groups II and III in an attempt to establish whether there are any differences in meaning.

O. Ashmol. 184 (Group II: Siptah/Tausret)

1 *dit diw n ꜣbd 2 šmw*	Distribution of rations for II Shemu
2 *pꜣ ꜥꜣ n ist ẖꜣr 5¾ ẖꜣr 1½ wḏꜣt=f ẖꜣr ¼*	The foreman, 5¾ *khar*, 1½ *khar*, his remainder ¼ *khar*.
3 *pꜣ sš ẖꜣr 2¾ ẖꜣr 1*	The scribe, 2¾ *khar*, 1 *khar*.
4 *s 17 wꜥ nb ẖꜣr 4½ ir.n ẖꜣr 68*	17 men, each 4½ *khar*, making 68 *khar*.
5 *pꜣ sꜣw ẖꜣr 2 pꜣ iry-ꜥꜣ ẖꜣr 1*	The guard 2 *khar*, the doorkeeper 1 *khar*,
6 *mnḥw s 2 wꜥ nb ẖꜣr ½ ir.n ẖꜣr 1*	2 youths, each ½ *khar*, making 1 *khar*,
pꜣ swnw ẖꜣr 1	The doctor 1 *khar*
7 *ḥmwt ẖꜣr 3*	Women servants, 3 *khar*.

O. DeM 186 (Group III: 20th Dynasty)

1 [...] *šmw s 18 wꜥ nb ¼ ir.n 4½*	[...] Shemu. 18 men, each ¼ making 4½.
2 [...] *wḏꜣt=f ꜣbd 4 prt ẖꜣr ⅜*	[...] his remainder IV Peret ⅜ *khar*.
3 [...] *pꜣ sš ẖꜣr 1 s 18 wꜥ nb ẖꜣr 1¼ ir.n 22½* [...]	[...] the scribe 1 *khar*, 18 men, each 1¼ *khar*, making 22½ [...],
4 [...] *18 wꜥ nb 1 ir.n ẖꜣr 18 mnḥw 3 wꜥ nb ẖꜣr* [...]	[...] 18 (men) each 1 *khar*, making 18 *khar*, 3 youths, each [...] *khar*. ...

O. DeM 379 (Group III: 20th Dynasty)

1 *ꜣbd 4 prt sw 25*	IV Peret Day 25.
2 *dit diw n ꜣbd 4 prt*	Distribution of rations for IV Peret.
3 *wnmy ẖꜣr 46⅝*	Right: 46⅝ *khar.*
4 *pꜣ iry-ꜥꜣ ẖꜣr 1½ dmḏ ẖꜣr 48⅛*	The doorkeeper 1 *khar.* Total 48⅛ *khar.*
5 *dmḏ ẖꜣr 63¾ ẖꜣr 110¾*	Total 63¾ *khar.* 110¾ *khar.*

O. Ashmol. 257 (Undated)

1 *pꜣ ꜥꜣ n ist ẖꜣr 5½*	The foreman, 5½ *khar.*
2 *s 14*	14 men
3 *wꜥ nb ẖꜣr 3 ẖꜣr 63¾*	each 3 *khar* 63¾ *khar.*
4 *s 4*	4 men
to the left of line 4: *dmḏ bty ẖꜣr 63¾*	Total emmer: 63¾ *khar*
5 *wꜥ nb ẖꜣr 3¼*	each 3¼ *khar,*
6 *mnḥw ẖꜣr 1 pn-tꜣ-wrt*	Youths 1 *khar,* Pentaweret

O. Ashmol. 184 and O. DeM 186 are instances where *ir.n* is included in a ration distribution text, and the meaning is that of a total. It serves as a total of a multiplication always in the form of a number of men multiplied by the ration received, in *khar,* "making" another value, the total, indicating its use as a running total for an individual component of ration lists. O. DeM 379 is one of a small number of examples in the ration corpus where *dmḏ* alone is used, and allowing for the values not adding up. In this example, there may be some additional information on a separate ostracon which relates to this delivery, so *dmḏ* appears to be a more generic term used for a total, and not restricted to either the grand total at the end of the list or the rations distributed on the preceding list. Despite being complete and a very short list, O. Ashmol. 257 appears to confuse matters somewhat. To the left of, and above, line 4 is written *dmḏ bdt* ("Total emmer"), which suggests that it was inserted after the record was written, perhaps as a means of clarification. Errors in the arithmetic do not help us, but only the scribe himself knew why *dmḏ bdt* was used instead of *ir.n*.

O. DeM 384, Col II (Undated)

1 *dit diw n ꜣbd 3 ꜣḫt*	Distribution of rations for III Akhet.
2 *pꜣ ꜥꜣ n ist ẖꜣr 2½*	The foreman 2½ *khar*
3 *pꜣ sš ẖꜣr 1¼*	The scribe 1¼ *khar*
4 *s 17 wꜥ nb ẖꜣr 2 ir.n 34*	17 men, each 2 *khar,* making 34
5 [...] *ẖꜣr 2*	[...] 2 *khar*
6 *nꜣ mnḥw ẖꜣr 6*	The youths, 6 *khar*
7 *ḥmt ẖꜣr 1½*	Woman servant, 1½ *khar*
8 *iry-ꜥꜣ ẖꜣr 1½*	Doorkeeper, 1½ *khar*
9 *dmḏ ẖꜣr 48¾*	Total: 48¾ *khar*
10 *dmḏ ẖꜣr 97½*	Total: 97½ *khar*

O. Munich ÄS 397 (Group III: Ramesses III)

1 *rnpt sp 28 ꜣbd 1 ꜣḫt ꜥrḳ di͗t di͗w n*	Year 28, I Akhet 30. Distribution of rations
2 *ꜣbd 2 ꜣḫt wnmy pꜣ ꜥꜣ n i͗st ḫꜣr 2*	for II Akhet. Right. The foreman 2 *khar*,
3 *pꜣ sš ḫꜣr ½*	the scribe ½ *khar*,
4 *s 20 wꜥ nb ḫꜣr ¾ i͗r.n ḫꜣr 15*	20 men, each ¾ *khar*, making 15 *khar*.
dmḏ ḫꜣr 17½	Total 17½ *khar*.
5 *wḥm pꜣ ꜥꜣ n i͗st ḫꜣr 2 pꜣ sš ḫꜣr 1*	Repeat. The foreman 2 *khar*, the scribe 1 *khar*,
6 *s 20 wꜥ nb ḫꜣr 1 i͗r.n ḫꜣr 20*	20 men, each 1 *khar*, making 20 *khar*,
ḥmt ḫꜣr 2 dmḏ ḫꜣr 25	servant 2 *khar*. Total 25 *khar*.
7 *dmḏ hꜣw nb n hrw pn ḫꜣr 42½*	Total of every expense for this day, 42½ *khar*.
8 *ꜣbd 2 ꜣḫt ꜥrḳ i͗w=f pꜣ ꜥꜣ n i͗st ḫꜣr 2*	II Akhet 30. His delivery. The foreman 2
pꜣ sš ḫꜣr ½	*khar*, the scribe ½ *khar*,
9 *s 20 wꜥ nb ḫꜣr 1¼ i͗r.n ḫꜣr 25*	20 men, each 1¼ *khar*, making 25 *khar*,
10 *ḥmt ḫꜣr 1 dmḏ hꜣw nb ḫꜣr 28½*	servant 1 *khar*. Total of every expense 28½ *khar*.

O. Munich ÄS 397 is an example of a substantial list recording ration deliveries for a group of workmen where both words are used together. The final amounts are recorded as a *dmḏ*. The same is true on O. DeM 384, but *dmḏ* is used twice in succession at the end of the text; *i͗r.n* is used as in the previous examples, here *dmḏ* is used to total the individual recipients' rations and also to add these to another value, certainly the corresponding ration total of the other side. On O. Munich ÄS 397, the final totals in lines 7 (the sum of totals in lines 4 and 6) and 10 (sum of totals in lines 8 and 9) are defined as *dmḏ hꜣw nb* and may be the only thing that differentiates different levels of total.

O. Munich ÄS 397 is one example of a document using an extended version of a total value. The use of *dmḏ hꜣw nb* may have a specific meaning, not only its use within texts but also in relation to the date of those texts. Only a small number of ostraca use the expression; while it seems far more prevalent in papyri, it is unfortunate that many examples of the latter are fragmented[39].

O. DeM 252 (Group III)

3 *[...] ḫꜣr 2 s 31 wꜥ nb ḫꜣr 2½*	[...] 2 *khar*, 31 men, each 2½ *khar*,
i͗r.n ḫꜣr 77½ [...]	making 77½ *khar* [...].
4 [...] *i͗ry-ꜥꜣ ḫꜣr ½ dmḏ hꜣw nb*	[...] doorkeeper ½ *khar*, total of all expenses:
bdt ḫꜣr 81[...]	emmer 81+ [...] *khar*.

O. DeM 380 (Group III: Ramesses IV)

4 *pꜣ ꜥꜣ n i͗st ḫꜣr ½*	The foreman, ½ *khar*
5 *pꜣ sš ḫꜣr ½*	The scribe, ½ *khar*

39 Given the condition of the papyri, there are examples which record dmD hAw nb after a ration distribution list, but the associated amounts and formatting is unclear. P. Turin 1906+1939+2047, rt. 3:4, 3:23, 4:3 (Group IV); P. Turin 2013+2050+2061, rt. 1:2, 1:6, x+2 (Group IV); P. Turin 2062, rt. I:6, I:10, II:8 (Group IV); P. Turin 2081+2095, rt. I:11, II:8. P. Turin 2013+2050+2061, rt.x+3, "Total of every expense 107¾ *khar*" follows on not from a list, but another use of the same expression.

6 *s 30 wꜥ nb ẖꜣr ¾ ir.n ẖꜣr 22½*	30 men, each ¾ *khar*, making 22½ *khar*
7 *s 1 ir.n ẖꜣr 1*	1 man, making 1 *khar*
8 [...] *dmḏ hꜣw nbt iryt m* [...]	[...] total of all expenses which were made [...]

O. DeM 383 (undated)

1 *pꜣ ꜥn ist* [...]	The foreman [...]
2 *pꜣ sš ẖꜣr 1½*	The scribe, 2½ *khar*,
3 *s 17 wꜥ nb ẖꜣr 2½*	17 men, each 2½ *khar*,
4 *ir.n ẖꜣr 42½*	making 42½ *khar*,
5 *mnḥ 3 wꜥ nb ẖꜣr 2 ir.n ẖꜣr 6*	3 youths, each 2 *khar*, making 6 *khar*,
6 *ḥmwt ẖꜣr 1½*	women servants 1½ *khar*.
7 *dmḏ hꜣw nb ẖꜣr 55*	Total of all expenses 55 *khar*,
8 *dmḏ ẖꜣr 111*	Total 111 *khar*.

O. DeM 388 (undated)

2 *s 21 wꜥ nb ẖꜣr 1¼* [...]	21 men, each 1¼ *khar* [...]
3 *ir.n 40 ir.n ẖꜣr 140* [...]	making 40, making 140 *khar* [...]
4 *ḥrp-srḳt s 1 ir.n ẖꜣr 1¼* [...]	scorpion-charmer, 1 man, making 1¼ *khar* [...]
5 *dmḏ hꜣw nb n hrw pn ẖꜣr 291¾*	Total of all expenses on this day 291¾ *khar*.

P. Turin 1884+2067+2071+2105 (Group IV: Ramesses IX)

rt. 2:12 *sš s 2 wꜥ nb ẖꜣr 2 ir.n ẖꜣr 4*	Scribe, 2 men each 2 *khar*, making 4 *khar*
iry-ꜥꜣ s 1 ir.n ẖꜣr 3	doorkeeper, 1 man, making 3 *khar*,
swnw s 1 ir.n ẖꜣr 2	doctor, 1 man, making 2 *khar*,
s 1 ir.n ẖꜣr 1¼ pꜣ ḥtpw-nṯr	1 man making 1¼ *khar*, the god's
ẖꜣr 1¼ dmḏ hꜣw nb	offerings 1¼ *khar*. Total of all
ẖꜣr 100 ẖꜣr 50	expenses 100 *khar*, 50 *khar*.

P. Turin 1932+1939 (Group IV: Ramesses X)

rt. 2:3 ... *s 11 wꜥ nb ẖꜣr 1½ ir.n ẖꜣr 16½*	11 men, each 1½ *khar*, making 16½ *khar*,
iry-ꜥꜣ s 1 ir.n ẖꜣr 2	doorkeeper, 1 man making 2 *khar*
pꜣ ḥtpw n Mrt-sgr [...]	the offerings for Meretseger [...]
rt. 2:4 *dmḏ hꜣw nbt n tꜣ rit wnmy*	Total of all expenses of the Right side:
it ẖꜣr 56¾	grain 56¾ *khar*.
rt. 2:5 *tꜣ rit smḥy ḥwtyw s 2 wꜥ nb ẖꜣr 3*	The Left side: captains, 2 men, each 3
ir.n ẖꜣr 6	*khar*, making 6 *khar*.
s 18 wꜥ nb ẖꜣr 2	18 men, each 2 *khar*
ir.n ẖꜣr 36 mnḥw s 7 wꜥ nb	making 36 *khar*. Youths, 7 men,
wꜥ nb ẖꜣr 1½	each 1½ *khar*.
rt. 2:6 *ir.n ẖꜣr 10½ iry-ꜥꜣ s 1*	making 10½ *khar*, doorkeeper, 1 man
ir.n ẖꜣr 2 dmḏ hꜣw nbt	making 2 *khar*. Total of all
n tꜣ rit smḥy it	expenses of the Left side: grain

ḫ3r 54½	54½ *khar.*

P. Turin 2081+2095 (Group III: Ramesses V)

rt. I:6 *p3 sš ḫ3r ¾ s 31 wꜥ nb ḫ3r ¾*	the scribe ¾ *khar*, 31 men each ¾ *khar*
ir.n ḫ3r 33¼ Ḥr-ms ḫ3r ¼	making 33¼ *khar*, Hormose ¼ *khar*,
dmḏ h3w nb it ḫ3r 25¼	Total of all expenses, grain 25¼ *khar.*

The evidence from the earlier ostraca is inconclusive as to the precise meaning of *dmḏ h3w nb*, since it is not fixed in position relative to other totals. In all likelihood it was used interchangeably with *dmḏ* as it almost always follows a ration distribution list. In contrast to today's accounting methods, where we use sub totals, totals and grand totals, often in different positions in the page, there seems to be no differential in the records between totals of different levels in the material at Deir el-Medina[40]. The meaning of *dmḏ* appears to be straightforward—a generic word indicating a total—and its use did not change over time[41] in the ration lists. So, based on the data available, *dmḏ* is best translated as a total or a grand total, whichever is the most suitable, but perhaps we do not totally understand its meaning. Towards the end of the Ramesside period, *dmḏ h3w nb* seems to be used more to indicate a final total, but the small number of examples is only an indicator of a possibility and its precise use remains unclear[42].

§3.2.4 *wḏ3t* (*ḏ3t*)

Twenty texts record the use of *wḏ3t* (almost certainly the successor to the Middle Kingdom *ḏ3t*) in ration contexts. More commonly used in wood and fish distribution records[43], its relative infrequency in ration lists facilitates examination as to its precise, and possibly varied, meanings within the rations material. To allow this, the relevant examples are reproduced and examined[44] where possible in order to allow us to get deeper than the typical translation of "balance", "remainder" or "deficiency"[45], and to allow an accurate rendering based on the data available, and furthermore, to ascertain whether *wḏ3t* is treated differently within rations and wood contexts[46]. Interestingly, neither of the words *spyt* or *mn* (both mean the same as *wḏ3t*) are used anywhere in

40 This is in slight disagreement with Ezzamel (1994: 236), who states that the words used in accounting not only existed in ancient Egyptian accounts, but that they were "technically precise and specific to accounting". This statement is for the most part true, but the use of *dmḏ* to denote a total on several levels is a notable and important exception.

41 Papyri exhibit the same features. Examples of *dmḏ h3w nb* include P. Turin 2081+2095, I:6 and 11, II:8 and 12 (*dmḏ* followed by an amount is commonplace). ir.n is used in the same formulaic manner as specified above on numerous occasions; cf. P. Turin 2013+2050+2061, rt. 1:2, 1:4 and 1:6.

42 Not within a rations context, a further and perhaps interchangeable use of *dmḏ* includes the phrase *dmḏ ꜥḥꜥ*, "total amount", as recorded on O. Cairo 25542, rt. 4, and O. Cairo 25607, vs. 3.

43 See Haring (2003b: 141-142) for a small selection of examples involving wood, fish, pottery and one relating to water.

44 Examples where *wḏ3t* is used, but it is impossible to get the sense of its meaning are: O. Ashmol. 111, vs. 1; O. Cairo 25698, 8 and 9; P. Turin 2015, 11; P. Turin 2081+2095, rt. I:3 and vs. II:7.

45 Faulkner (1962: 318).

46 See Janssen (2003: 12-24) for a discussion on wood and the associated quota system.

the rations documentation; *spyt* and *wḏ3t* are both used in P. Louvre E3226, there are examples of alternating totals[47].

O. Ashmol. 184 (Group II: Siptah/Tausret)

[2] *p3 ꜥ3 n ist ḫ3r* <u>*5¾*</u> *ḫ3r 1½* *wḏ3t=f ḫ3r ¼*	The foreman <u>5¾</u> *khar*, 1½ *khar*, his balance ¼ *khar*.

O. Cairo 25689 (Group III: 20th Dynasty)

[7] (list) *dmḏ ḫ3r 71¼ wḏ3t ḫ3r 8¾ 28* [...]	Total 71¼ *khar*. Balance 8¾ *khar*, 28 [...]

O. DeM 177 (Group II: Amenmesse)

[9] *rdyt r diw n n3 rmṯ ist 9*	What was given on account of the rations for the 9 workmen.
wḏ3t n 3bd 1 prt	Balance for I Peret .

O. DeM 329 (Group III: 20th Dynasty)

[6] (list) *dmḏ ḫ3r 68¾ wḏ3t ḫ3r 1*	Total 68¾ *khar*. Remainder 1 *khar*.

O. DeM 640 (Undated)

[1] [*šsp*] *diw 2 13/16, 1*	[Receiving] rations 2 13/16, 1
[2] [...] *ḫ3r 1 11/32 iw 27/32*	[...] *khar* 1 11/32, Delivered 27/32
[3] *p3-nḥs ḫ3r 1¼+1/16+1/32* <u>*½*</u> *iw ½+*<u>*½*</u> *wḏ3t ¾+1/16+1/32*	Panehsy 1 11/32 + <u>½</u> *khar*; delivered ½ + <u>½</u>. Remainder 27/32.
[4] *pn-nst-t3wy ḫ3r ½*	Pennesetawy ½ *khar*
[5] *imn-m-ipt ḫ3r 1¼*	Amenemipet 1¼ *khar*

O. DeM 839 (Undated)

[1] *rdyt r diw n p3 ꜥ3 n ist ḫ3r 2*	What was given on account of rations to the foreman, 2 *khar*.
[2] *wḥm rdyt n 3bd 1 prt ḫ3r 1 wḏ3t ½*	Repetition of what was given for I Peret, 1 *khar*. Remainder ½

The remainder amounts on O. Ashmol. 184 and O. Cairo 25689 are part of standard ration distribution lists, so the balance in both examples was probably an arrears owed from a previous month. The totals from the list of recipients can be added up, and if they are correct, the balance was likely to be an amount from a previous period not recorded on this ostracon. The rations given to the recipients listed on O. DeM 329 add up correctly and total 68¾ *khar*. The remainder is stated in line 6 as 1 *khar*, but what this relates to is not clear, though it must have something to do with deliveries on a different ostracon. Unlike the other examples, the balance is written in isolation, so it may well be a reminder to deliver the 1 *khar* at the earliest opportunity. Occasionally it

47 Megally (1977: 48 and note 2). For *mn*, see *ibid.*,78-82, and for *spyt*, see *ibid.*, 82-86. The periods and frequency of use of all three phrases is a definite avenue for further research.

is clearly stated that the remainder relates to an arrears from a previous month, such as O. DeM 177, which is dated II *prt* 13 and which details the arrears of three individuals. The remainder is clearly stated as the amount that was not delivered to Panehsy on O. DeM 640, but the amounts are very precise which would suggest that they may have been balancing or arbitrary figures; a similar interpretation can be made from the small amount recorded as a remainder on O. DeM 839, especially given that the text itself is so brief.

O. DeM 186 (Group III: 20th Dynasty)

[2] [...] *wḏ3t 3bd 4 prt ḫ3r ⅜*	[...] Remainder, IV Peret ⅜ *khar*.

O. DeM 381 rt. (Group III: Ramesses IV)

[9] (list) *dmḏ ḫ3r 92 wḏ3t ḫ3r 1*	Total 92 *khar*. Remainder 1 *khar*.

O. DeM 10034 (Group III: Ramesses III)

[1] *3bd 3 prt sw 25 dit diw in*	III Peret 25. Distribution of rations by the
sš imn-nḫt sš Ḥri	scribe Amenakht and the scribe Hori,
[2] *ḫ3r 50¾ dmḏ 66¾ 61¾*	50¾ *khar*. Total 66¾, 61¾.
(*sw*) *27 ḫ3r 180¾ wḏ3t ḫ3r 66¾*	(Day) 27. 180¾ *khar*. Remainder 66¾ *khar*.

Both O. DeM 381 and O. DeM 10034 record totals but there are no accompanying distribution lists. If the remainders on O. DeM 10034 relate to three individual deliveries, then the second one was omitted and as a result was an arrears. The total delivered on O. DeM 381 to the individual recipients adds up to 98¾ *khar*, so the total is itself incorrect. The 1 *khar* remaining is either an arrears or a reminder to deliver a shortfall. The start and ends of the lines in O. DeM 186 are lost, including the link between the balance and the preceding list, so all we know is that the balance related to an individual month.

O. Ashmol. 277 (Undated)

[1] *sš ipw*	Scribe Ipuy
[2] *wḏ3t n p3 diw*	Balance of the rations,
[3] *it ḫ3r ½*	Grain, ½ *khar*,
[4] *bnri ḫ3r 2¾*	Dates, 2¾ *khar*.

The brief O. Ashmol. 277 is an unusual example, since it records the delivery of rations and offering supplies for a temple. It appears to be a memorandum written as a reminder, it can equally be speculated that it may be an extra delivery made to complete an earlier quota. Therefore *wḏ3t* may be translated as a balance or arrears even though one fits the memorandum context and the other fits the additional delivery.

O. Turin 57072 rt. (Group III: Ramesses III)

[rt. 2] *rnpt sp 28 3bd 4 šmw ʿrḳ*	Year 28, IV Shemu, last day.
hrw pn nḥm gs n p3y (=i) diw	This day, taking away half (my) rations

3 [...] *rḫ.tw tꜣy=i wḏꜣt*	[...] inform you of my balance.
4 *ꜣbd 4 šmw iw bdt ẖꜣr 4⅝*	IV Shemu. Delivered: emmer 4⅝ *khar*,
wḏꜣt ẖꜣr ⅞	balance ⅞ *khar*.
5 *pꜣ ḥryw-rnpt wḏꜣt ẖꜣr 23/32*	The Epagomenal days, remainder 23/32 *khar*.
6 *ꜣbd 1 ꜣḫt iw ẖꜣr 4⅝ wḏꜣt ẖꜣr ⅞*	IV Akhet. Delivered: 4⅝ *khar*, balance ⅞ *khar*.
7 *ꜣbd 2 ꜣḫt iw ẖꜣr 4⅝ wḏꜣt ẖꜣr ⅞*	IV Akhet. Delivered: 4⅝ *khar*, balance ⅞ *khar*.
8 *ꜣbd 3 ꜣḫt iw ẖꜣr 5¼ wḏꜣt ẖꜣr ¼*	IV Akhet. Delivered: 5¼ *khar*, balance ¼ *khar*.
9 *ꜣbd 4 ꜣḫt iw ẖꜣr 5 wḏꜣt ẖꜣr 35/64*	IV Akhet. Delivered: 5 *khar*, balance 35/64 *khar*.
10 *ꜣbd 1 prt iw mḥ*	I Peret. Delivered. Complete.
11 *ꜣbd 2 prt iw ẖꜣr 1½ wḏꜣt ẖꜣr 4*	II Peret. Delivered: 1½ *khar*, balance 4 *khar*.
12 *ꜣbd 3 prt m wḏꜣt ẖꜣr 1½*	III Peret. As balance, 1½ *khar*.
13 *ꜣbd 4 prt iw ẖꜣr 5 wḏꜣt ẖꜣr* [½]	IV Peret. Delivered: 5 *khar*, balance [½] *khar*.
14 *rnpt sp 29*	Year 29
15 *ꜣbd 1 šmw iw ẖꜣr 3 wḏꜣt* [*ẖꜣr 2½*]	I Shemu. Delivered: 3 *khar*, balance [2½ *khar*].
16 *ꜣbd 2 šmw iw ẖꜣr 5 wḏꜣt ẖꜣr* [½]	II Shemu. Delivered: 5 *khar*, balance [½] *khar*.
17 *ꜣbd 3 šmw iw ẖꜣr 5 wḏꜣt ẖꜣr* [½]	III Shemu. Delivered: 5 *khar*, balance [½] *khar*.
18 *ꜣbd 4 šmw iw ẖꜣr* [*4 wḏꜣt ẖꜣr 1½*]	IV Shemu. Delivered: [4] *khar*, [balance 1½ *khar*].
19 *m ꜣbd 1 ꜣḫt iw mḥ*	In I Akhet. Delivered. Complete.
20 *ꜣbd 2 ꜣḫt* [...]	II Akhet. [...]

vs. 1 *rnpt sp 29 ꜣbd 3 prt iw m pꜣ*	Year 29, III Peret. Delivered as the
diw bty ẖꜣr 3¾	rations of emmer, 3¾ *khar*.
2 *wḏꜣt r ẖꜣr 1¾*	Balance on account of 1¾ *khar*.
ꜣbd 4 prt iw m pꜣ diw ẖꜣr 2	IV Peret. Delivered as the rations, 2 *khar*,
wḏꜣt r ẖꜣr 3½	balance on account of 3½ *khar*.
3 *rnpt sp 30* [...]	Year 30 [...]
4 *ꜣbd 1 šmw iw ẖꜣr 3½ wḏꜣt ẖꜣr 2½*	I Shemu. Delivered 3½ *khar*, balance 2½ *khar*.
5 *ꜣbd 2 šmw iw ẖꜣr 3¾ wḏꜣt ẖꜣr 1¾*	II Shemu. Delivered 3¾ *khar*, balance 1¾ *khar*.
6 *ꜣbd 3 šmw iw ẖꜣr 5*[½] *mḥ*	III Shemu. Delivered 5[½]. Complete.
7-9 (*unconnected*)	

O. Turin 57072 is perhaps the most enlightening text when the content is examined in detail, and a large extract is worth reproducing[48] since there are some subtle differences in vocabulary used. It details the rations received by one individual workman over a period of time, recording monthly deliveries from IV *šmw* of Year 28 through to II *ꜣḫt* of Year 29 (these go through to III *šmw* of Year 30 if the missing portion at the bottom of the recto and top of the verso contained the missing months[49]), and included the accompanying remainder amounts. When the deliveries and balances are written out in tabular form, the result is similar to the appearance of a stock

48 O. Turin 57072 is examined in considerable detail by Janssen (1979) within the context of the Year 29 strikes. Although the translation here of *iw* has been written as "delivered", "entered" is perfectly acceptable.
49 There are four delivery lists dated to this period: O. DeM 738 (III *šmw* 4); O. DeM 10032 (III *ꜣḫt* 11); O. DeM 10033 (III *šmw* 5); and O. Cairo 25592 (*dni* for III *šmw* 4),

ledger, with the remainder being an arrears or shortfall. Unfortunately, only by an examination of the original document can we show whether the document was written up in one sitting or added to each month. Such information would undoubtedly add to our knowledge of accounting at this time. All units are in *khar*.

Year	Date	Delivered	Balance	Total	
28	IV *šmw*	4⅝	⅞	5½	
	Epag. days	-	23/32	23/32	
	I *ꜣḫt*	4⅝	⅞	5½	
	II *ꜣḫt*	4⅝	⅞	5½	
	III *ꜣḫt*	5¼	¼	5½	
	IV *ꜣḫt*	5	½	5½	
	I *prt*	5½	-	5½	(*mḥ*)
	II *prt*	1½	4	5½	
	III *prt*	(4)	1½	5½	
	IV *prt*	5	½	5½	
29	I *šmw*	3	[2½]	5½	
	II *šmw*	5	[½]	5½	
	III *šmw*	5	[½]	5½	
	IV *šmw*	4?	[1½?]	5½	
	I *ꜣḫt*	5½	-	5½	(*mḥ*)
	III *prt*	3¾	1¾	5½	
	IV *prt*	2	3½	5½	
30	I *šmw*	3½	2½	5½	
	II *šmw*	3¾	1¾	5½	
	III *šmw*	5½	-	5½	

In this section of the text, there is only an implication of who received the rations, since the delivery plus the balance or remainder equals 5½ *khar*, which was the monthly emmer ration for a foreman or a scribe. This suggests that the recipient was one of these higher ranked individuals. The apparent contradiction by the presence of the 3 captains (*ḥwtyw*) in line 7 can be disregarded since the last three lines on the verso are not related to the text[50]. Throughout this example, the *wḏꜣt* is in effect a balance or remainder but these concepts do not quite capture the precise meaning, so perhaps a better rendering of *wḏꜣt* here would be "arrears" or "owed".

Some of the documents clearly have *wḏꜣt* but they are either damaged to a large enough degree to make interpretation difficult, while others have ration amounts that can not be linked with any balance or remainder. O. DeM 377 rt. is a lengthy delivery list but unfortunately the start of lines 12 and 13 are lost. The balance of 4 *khar* in line 12 and the total (*dmḏ*) of 102 *khar* in line 13, as well as another amount of 23½ *khar* in line 13 can not be tied up with each other or the total of 84¾ or the additions of 81¼ *khar*. A balance is recorded in line 9 of O. Cairo 25809 rt., though

50 Janssen (1979: 301). He also points out (*ibid.*, 303) the error in the delivery in I *šmw* is a transcription error either by López (1978) or the scribe, since the balance is clearly 2½.

many of the amounts are lost. Whilst the verso is fragmented, line 3 records *wḏ3t*, followed by  which is probably a determinative rather than a total as the text ends there. O. IFAO 265, vs. 1, records a day 30 and a balance of 200 which can not be connected with either the recto or the rest of the verso. O. Strasbourg H117, 3, records a total of 18 and remainder of 6, but what this relates to is not known since the rest of this short document relates to dates and offering bread. Lines 3:8 to 3:10 of P. Turin 1906+2939+2047 rt. record amounts which total 60⅛, confirmed as a total in line 3.10. Allowing for the calculation error in line 3:9 of ¾, the *wḏ3t* of ⅜ does not tie in with the rest of the figures, so the best we can do is translate it as a balance.

Most of the examples consist of a list of recipients followed by a total and then the *wḏ3t*. In modern western accounting, a "balance" can either mean a balancing item, or an amount carried forward from one month to the next in order to facilitate transactions between two periods. It can also mean an amount which is used in another set of accounts which would link different records, such as components of an assets register as part of a balance sheet in company accounts. This does not seem to be the case in Deir el-Medina, although there is not enough evidence to discount this completely. In many cases it is not clear exactly what *wḏ3t* refers to but one suggestion is that these balances were a written reminder to the person delivering the commodity following an oral request to complete the quota. This seems more appropriate to commodities where quotas were given, but does not explain the presence of balances or remainders in the ration accounts. On the basis of the material examined, and like so many ancient Egyptian words, the precise rendering of *wḏ3t* varies as to the context of the text, and can be taken to mean "balance", "remainder", "arrears" or "owed".

§3.2.5 *ẖry-ḥ3t*

This word is very rarely used in the records, and is traditionally translated as "previously"[51]. Closer examination suggests that it has a more precise meaning in an accounting context, perhaps even in an attempt to make the accounts more concise[52].

P. Turin 2013+2050+2061 (Group IV: Ramesses IX):

rt.2.4 *p3 sš-ḳd ḥry ẖ3r 1 s 62*	The chief draughtsman 1 *khar*, 62 men,
wꜥ nb ẖ3r ½ ir.n ẖ3r 31	each ½ *khar*, making 31 *khar*,
rt.2.5 *ẖry-ḥ3t wꜥ nb ẖ3r 1½ dmḏ ẖ3r 2*	previously each 1½ *khar*, total 2 *khar*,
ir.n ẖ3r 122	making 122 *khar*.

There is no connection between the totals as nothing on the papyrus can be allocated the stated ration rates. However, the sense in an accounting concept is one fundamental to modern day accruals and double entry bookkeeping, of a value being brought forward. The meaning here appears to be that the workforce, probably complete at sixty-two men, had been paid part of their rations earlier (for which no evidence is forthcoming) and the remainder was delivered later[53].

51 Lesko (2002: 297, 386).

52 Megally (1977: 86), although the examples quoted are few in number.

53 Compare with P. Turin 1884+2067+2071+2105, rt. 3:9 (Group IV: Ramesses IX), which states totals of lamp wicks. The sense of *ẖry-ḥ3t* in this case is undoubtedly that some wicks were delivered previously

There is no use of *wḏꜣt* which suggests that a more generic meaning of "arrears" is not what is meant in this example. An alternative sense implied by *ẖry-ḥꜣt,* is that of the workmen being given a pay rise, but this is improbable with no evidence anywhere to support this.

§3.2.6 *ʿḥʿ*

There are number of varied meanings for this word, but in numerical contexts it is usually translated as "amount"[54]. In the Deir el-Medina corpus itself, its use is relatively frequent for other commodities such as water, varieties of oil, gypsum and bread[55], but the use of *ʿḥʿ* in a rations context is rare and is confined to isolated examples. Of greater interest is not so much the word itself, but its placement within the document and the use of other accounting terminology in close proximity to *ʿḥʿ*, especially *wp st*. Unfortunately, the small number of examples is insufficient to observe whether any changes in use occurred over time.

O. Ashmol. 108 rt. (Undated)

1 *ʿḥʿ it rdyt r*	Amount of grain which was given to the effect
nty sš ḥwy dit [...]	that the scribe Huy [...].
2 *diw n ꜣbd 3 šmw nty m* [...]	Rations for III Shemu which were in [...]
ẖꜣr 39¾	39¾ *khar*.
3 *wḥm rdyt n=f ẖꜣr 74*	Repetition of what was given to him; 74 *khar*,
dmḏ ẖꜣr 113¾	total 113¾ *khar*.

O. DeM 843 (Group II: Ramesses II)

1 *ʿḥʿ n rmṯ ist*	Amount for the crew
2 *nty r mḥ pꜣy=i diw*	which is to complete my rations:

3-15 *(List of names and amounts of 1¼ and 1½ khar)*

O. Turin 57429 (Group I: Ramesses II)

6 *ʿḥʿ ẖꜣr 48¼, <u>21¼</u> dmḏ 69½*	Amount: 48¼, <u>21¼</u> *khar*, total 69½.
wp st	Details of it:

7-9 *(List of names starting with the foreman in standard ration list format)*

O. DeM 662 (Group III: Ramesses III)

1 *rnpt sp 19 ꜣbd 3 šmw sw 6*	Regnal Year 19, III Shemu 6.
hrw pn n dit wꜣḏw	This day of distribution of vegetables
2 *n tnt-niwt ʿḥʿ n bty*	for Tinetniut(?). Amount of emmer:
ẖꜣr 9 wp st	9 *khar*. Details of it:

---

with no question of accruals.

54 Lesko (2002: 76), but see also Valbelle (1977: 131-132), who relates it to something absent, albeit outside a rations context. Helck (1974: 127) renders the meaning as "zusammenfassende Aufstellung" (summary statement).

55 Examples of each, in order, include O. Cairo JE 72457, vs. 3; O. Cairo 25742, 6; O. Cairo 25755, vs. 5; and O. DeM 10007, 3 (*ʿḳw*).

[3] *p3 i3w ḫ3r 3*	The old man 3 *khar*,
[4] *p3 swnw*	The doctor.

In two of the four examples, *ꜥḥꜥ* appears at the start of the first line, as a header, which would seem like the most appropriate place. Despite this, and also with the last part of the line being lost, the first line of O. Ashmol. 108 recto appears to duplicate what follows, since the following line, which includes an amount, could also be taken as a heading. In addition, further emphasis is provided by *wp st* in line 4, and the next lines commonly use *rdyt*, providing the impression of sub-sections in the text. The amounts of lines 4-6 are recorded on each line and totalled in line 7. Why the text is split up in this way is unclear and somewhat confusing. O. DeM 843 is more straightforward, *ꜥḥꜥ* is used as a heading of a document that may be a memorandum to the writer, given his reference to "completing my rations" as part of a quota. Unlike wood, fish and other consumables delivered from outside the village, there is no evidence for rations being delivered in quotas, so what this text may represent is what the writer was responsible for. The individual ration amounts are unusual and would suggest additional rations, but the payments are stated as *diw*.

By the style of the content, O. Turin 57429 seems to have been written in two parts, but this can not be confirmed without viewing the original ostracon. Line 6 records *ꜥḥꜥ* followed by amounts in *khar* and emphasised by *wp st*, then specifically broken down in sections in the standard ration format. O. DeM 662 is included as it records an amount of emmer probably split between at least three individuals; this may or may not relate to rations. Again, there seems to be a relationship between *ꜥḥꜥ* "amount" and *wp st* "details of it", perhaps one of emphasis, but recording an "amount" does not appear unusual.

Further uses of *ꜥḥꜥ* are present in non-rations contexts; the rendering of "amount" is still correct, but it has a number of uses which depend on other words used within the phrase. These have been examined by Megally[56], who concludes that *dmḏ ꜥḥꜥ* is itself a repetition, whist comparing the format of phrases incorporating *îw*, *šsp* and *ꜥḥꜥ*, all of which seem very much interchangeable. Therefore, *ꜥḥꜥ* is one example where a word is used more in one area of accounting than another, and seems to be more prevalent in accounts detailing deliveries of commodities such as fish, wood and copper than ration payments. Its use in these contexts, where the consumables were brought in from outside, may have been limited to the 20th Dynasty[57], but despite there being fewer usages within ration accounting, this latter subset does indicate that the use of *ꜥḥꜥ* was not restricted to the 20th Dynasty. Even if the volume of evidence is limited, these few examples add to our knowledge by revealing that *ꜥḥꜥ* was used in the 19th Dynasty even if any detailed examination of any change in use or meaning is still not possible.

§3.2.7 *wḥm*

The standard meaning of *wḥm* is "again", "repeat" or "report"[58] primarily used in a verbal sense.

---

56 Megally (1977: 58-59).

57 Suggested by Haring (2003b: 140-141), who rightly adds that there is not sufficient surviving material to prove this to be correct.

58 Lesko (2002: 108).

There are a handful of examples in the rations corpus from Deir el-Medina covering the whole of the Ramesside period, but only upon closer examination of each context can suggestions of the exact use be made.

O. Ashmol. 111 rt. (Group II)

1 *rnpt sp 4 ꜣbd 4 šmw sw 9*	Regnal Year 4, IV Shemu 9.
wḥm diw wp=sn	Report. Rations. Detail of them:
2-3 (*A list of rations*)	

O. Ashmol. 111 rt. has *wḥm diw* written in red, which indicates a heading and therefore in this instance eliminates the use of "again" as a translation. The sense here is surely a report which highlights the different ration components, namely the *diw* here and the *dni* on line 4, both of which are written in red. One possibility is that this was an early way of showing both ration classes on the same document, but this is highly unlikely since it is known that emmer was specified in red and barley in black.

O. DeM 839 (Undated)

1 *rdyt r diw n pꜣ ꜥꜣ-n-ist ẖꜣr 2*	What was given as rations to the foreman: 2 *khar.*
2 *wḥm rdyt m ꜣbd 1 prt ẖꜣr 1*	Also. What was given for I Peret: 1khar.
ḏꜣt ½	Balance ½.

There seems to be no notion of reporting in any sense in this short example, which is complete in its two lines, so the report would have been very brief indeed. Instead, the allusion here is more one of "in addition to" what was written in line 1; not the same meaning as "again" but perhaps "also".

O. DeM 852 vs. Col. II (Group II: Ramesses II)

1 *dmḏ wḥm 1 ẖꜣr 10*	Total, in addition to 1, 10 *khar.*
2 *iw 2½ wḥm 4*	Delivered 2½, again, 4.
3 *rwi n nn ipt 1*	Reimbursed to them, 1 *oipe.*
4 *iw 4¼ wḥm 2 dmḏ 6¼*	Delivered 4¼, again 2. Total 6¼.

This somewhat confusing ostracon gives us another insight into recording techniques. Grandet[59] has translated *wḥm* in line 1 as "added", referring to the total of 1 *khar* recorded on verso I, 6-9. This seems logical, as it would tie in with the same meaning as that on O. Ashmol. 111. The meanings in lines 2 and 4 are clearly the same, and here "again" is a good fit, since it refers to the same bringing forward mechanic noted in line 1. In line 2, the 2½ relates to the 1 *khar* in line 1 being added to the 1½ *khar* recorded in lines 2 to 5 in Column 1. It is not clear where the 2 *khar* in line 4 comes from.

59 Grandet (2003: 33).

O. Munich ÄS 397 (Group III: Ramesses III)

1-4 (*Date followed by delivery list*)

5 *wḥm dmḏ p3 ꜥ-n-ist ẖ3r 2* — Report. Total. The foreman, 2 *khar*,

p3 sš ẖ3r 1 — the scribe 1 *khar.*

6-7 (*A list of rations follows*)

8-10 (*A list of rations follows*)

The use of *wḥm* is more like that used on O. Ashmol. 111, where the term is part of a heading contained within the text itself. This ostracon contains four delivery lists on the same surface, and the second is the only time where *wḥm* is used. Why this should be so is unknown, but it does highlight the variations contained not only within ostraca from the same time period, but variations contained within the same document.

P. Turin 1960 vs. (Group IV: Ramesses IX)

1:1-4 (*Some text lost, but records a delivery list*)

1:5 *wḥm rdyt.n=sn* — Again (or report). What they had been given.

1:5-6 (*A list follows*)

1:7-9 (*A delivery list*)

1:10 (*wḥm followed by list*)

These two examples are similar to a discussion made by Megally[60], where it is suggested that the *wḥm rdyt n=f* formula indicates something which had been given at a different and separate time. While this appears to be logically sound, in isolated rations examples it is difficult to confirm or deny this statement. Both "again" or "report" are appropriate renderings of *wḥm* here, with the latter in the sense of repeating.

P. Turin 2062 vs. (Group IV: Ramesses IX)

Lines 7 and 8 both read *wḥm* followed by short lists. Parts of the text are lost so it is impossible to ascertain whether other short lists recorded on the verso contain *wḥm* or not. Based on what is legible, the use appears to be identical to that employed in the verso of P. Turin 1960.

P. Turin 2081 rt. (Group III: Ramesses III)

1:3 (*A list followed by*):

wḥm Ḥr-ms ẖ3r ½ dmḏ 1¼ — Again, Hormose ½ *khar*. Total 1¼.

ḥmwt ẖ3r 2½ — Women servants 2½ *khar*.

1:4 (*Lost*)

1:5 (*A different delivery list dated to Day 24*)

The reason for including *wḥm* prior to Hormose in this instance, and not where he receives rations in rt. 6, is unknown. This particular Hormose was in a position of some authority, but

60 Megally (1977: 67).

whether he was a scribe or had some other function within the community is unclear[61].

Closer examination of the handful of instances where *wḥm* is used in a rations context seems to suggest that the sense implied by its usage could be varied. On one hand, the notion is that of a sub-heading, signifying "a report" in terms of someone repeating or giving someone else a list of deliveries; on the other, a more simple meaning of "again" seems to be more appropriate. The term is used throughout the Ramesside period, but even so this small number of examples can not confirm that its use was constant during the whole of this period.

§3.3 Conclusion

The subject of vocabulary used within sets of texts is extensive, and while taking such terminology solely in a ration context narrows the scope considerably, there is still enough subject matter to warrant its own section to allow the focus to be on specific words and phrases and also on profound changes over the course of the Ramesside period. The effectiveness of such scrutinisation depends upon the number of examples present in the available material, and this in turn can facilitate one avenue of further study, which could be a comparison between the use of words in accounting documents and the same words in texts of others genres such as letters and legal records.

In the rations material, terminology and vocabulary comes under two broad classes: words which are usually, but not always, used as headers, and those which are specifically used in an accounting context. There is usually little doubt about how words in the former category should be read. There are some variations of what appears to be a standardised set of expressions, which indicates that the scribes followed a generalised format, but were still allowed some degree of individuality. Words and expressions used in ration accounts need as many examples as possible to be tested against the generally accepted meaning in order to render an accurate sense, and this may also vary as to the context and the date of the document. There are many variations of formulae used in headings or sub-headings within documents, some of these are slight, with a large number of deliveries solely being recorded as *m-drt* an individual.

It is probable that certain words were used with a greater degree of frequency, depending on whether the records were from the 19th or the 20th Dynasty. We are unfortunately hampered by the lack of surviving evidence in many cases, but there are suppositions which can be made. Some seem logical, such as the increased use of *pꜣ dit diw* with the definite article during the 20th Dynasty, and the popularity of *rdyt* in the 19th Dynasty. Other vocabulary, such as *ꜥḥꜥ*, may have no definitive pattern in a rations context, but expanding the scope of the study into other fields would reveal a tendency towards a later use rather than an earlier one.

There seem to be no strict rules as to the precision of the terminology used, and the order in which they occurred. Instead scribes were allowed a slight variation in the vocabulary necessary to suit their exact requirements. Words relating to ration accounting often have their expected meaning, but not always, and the meaning of a given word can depend on its position within the text and any presence of other accounting based words and phrases. Words such as *wp st* and *dmḏ* do not always convey the same meaning and can even have different meanings within the same text. Sometimes there are subtle variations in the sense of individual words, such as the use of *wḏꜣt*. Other expressions, such as *dmḏ hꜣw nb* and *ḫry-ḥꜣt*, are used sparingly and may even

61 None of the individuals with this name discussed by Davies (1999) configure to this individual.

change meaning over time, as seems to be the case with *dmḏ h3w nb*. However, the relatively infrequent use of some accounting words does not always allow any meaningful analysis on changes over time.

CHAPTER 4

CHRONOLOGY OF THE DELIVERY DATES

It is fortunate for scholars today that the scribes at Deir el-Medina dated many of their documents, since a wealth of information relating to a multitude of village matters can be examined and assessed including in a ration context, patterns of ration delivery and any associated absences, the layout and composition of the documents and how they changed over time, and the checking of an "ideal" delivery time against the entire corpus of dated documents, if such a concept existed. One of the main aims in taking as complete a list of documents as possible and looking at the individual dates is to speculate as to the patterns of delivery, not only showing any clustering within the month but also to get behind the reasons as to why this should occur, as well as investigating the likelihood of a regular day when rations were delivered.

It is not clear what the official day of payment was for the rations, or even whether there was one, but the suggestion that the 28th of the previous month[1], which is perhaps more akin to modern Western wage patterns, is not substantiated by the evidence. This delivery date is probably better viewed as an ideal for our convenience rather than practice[2], as it is easy to believe that rations tended to be delivered on specific days of the month. How accurate this possibility is can only be revealed in the following discussion, with a detailed breakdown, sifting through and arranging the data, and using it to produce tables and graphs to enable accurate visual and statistical conclusions. The only scholar to attempt anything of this sort has been Antoine (2009). However, the present study takes matters further by expanding the available material and makes fewer general assumptions. Antoine uses a greater range of variables, such as social disturbances, the season of delivery and fluctuations in grain price, and attempts to link these with grain delays. The former does not appear to be particularly valid on the grounds that fourteen examples of

1 The statement made by Žába (1952: 644-645) is based on three selected examples, and is not made within a rations context. See also Antoine (2009: 3 and n. 2), who bases his study of the delays in grain rations on the assumption that *diw* were expected to be issued on the first day of the month. His study is concerned with arrears and includes Journals where no rations are delivered, but this is stated to be not as a result of scribal omission (p. 9).

2 Janssen (1975: 464). This does not discount the possibility that calculations may have started from the 1st of the month.

adverse social events, such as the crew "passing the wall", are far too few to generate any accurate result. The latter is limited to specific time periods because any rise in the price of emmer or barley throughout the Ramesside period can not be pinpointed accurately except from the mid 20th Dynasty,[3] or the time of Ramesses VII onwards[4]. Undoubtedly delays in grain rations did exist[5], but the degree of any such delay is very difficult to assess because there is no indication what the base point was in terms of the day of delivery and what was regarded as "late"; instead a more general approach is adopted here in examining variances with emphasis placed on the months of delivery.

The documents which contain one or more dates in the text have been separated into three groups; those which contain no day or month or include only a regnal year are not included at this point. The first group is tabulated in Table 1, which shows 104 examples of basic rations (*diw*) being distributed, and this group includes examples where either a date of delivery or the period to which the delivery related was recorded. Table 2 shows the corresponding information for thirty-one examples recording details of additional ration payments (*dni*). If a text can be dated with certainty to a particular pharaoh, this will be included in the evaluation since it is important to show the periods which we have material for; however, where the date of a document is uncertain, it is shown in the relevant table in italics. Both groups consist primarily of ostraca, but a papyrus is included within this first group if it is known with certainty that its date is prior to the reign of Ramesses IX. The majority of documents specifically state whether the recording is of *diw* or *dni*, but there is some slight uncertainty noted in three ostraca: O. DeM 712, O. DeM 10039 rt., and O. DeM 10040. These are included in Table 1 despite there being no label as such; the amounts suggest *diw* and not *dni* albeit not entirely conclusively[6].

The last group, tabulated in Table 3, consists of papyri dating from the late 20th Dynasty reigns of Ramesses IX to Ramesses XI. These are treated as a separate group in order to facilitate a comparative discussion on ostraca and papyri as media of recording in terms of content and vocabulary, and the hopeful possibility of looking into changes over time in recording techniques. Despite their length, the number of papyri in this category is relatively small and only two indicate a clear mention of *dni*. Therefore documents recording either *diw* or *dni* are included together as one subset and not two.

3 Černý (1934: 176-177).

4 Janssen (1975a: 114, 122). The problem here, of course, is that we have no concrete dating evidence from the reign of Ramesses VII, or those kings either side, so as a result any correlation between grain prices and season are inconclusive (*ibid.*, 126-127).

5 Valbelle (1985: 149).

6 These are dated examples where the classification of rations is not noted. In addition, there are many more examples of non-dated texts where the same absence of information exists. These are: O. Ashmol. 20; O. Ashmol. 72; O. Ashmol. 257; O. Ashmol. 277; O. BM EA 50726; O. Cairo 25620; O. Cairo 25643 rt.; O. Cairo 25689; O. Cairo JE 72455; O. Cairo JE 72457; O. DeM 149; O. DeM 181; O. DeM 182; O. DeM 188; O. DeM 189; O. DeM 369 (Year 4 but no month or day); O. DeM 370; O. DeM 383; O. DeM 577; O. DeM 591; O. DeM 640; O. DeM 661; O. DeM 735; O. DeM 740; O. DeM 741; O. DeM 837 (Year 56 but no month or day); O. DeM 838; O. DeM 843; O. DeM 850; O. DeM 10031; O. DeM 10035; O. IFAO 265; O. Michaelides 34; O. Michaelides 65; O. Qurna 656/4; O. Qurna 659/4; and O. Turin 57429. O. DeM 707 records small, unclassified amounts, but even so is assumed to be *diw*. O. DeM 852 rt. records a delivery of *diw*, but consisting of dates and not grain.

Table 1. Documents recording the delivery of basic ration wages (*diw*)

Document	King	Season	Day	Date of delivery	Period Covered
O. Ashmol. 11 vs.*	*Ramesses V*	Akhet I	3	Yr 2 I *3ḫt* 3	-
O. Ashmol. 21	-	Shemu IV	3	Yr 3 IV *šmw* 3	-
O. Ashmol. 107	*Ramesses IV*	-	-	-	III *šmw*
O. Ashmol. 108	-	-	-	-	III *šmw*
O. Ashmol. 111	Seti II/Siptah	Shemu IV	9	Yr 4 IV *šmw* 9	III *šmw*
O. Ashmol. 131 vs.	*Ramesses VI*	Peret II	5	Yr 2 II *prt* 5	IV *3ḫt* - II *prt*
O. Ashmol. 184	Siptah/Tausret	-	-	-	III *šmw*
O. Ashmol. 200	Ramesses II	Peret I	3	Yr 30 I *prt* 3	-
O. Ashmol. 262	-	Akhet II	-	Yr 4 II *3ḫt*	I *3ḫt* 5
O. Ashmol. 274	*Ramesses III*	Peret IV	10	IV *prt* 10	-
O. Ashmol. 1139	-	-	-	-	II *šmw*
O. Berlin 10661	*20th Dynasty*	-	-	Yr 12	II *šmw* - IV *šmw*
O. Berlin 11249	*20th Dynasty*	-	-	-	I *prt*
O. Berlin 12294	Ramesses II	Shemu IV	21	IV *šmw* 21	IV *šmw* – II *3ḫt*
O. Berlin 12631 rt.*	Ramesses IV	Shemu IV	11	Yr 1 IV *šmw* 11	-
O. Berlin 12633 rt.*	Ramesses III	Peret IV	21	(Yr 25) IV *prt* 21	-
O. Berlin 14210	*Ramesses III*	-	-	-	II *prt*
O. Berlin 14219	*20th Dynasty*	Peret IV	2	IV *prt* 2	I *šmw*
O. Berlin 14264 rt.	*20th Dynasty*	Shemu III	3	III *šmw* 3	-
O. Berlin 14302 vs.	Ramesses IV	Akhet IV	12	Yr 3 IV *3ḫt* 1	II *3ḫt*
O. Berlin 14842 rt.	Late 19th Dynasty	Peret IV	6	IV *prt* 6	-
O. Berlin 14842 vs.	Late 19th Dynasty	Akhet IV	1	Yr 3 II *3ḫt* 12	-
O. BM EA 50739	Late 19th Dynasty	-	-	-	III *šmw*
O. Cairo 25280	*Ramesses IV*	Akhet III	4	Yr 6 III *3ḫt* 4	-
O. Cairo 25533 vs.*	-	Peret III	19	III *prt* 19	-
O. Cairo 25608	*Mid 20th Dynasty*	Shemu I	-	I *šmw*	II *šmw*
O. Cairo 25685 rt.	*Late 20th Dynasty*	Peret IV	-	IV *prt*	III *prt* – IV *prt*
O. Cairo 25698	*20th Dynasty*	Akhet I	20	Yr 3 I *3ḫt* 20	-
O. Cairo 25809 rt.	Ramesses II	Peret I	2	Yr 38 I *prt* 2	-
O. DeM 32*	Ramesses III	Shemu IV	21	Yr 25 IV *šmw* 21	-
O. DeM 34*	Ramesses III	Peret IV	13	Yr 27 IV *prt* 13	-
O. DeM 38*	Ramesses III	Shemu II	11	Yr 32 II *šmw* 11	I *šmw*
O. DeM 42*	Ramesses IV	Akhet III	15	Yr 1 III *3ḫt* 15	III *3ḫt*
O. DeM 43*	Ramesses IV	Peret I	13	Yr 1 I *prt* 13	I *prt*

Document	King	Season	Day	Date of delivery	Period Covered
O. DeM 44*	Ramesses IV	Shemu III	28	Yr 2 III *šmw* 28	III *šmw* – IV *šmw*
O. DeM 45*	Ramesses IV	Akhet II	19	Yr 2 II *ꜣḫt* 19	II *ꜣḫt* – III *ꜣḫt*
O. DeM 141	*20th Dynasty*	-	-	-	III *prt*
O. DeM 153 rt.*	Ramesses III	Shemu I	5	Yr 31 I *šmw* 5	IV *prt*
O. DeM 153 vs.*	Ramesses III	Shemu I	27	Yr 32 I *šmw* 27	I *šmw*
O. DeM 156*	Ramesses III	Shemu IV	5	Yr 28 IV *šmw* 5	-
O. DeM 159*	Ramesses III	Peret I	6	Yr 31 I *prt* 6	IV *ꜣḫt*
O. DeM 162*	*Ramesses IV*	-	-	-	I *šmw*
O. DeM 177	*Amenmesse*	Peret II	13	Yr 1 II *prt* 13	I *prt* - IV *prt*
O. DeM 179	*Merenptah*	-	-	-	IV *ꜣḫt*
O. DeM 180	*Ramesses IV*	Akhet IV	9	IV *ꜣḫt* 9/10	-
O. DeM 184	*20th Dynasty*	Peret II	10	Yr 4 II *prt* 10	III *prt* – IV *prt*
O. DeM 186	*20th Dynasty*	Shemu I	-	(I) *šmw*	IV *prt*
O. DeM 252	*20th Dynasty*	Peret III	13	Yr 5 III *prt* 13	-
O. DeM 272	*20th Dynasty*	-	-	-	I *prt*
O. DeM 276	*Ramesses III*	Akhet I	20	I *ꜣḫt* 20	-
O. DeM 288	*19th Dynasty*	-	-	-	II *šmw*
O. DeM 312	-	-	-	-	IV *prt*
O. DeM 329	-	Shemu IV	-	IV *šmw*	-
O. DeM 345	*20th Dynasty*	Akhet IV	10+?	IV *ꜣḫt* 10 (+?)	IV *ꜣḫt*
O. DeM 371	-	-	-	-	I *ꜣḫt*
O. DeM 374	*19th Dynasty*	-	-	-	IV *prt*
O. DeM 375	*Siptah*	-	-	-	II *prt*, IV *prt* -I *prt*
O. DeM 376	*Siptah*	-	-	-	II *šmw* - III *šmw*
O. DeM 377	*20th Dynasty*	-	-	-	III *prt*
O. DeM 378	-	Shemu I	18	I *šmw* 18	-
O. DeM 379	*20th Dynasty*	Peret I	25	IV *prt* 25	IV *prt*
O. DeM 380	Ramesses IV	Shemu IV	27	Yr 2 IV *šmw* 27	III *šmw*
O. DeM 381 rt.	Ramesses IV	Peret II	22	Yr 4 II *prt* 22	-
O. DeM 381 vs.	Ramesses IV	Peret II	12	Yr 4 II *prt* 12	-
O. DeM 382	*Ramesses III*	-	-	-	II *prt* - III *prt*
O. DeM 384	Ramesses III	-	-	-	II *ꜣḫt* - III *ꜣḫt*
O. DeM 386	*20th Dynasty*	Peret III	6	III *prt* 6	III *prt*
O. DeM 427*	Ramesses III	Akhet I	2	Yr 28 I *ꜣḫt* 2	-

Document	King	Season	Day	Date of delivery	Period Covered
O. DeM 611	Siptah	Shemu III	19	Yr 1 III *šmw* 19	I *prt*
O. DeM 621 rt.	Ramesses II	Shemu I	12+?	I *šmw* 12 (+?)	I – II *šmw*
O. DeM 638	-	-	-	-	II *ꜣḫt*
O. DeM 707	*Ramesses IV/VI*	Akhet II	5	Yr 6 II *ꜣḫt* 5	-
O. DeM 712	-	-	-	-	I *ꜣḫt*
O. DeM 734	-	-	-	-	I *ꜣḫt*
O. DeM 736	-	Akhet II	6	II *ꜣḫt* 6	-
O. DeM 737	-	Akhet I	12	I *ꜣḫt* 12	-
O. DeM 738	Ramesses III	Shemu III	4	Yr 29 III *šmw* 4	-
O. DeM 739	-	Akhet I	3	I *ꜣḫt* 3	I *ꜣḫt*
O. DeM 839	-	-	-	-	I *prt*
O. DeM 840	-	Shemu II	24	II *šmw* 24	-
O. DeM 841	-	-	Epag	-	-
O. DeM 842	Ramesses III	Epag. 3	-	Yr 24 Epag.3	-
O. DeM 845	-	-	-	-	II *ꜣḫt*
O. DeM 846	*Late 19th Dynasty*	-	-	-	I *šmw* - II *šmw*
O. DeM 848	-	Akhet II	2	II *ꜣḫt* 2	-
O. DeM 849	-	Peret I	1	I *prt* 1	-
O. DeM 852 vs.	Ramesses II	Akhet I	5	I *ꜣḫt* 5	I *ꜣḫt*
O. DeM 10032	Ramesses III	Akhet I	11	Yr 29 I *ꜣḫt* 11	-
O. DeM 10033	Ramesses III	Shemu III	5	Yr 29 III *šmw* 5	-
O. DeM 10034	*20th Dynasty*	Peret III	25	III *prt* 25	-
O. DeM 10036	-	-	-	-	I *ꜣḫt*
O. DeM 10039 rt.	-	Shemu III	13	Yr 2 III *šmw* 13	IV *ꜣḫt* and I *prt*
O. DeM 10040	-	-	-	-	III *šmw* 29
O. DeM 10161 rt.	Ramesses III	Shemu III	-	III *šmw*	-
O. DeM 10161 vs.	Ramesses III	Shemu III	-	III *šmw*	-
O. DeM 10163	Ramesses II	-	-	-	-
O. DeM 10164	Siptah	Peret III	20	Yr 1 III *prt* 20	II *prt*
O. DeM 10165	Siptah	Akhet III	10+?	III *ꜣḫt*	III *ꜣḫt*
O. IFAO 300 rt.	Ramesses III	Peret III	19	(Yr 27) III *prt* 19	-
O. Michaelides 73	Ramesses III	Peret III	26	Yr 31 III *prt* 26	III *prt*
O. Munich ÄS 397	Ramesses III	Akhet I	30	Yr 28 I *ꜣḫt* 30	II *ꜣḫt*
O. Munich ÄS 397	Ramesses III	Akhet II	30	Yr 28 II *ꜣḫt* 30	-
O. Prague H14*	Ramesses III	Akhet III	10	Yr 31 III *ꜣḫt* 10	-
O. Strasbourg H110 rt.	*Late 19th Dynasty*	Akhet IV	18	IV *ꜣḫt* 18	III *ꜣḫt* and I *prt*

Document	King	Season	Day	Date of delivery	Period Covered
O. Strasbourg H110 vs.	*Late 19th Dynasty*	Akhet IV	18	IV *ꜣḫt* 18	I *prt*
O. Strasbourg H117[1]	Ramesses III	Peret IV	26	Yr 14 IV *prt* 26	-
O. Turin 57072	Ramesses III	All	-	Yr 28-30	-
O. Turin 57475*	Ramesses III	Akhet III	12	(Yr 25) III *ꜣḫt* 12	-
O. UC 39648*	Ramesses III	Akhet I	19	Yr 25 I *ꜣḫt* 19	-
O. Varille 39	Ramesses III	Peret II	17	Yr 29 II *prt* 17	II *prt*
P. Turin 1880	Ramesses III	Peret II	17	Yr 29 II *prt* 17	II *prt*
P. Turin 1885*	*Ramesses IV*	Akhet I	18	I *ꜣḫt* 18	-
P. Turin 2081+2095	*Ramesses V*	Akhet II	16	II *ꜣḫt* 16	II *ꜣḫt*

Notes to Table 1:

1. The writing on O. Strasbourg H117 is unclear, thus it is treated as internal.
2. The dates of documents attributed to reigns in italics are not certain or are very general, and have been taken after scholars such as Černý, Kitchen and Helck, as entered into the Deir el-Medina Database.
3. Texts recording possible ration deliveries from outside are highlighted in bold.
4. Documents from the Journal of the Necropolis are denoted by an asterisk.

Table 2. Documents recording the delivery of additional ration wages (*dni*)

Document	King	Season	Day	Date of delivery	Period Covered
O. Ashmol. 48	-	-	29	Day 29	IV *šmw*
O. Ashmol. 111	Seti II/Siptah	Shemu IV	9	Yr 4 IV *šmw* 9	III *šmw*
O. Ashmol. 200	Ramesses II	Akhet I	3	Yr 30 I *ꜣḫt* 3	-
O. Ashmol. 262	-	Akhet II	-	Yr 4 II *ꜣḫt*	I *ꜣḫt*
O. BM EA 50739	*Late 19th Dynasty*	-	-	-	III *šmw*
O. Cairo 25517γ	Siptah	Shemu IV	9	IV *šmw* 9	I *prt*
O. Cairo 25592	Ramesses III	Akhet II	2	Yr 29 III *ꜣḫt* 2	-
O. Cairo 25620	*20th Dynasty*	-	-	-	I *prt*
O. Cairo 25685 rt.	*Late 20th Dynasty*	Peret IV	28	IV *prt* 28	III *prt* - IV *prt*
O. Cairo 25685 vs.	*Late 20th Dynasty*	Shemu I	7	I *šmw* 7	IV *prt*
O. Cairo JE 72455	-	Peret II	3	II *prt* 3, III/IV *prt*	-
O. DeM 179	*Merenptah*	-	-	-	IV *ꜣḫt*
O. DeM 184	*20th Dynasty*	Peret II	10	Yr 4 II *prt* 10	III *prt* - IV *prt*
O. DeM 252	*20th Dynasty*	Peret III	13	Yr 5 III *prt* 13	-
O. DeM 374	*19th Dynasty*	-	-	-	I *šmw*, II *prt*, IV *ꜣḫt*
O. DeM 382	*Ramesses III*	-	-	-	I *prt*
O. DeM 385	*20th Dynasty*	-	-	-	II *ꜣḫt*

Document	King	Season	Day	Date of delivery	Period Covered
O. DeM 427*	Ramesses III	Akhet I	5	I *ꜣḫt* 5	IV *šmw*, I *ꜣḫt*
O. DeM 737	-	Akhet I	12	I *ꜣḫt* 12	I *ꜣḫt* 21
O. DeM 845	-	-	-	-	II *ꜣḫt*
O. DeM 849	-	Peret I	1	I *prt* 1	-
O. DeM 10162 rt.	-	-	-	-	-
O. Strasbourg H110 rt.	*Late 19th Dynasty*	Akhet IV	18	IV *ꜣḫt* 18	III *ꜣḫt* – II *prt*
O. Strasbourg H110 vs.	*Late 19th Dynasty*	Akhet IV	18	IV *ꜣḫt* 18	IV *ꜣḫt* – II *prt*
O. UC 39626 vs.*	Ramesses III	Akhet II	23	Yr 25 II *ꜣḫt* 23	II *ꜣḫt*
O. UC 39661	*20th Dynasty*	Akhet II	5	II *ꜣḫt* 5	I *ꜣḫt*
O. Valley of Queens 6	Ramesses II	Shemu III	1	Yr 42 III *šmw* 1	-
P. Bib. Nat. 237 Cart.1	*Ramesses VI*	Akhet II	20	II *ꜣḫt* 20	II *ꜣḫt*
P. Turin 2081+2095	*Ramesses V*	Akhet II	16	II *ꜣḫt* 16	I *ꜣḫt*
P. Turin 2081+2095	*Ramesses V*	Akhet II	21	II *ꜣḫt* 21	II *ꜣḫt*
P. Turin 2081+2095	*Ramesses V*	Akhet III	2	III *ꜣḫt* 2	II *ꜣḫt*

Table 3. Papyri from Ramesses IX – Ramesses XI

Document	King	Season	Day	Date of delivery	Period Covered
P. Turin 1884 + 2067 + 2071 + 2105	Yr 16 Ramesses IX	Akhet I	26	I *ꜣḫt* 26	-
P. Turin 1898 + 1926 + 1937 + 2094	Yr 3 Ramesses X	Peret IV	29	IV *prt* 29	-
P. Turin 1898 + 1926 + 1937 + 2094	Yr 3 Ramesses X	Shemu I	28	I *šmw* 28	-
P. Turin 1906 + 1939 + 2047	Yr 7 Ramesses IX	Akhet III	17	III *ꜣḫt* 17	-
P. Turin 1906 + 1939 + 2047	Yr 7 Ramesses IX	Akhet III	25	III *ꜣḫt* 25[1]	-
P. Turin 1932 + 1939	Yr 19 Ramesses IX	Akhet III	7	III *ꜣḫt* 7	-
P. Turin 1932 + 1939	Yr 19 Ramesses IX	Akhet IV	9	IV *ꜣḫt* 9	-
P. Turin 1960 + 2071	Ramesses IX	-	-	-	-
P. Turin 2002	Ramesses IX	-	-	-	-
P. Turin 2013 + 2050 + 2061 (dni)	Yr 6 Ramesses IX	Akhet II	4	II *ꜣḫt* 4	II *ꜣḫt*
P. Turin 2013 + 2050 + 2061	Yr 6 Ramesses IX	Akhet II	4	II *ꜣḫt* 4	III *ꜣḫt*
P. Turin 2013 + 2050 + 2061	Yr 6 Ramesses IX	Akhet II	30	II *ꜣḫt* 30	II *ꜣḫt*
P. Turin 2013 + 2050 + 2061	Yr 6 Ramesses IX	Akhet III	16	III *ꜣḫt* 16	-
P. Turin 2015	Yr 2	Shemu IV	26	IV *šmw* 26	-
P. Turin 2018[2]	Yr 8 Ramesses XI	-	-	-	-
P. Turin 2062	*Ramesses IX*	-	-	-	III *šmw*
P. Turin 2097+2105	Yr 20 Ramesses XI	Shemu I	30	I *šmw* 30	-

Document	King	Season	Day	Date of delivery	Period Covered
P. Turin 2097+2105	Yr 20 Ramesses XI	Shemu II	28	II *šmw* 28	-
P. Turin 2097+2105	Yr 20 Ramesses XI	Shemu III	28	III *šmw* 28	-
P. Turin PN109	*Ramesses IX*	Shemu IV	26	IV *šmw* 26	IV *šmw*

Notes to Table 3:

1 The verso is headed *it m it* (barley) and followed by a fragmented list. Verso 2:12 records a delivery on III *3ḫt* 2, but since it is highly dubious whether the delivery classed as ration payments, it has not been included in the analysis.

2 P. Turin 2018 is a series of grain accounts. On rt. A1, the date of delivery (? *3ḫt* 15?), where rations are stated, is doubtful. Both rt. A4:1-2 and vs. A1:17 are undated, even though the period the rations relate to is given. Vs. B1:2 records the distribution of rations on a Day 16. These fragmented records are noted here, but for the purposes of the analysis, they are not included.

The vast majority of the documents undoubtedly relate to rations being distributed once the grain has reached the village, but there are three records which *may* relate to deliveries from outside; however all three are doubtful and need some examination. O. DeM 712 seems to be the most clear-cut of the three, on the basis that the small amounts of emmer were delivered (*iw*) to an unspecified recipient or location. Similarly, O. DeM 380 appears to be a delivery from outside, since grain was explicitly stated to have been brought by (*in*) the scribe Hori to the Enclosure (line 2 reads *inyt in sš Ḥri r p3 ḫtm*). Despite the specific use of this word, it is difficult to believe that a scribe would bring grain to the village, so unless he either accompanied it on its journey, or more likely supervised the delivery, the doubt remains. The last example is O. DeM 288, which continues after the initial date with *in* [...] *gmyt im* "brought [...] which was found there", possibly implying some grain was found somewhere and brought to the village as part of temple offerings. This is more confusing, especially since a few damaged signs in the middle of line 1 hinders any interpretation. However, the grain appears to be part of temple offerings; in addition this grain "was found there", wherever "there" was. No added value can be provided by treating these examples separately, so despite the ambiguity, they will be treated as standard ration distribution lists.

Of interest are the documents from which delivery patterns can be extracted. Where the individual days are recorded, texts can show the presence or absence of a strict delivery schedule, and these are tabulated in Tables 4 and 5 for *diw* and *dni* respectively, which are discussed in due course. Documents which record a variance between the date of issue, and the month(s) to the delivery related, can provide figures as to the proportion of deliveries which were in arrears, on time or in advance. Only then will it be possible to attempt to get behind these figures and suggest possible explanations for any significant results. Not including the doubtful day on O. DeM 10165, out of the 104 basic ration examples, forty-two have both dates recorded (a total of sixteen out of thirty-one for *dni*). Two of these need further explanation. O. DeM 621 is a lengthy composition dated to I *šmw* but has deliveries to both sides dated to I *šmw* and II *šmw*, although the note relating to III *prt* (rt. 5) is merely a small total and can be disregarded from the analysis. The date recorded on O. DeM 186 is broken, but it is highly probable that the first month of *šmw* is the correct month. In addition to this, O. Turin 57072 is included in Table 1, but without any dates, on the basis that it records the monthly rations delivered, and the associated balances, to a single individual over the course of more than a year. This document serves more as a private set of accounts for this workman rather than revealing any specific details of deliveries. Further examination of the writing itself may indicate whether the ostracon was written in one sitting or added to during the noted periods.

Where a document is fragmentary to the extent that dates or days are either missing or uncertain, such as O. IFAO 265 which may or may not be dated to Day 30, it is not included. The composition and writing of O. Berlin 14264 strongly suggests that the recto and verso record two lists delivered and recorded at the same time, so it will be treated throughout as one example rather than two. There are also other absentees from the tables: O. DeM 388 records an undated ration delivery, but a separate delivery to one of the temples is dated and there is no indication of whether the deliveries were on the same day or not. O. DeM 852 rt. relates to the delivery of *diw*, but the records are of dates (*bnri*) and not of grain, and hence are outside the scope of the present study.

A further problem is encountered upon examination of the variances[7], where a variance can be defined as any deviation between the period to which the delivery or distribution relates, and the date of the document. In the event that a single document has one or more months to which the deliveries relate, for example O. DeM 177, there is the question of how the variances of such documents should be treated. One possible solution would be to analyse the ration texts in a broad manner, thus creating groups where the variances are merely positive, negative or zero, ignoring absolute values, but there would still be considerable overlapping. The other option is to treat each month as a specific example, but this could get too cumbersome and place weight statistically onto documents with a wide range of delivery dates. These documents will undoubtedly come into their own once the reasons for their content and extended delivery schedules are examined. Therefore some kind of compromise is proposed, where an example can be split, but only if the magnitude, in mathematical terms, of the variances is distinct. To clarify, any sequence of delivery dates which is two months or longer[8] will be treated as one example if both months show only a positive variance or only a negative variance. The documents which record a date of issue and period of delivery can then be extracted and expanded to include the variances, and these are tabulated in Tables 11 (*diw*) and 12 (*dni*).

§4.1 Day, month and season of delivery

Before we can attempt to explain fully the distributions based around days, decades and seasons, we must take into account what type of document is being dealt with, or in other words, whether the record is a Journal text, a general notice of delivery or distribution—and these often overlap—or an account of the distribution of rations among members of the workforce. This line of approach will also require some investigation into any absences of delivery within the Journal,

7 Compare the methodology used here with that of Antoine (2010: 225), who identifies the problem and adopts the solution that any duplication is *dni*.

8 Therefore, as an example, O. DeM 177 is dated to II *prt* 13, and the deliveries are dated between I *prt* and IV *prt* and is therefore a positive variance. This subject is discussed in §4.5.

and therefore whether records were always kept. Clearly this was not done every time, as shown by the significant periods of non-delivery in the detailed calendar in Appendix 1. A more complete attempt to explain the reasons behind this may only be attempted when the original hieratic writing is taken into account, primarily because it may show the frequency of one scribe writing multiple documents.

Table 4 shows the data for *diw* which are split up into categories according to the delivery day, so a more detailed examination of delivery patterns can be performed on the relevant groups of texts. Two exercises will be carried out; firstly on the mid 20th Dynasty material covering the period from late Ramesses III through to Ramesses V, and secondly by taking all the material up to and including the mid 20th Dynasty as a single group, including the undated examples. The reason for this approach is simply that the number of texts from the 19th Dynasty is relatively low, so comparing the other results can enable us to estimate whether or not these documents had a significant impact on the final outcome. In addition, things can get somewhat cumbersome with too many sets of data being used concurrently, so in order to facilitate comparison with the later papyri, the data from both periods will be combined with the undated material to produce a larger sample size which will ensure a greater degree of accuracy to the results. This is not performed on the texts recording *dni* due to the limited number of examples.

Table 4. Basic rations: days of delivery of basic rations[9]

Day (Decade 1)	**1**	**2**	**3**	**4**	**5**	**6**	**7**	**8**	**9**	**10**	**Total**
19th Dynasty	1	1	1	0	1	1	0	0	1	0	6
Mid 20th Dyn.	0	2	2	2	5	2	0	0	1	3	17
Undated	1	1	2	0	0	1	0	0	0	0	5
Day (Decade 2)	**11**	**12**	**13**	**14**	**15**	**16**	**17**	**18**	**19**	**20**	
19th Dynasty	0	0	1	0	0	0	0	2	1	1	5
Mid 20th Dyn.	3	3	3	0	1	1	2	1	3	2	19
Undated	0	1	1	0	0	0	0	1	1	0	4
Day (Decade 3)	**21**	**22**	**23**	**24**	**25**	**26**	**27**	**28**	**29**	**30**	
19th Dynasty	1	0	0	0	0	0	0	0	0	0	1
Mid 20th Dyn.	2	1	0	0	2	2	2	1	0	2	12
Undated	0	0	0	1	0	0	0	0	0	0	1

9 O.DeM 345 (20th Dynasty), O.DeM 621 rt. (Ramesses II) and O.DeM 10165 (Siptah) are all damaged, but it is clear that the deliveries were made in the middle decade of the month. They are included in the total for Decade 2, but not within the individual days.

The first section of analysis will be carried out on the earlier material, comprising mainly ostraca, which survive in greater number than the later papyrus documents. Fortunately, much of the surviving Journal material during the late years of Ramesses III and the first years of Ramesses IV was written by the same scribe[10], so at least during this period the effect of different scribes composing the Journals can be reduced. Of course, these documents did not run concurrently, and additional material from the French Institute, the Turin collection and others, was also a component of the Journal. The Journal in Year 1 of Ramesses IV can highlight this, since there is a five-month series of documents written by this scribe. Ration deliveries are recorded on O. DeM 42 and O. DeM 43, but this is not the case on either O. DeM 41 or O. DeM 47, and in addition, when the period of time is extended back to Year 25, there is a considerable variety of vocabulary used in the ration entries within the Journal alone[11], with these variations not following a strict chronological order. As a result, the scribe was not consistent in his methods, so there must have been other reasons for the absences in recording ration deliveries, which will be examined in due course. It would be expected that basic rations would have been delivered to a schedule, whether it be weekly or monthly, with the deliveries for additional rations being more variable.

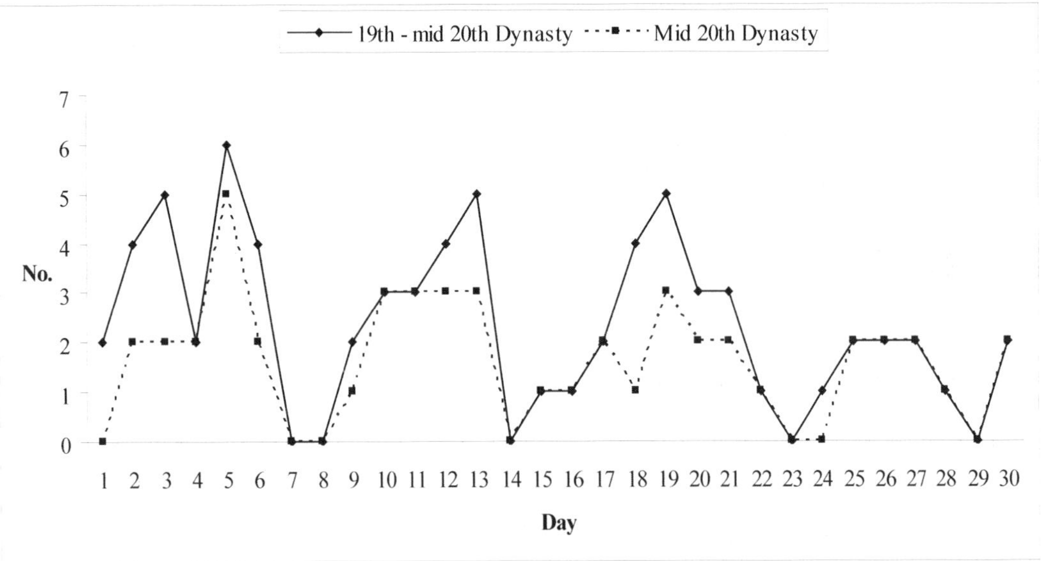

Figure 1. A comparison of *diw* between the two periods from the 19th to the mid 20th Dynasty and solely the mid 20th Dynasty

If the data from the middle of the 20th Dynasty are taken to be one group and all the examples from the 19th Dynasty and those which are undated and included in Table 4 are added together as the other group, it reveals the distribution as shown in Figure 1. Allowing for O. DeM 345,

10 O. DeM 32 to O. DeM 47 were written by the same scribe; see Donker van Heel (2003: 73-76) for a detailed case study on this group of Journal texts.

11 *pȝ dit diw* (O. DeM 32; O. DeM 34), *iw=tw dit diw* (O. DeM 38; O. DeM 43), *dit diw* (O. DeM 42; O. DeM 45), *pȝy=w diw* (O. DeM 44).

O. DeM 621 and O. DeM 10165 as imprecisely dated, and O. DeM 842 recording a delivery on an epagomenal day, there are still forty-eight out of the seventy examples which relate to the narrower period, so we should not expect there to be too much of a variation. This is borne out by Figure 1 in general, although the first three days of the month provide a noticeable contrast. This difference must be considered insignificant due to the small sample size and the additional observation that most of these fall into the "undated" category. Unfortunately, there is just not enough evidence to make any suggestions relating to the 19th Dynasty in isolation, but even so, this short exercise serves to justify the inclusion of the numerically larger and wider group as the basis for further analysis and comparisons between the periods where the ostracon was the primary medium of recording and that where papyrus was predominant. This is presented in Table 5, showing the number of examples that record each day of the month as the delivery date for basic rations. The longer period from the 19th Dynasty to the reign of Ramesses V can be taken as the benchmark for investigation; out of the 104 examples relating to basic ration deliveries, the seventy-three examples producing Table 5 record both a day and season of delivery. The writing of the days on O. DeM 345, O. DeM 621 rt. and O. DeM 10165 are damaged, but it is still clear that the delivery in these cases was made in the middle decade of the month. In addition, a further eight examples only record the month of delivery, but no day.

Table 5. 19th - mid 20th Dynasty: days of delivery of basic rations

Day (Decade 1)	**1**	**2**	**3**	**4**	**5**	**6**	**7**	**8**	**9**	**10**	**Total**
No. of examples	2	4	5	2	6	4	0	0	2	3	28 (6)
Day (Decade 2)	**11**	**12**	**13**	**14**	**15**	**16**	**17**	**18**	**19**	**20**	
No. of examples	3	4	5	0	1	1	2	4	5	3	31 (10)[12]
Day (Decade 3)	**21**	**22**	**23**	**24**	**25**	**26**	**27**	**28**	**29**	**30**	
No. of examples	3	1	0	1	2	2	2	1	0	2	14 (5)

On the face of it, there appears to be little that stands out, except perhaps there being fewer deliveries in the final decade of the month. It did not appear to matter whether the delivery was made during the week or at the weekend (Days 9 and 10 of each decade), and neither were there any particular times during the week where deliveries were consistently higher or lower than any other. The most frequent delivery days were Days 3, 5, 13 and 19, where five out of seventy-three examples[13] show a delivery having been made (six deliveries recorded on a Day 5). Further examination is necessary, bringing in criteria such as season and document type, in order to prove these days may well be more significant than is suggested at first glance.

Overall, the number of examples is very low, given that the period to which most, but not all, of the material relate is relatively short at eight or nine years, so perhaps we should not expect any

12 See n. 9.

13 O. DeM 842 is not included in the table as it is dated to the epagomenal days.

significant results. However, more striking results are revealed if the same exercise is carried out on the documents from the Journal, of which there are seventeen texts mentioning the delivery of rations. These entries take the form of a notification rather than anything more substantial, and despite this, the deliveries were not recorded as being from outside the village[14]. Despite the results for the individual days showing nothing out of the ordinary, what stands out is the decade of delivery recorded in the Journal. These are shown in brackets in Table 5, and about half the Journal documents (10 out of 21) relate to the middle decade of the month. About a third (32%) of all documents relating to the middle decade are from the Journal, while this figure is 21% for the first decade and 36% for the last. It is surely a fair assumption that this sample would be a sound representation of the overall documentation, whether lost or incomplete, so there must be some reason behind this significant result. The presence of fewer journal documents from the first decade of the month recording ration deliveries would imply that the assumption of rations being paid on the first day of the month is incorrect, especially given that there are many journals with a complete absence of such records and the belief that the scribe did not fail to record ration payments[15] is a complete fallacy. Like today's accountant, ancient scribes certainly did make mistakes and omissions of both individual words and entire sections and lines were not infrequent.

For additional rations (*dni*), twenty-four examples record either the day or month of delivery, and of these, twenty-two record both. The individual breakdown of additional ration deliveries is shown in Table 6, and the results are similar to those for basic rations. There is not enough material available to discern patterns over time on a daily basis, and assuming this small sample to be a representative distribution of whole, the decade of delivery has a more marked distribution. Over half (64%) of the available evidence points to supplements in rations being given in the first half of the month, with only four instances of a delivery in the last decade of the month. This seems to contradict what may be expected—that additional rations were delivered on a more random basis—but until more evidence is forthcoming it cannot be proved that there was a tendency for *dni* to be distributed earlier in the month.

Table 6. Additional rations: days of delivery of additional rations

Day (Decade 1)	**1**	**2**	**3**	**4**	**5**	**6**	**7**	**8**	**9**	**10**	**Total**
No. of examples	2	2	2	0	2	0	1	0	2	1	12
Day (Decade 2)	**11**	**12**	**13**	**14**	**15**	**16**	**17**	**18**	**19**	**20**	
No. of examples	0	1	1	0	0	1	0	2	0	1	6
Day (Decade 3)	**21**	**22**	**23**	**24**	**25**	**26**	**27**	**28**	**29**	**30**	
No. of examples	1	0	1	0	0	0	0	1	1	0	4

14 As seen in Chapter 3, the vocabulary used in the Journal is similar to that used elsewhere and exhibits variations within the documents.

15 Antoine (2010: 224).

A non-parametric statistical test, where no assumptions are made on any of the variables, can be performed on the two sets of data, if they are treated as samples from the whole population of ration deliveries, which were made during the Ramesside period. The Mann-Whitney U test tests the hypothesis that the *diw* and *dni* come from the same population, in other words, there is no difference between the two distributions. This treats each delivery as an observation and pairs off the day of the delivery with the type of ration (the groups being denoted arbitrarily as 0 for *diw* and 1 for *dni*), and then assigns ranks to the frequency of delivery of any given day within the complete set of observations. Finally, the U statistic is calculated, here using SPSS software. In this instance, it works out at 0.355, which is not significant using a 5% significance level[16], and this would suggest that there is no relationship between the delivery patterns of the two categories of rations. Bearing in mind the small sample size, the test supports the view that there is no real pattern to the days of delivery. Unfortunately, when it comes to splitting the records into decades, the small sample renders these types of tests inappropriate as the results would not be reliable.

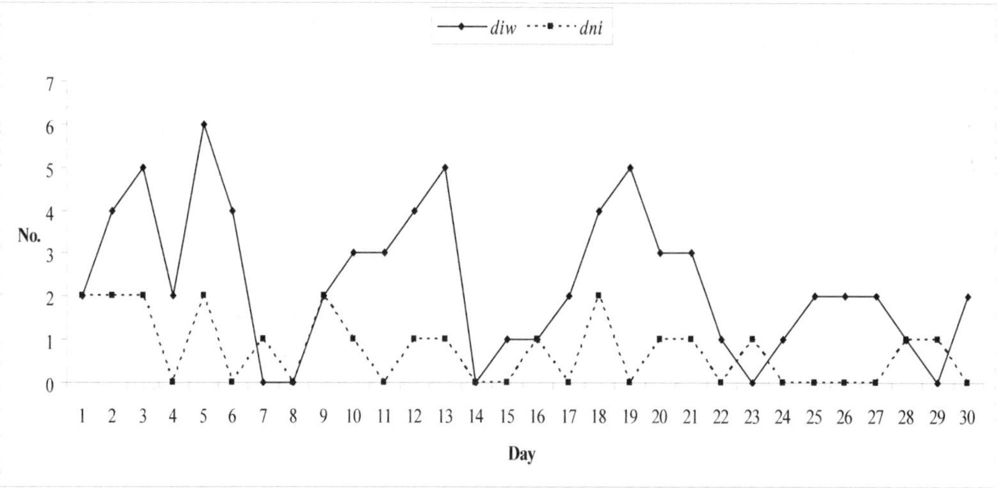

Figure 2. Days of delivery of *diw* and *dni* from the 19th to the mid 20th Dynasty

It is not unsurprising that in statistics, the bigger the sample, the more reliable the test is. Here, the number of examples is not great, so although the test carried out and the table provide a broad agreement, neither can provide a really detailed scrutiny of patterns of delivery on a daily basis. Therefore, in order to put this supposition to further scrutiny, a line diagram showing the information in Tables 5 and 6 can aid to attempt an explanation for any correlation between the two categories of rations. The line diagram shown in Figure 2 provides a clear visual representation of the deliveries, by day, of *diw* and *dni*, recorded in the surviving material from the 19th and the first half of the 20th Dynasty. The corpus of surviving documents is not vast, particularly so for *dni*, so any conclusions arrived at would have to be taken tentatively, assuming that the material used

16 See Conover (1980) and Hollander & Wolfe (1976) for terminology in the field of statistics, and details and examples of a number of statistical tests available. The significance level of a test is the probability of rejecting the null hypothesis (an initial statement made about a distribution) when it is actually true.

here is representative of the administration throughout the period being examined.

As can be seen in Figure 2, there are clear peaks for the distribution of *diw*, even though those for *dni* are not so prevalent there are instances of increased activity for the latter also. There does appear to be at least some degree of correlation between the timing of deliveries, for example the *diw* deliveries on days 2 to 6 with the *dni* deliveries at around day 9; and *diw* deliveries on days 10 to 13 with the *dni* deliveries around day 18, and the *diw* deliveries on days 18 to 21 may affect the *dni* deliveries in the first few days of the month. Incidentally, only three documents record two *diw* deliveries in a given month[17], but it is not always clear which months the deliveries related to, and such additional information is lacking in about half of the Journal entries. Figure 2 suggests that there may have been some regularity in the ration delivery system; not once a month but once a week, but since the data covers a small amount of surviving material over a period of over fifty years, it remains unlikely.

However, there are problems in interpretation. Firstly, there is the survival of the material, especially concerning *dni*, with the small sample from which these results are inferred which makes it a certainty that this will limit the reliability of any statistical tests. Secondly, and perhaps more importantly, with *dni* being *any* additional delivery in a given month, the lag in timing was unlikely to have been such a short period. In other words, it is not possible to say which initial ration delivery the supplements were part of. If there was a tendency for additional rations to be delivered during the first or second decade, after three weeks have passed and supplies have run low, an additional delivery may have kept the workmen going until the next basic ration instalment. Similarly, the *dni* could be regarded as an early month top-up, but only in unusual and exceptional cases is there any indication that a *dni* delivery *may* have followed a set *diw* delivery[18], so despite Antoine's suggestion to the contrary[19], although it may be true, there is no evidence to support this.

It would be possible to examine the ration patterns by splitting the distribution lists to the workmen from the notification entries of delivery in the Journal, and search for any patterns especially in attempting to state how long the grain remained in the *ḫtm*, but we would undoubtedly be reliant on chance survival of distribution and Journal records for the same period. There is certainly no evidence of any stock accounting at the *ḫtm*, or anywhere else. Therefore, we are unable to ascertain whether or not the ancient Egyptians used a FIFO[20] system of stock movement. This absence of evidence seems to imply that grain rations were handed out soon after they were delivered to the village, as they became available.

Antoine has conducted an independent examination on his own data concentrating on vari-

17 O. Berlin 12631, O. DeM 34 and O. DeM 153. The day numbers in one delivery notification in the first two examples are lost due to damage, which makes stating delivery months impossible.

18 Even from examples such as O. DeM 737, which record *diw* and *dni* deliveries with their dates, there is no indication that the latter related to the former.

19 Antoine (2010: 227) states that there are two instances (O. DeM 427 and P. Turin 2013+2050+2061, rt. x+4) where a recorded *dni* delivery follows the corresponding *diw* payment. On O. DeM 427, vs. 9, no month is specified for the *diw*, and the same is true for P. Turin 2013+2050+2061, where in addition the deliveries are not necessarily in the order they were made.

20 First in first out; older stock gets moved out before newer. Accounting conventions and procedures will be examined in Chapter 6.

ances and delay in ration payments[21], and one of his results uses the Kruskal Wallis test to show that the delay was significantly longer (p=0.004) for a *dni* distribution (33.00 ± 8.61 days) than for *diw* (21.5 ± 16.52 days). While the statistical methodology is sound, and result is more than likely correct, the analysis suffers from two main flaws. Firstly, it can not be assumed that both types of ration delivery would be taken as being on the 1st of the month, and *dni* is particularly problematic. There is no indication in the textual record when a *dni* delivery was due, as by its definition this is an undefined variable. Secondly, any absence of recording was equated with a non-delivery, and this is incorrect as scribes did not account for, nor did they record, everything. It would make sense to expect the *diw* to be paid once a month, but attempting to make any kind of analysis on delays would be almost impossible since there is no starting point upon which to base the periods of delay.

Table 7. Basic rations: month and season of delivery of basic rations

Season		Month			Total
ꜣḫt	I	II	III	IV	
No. examples	11 (4)	6 (1)	5 (3)	6	29 (8)
prt	I	II	III	IV	
No. examples	4 (2)	7	7 (1)	8 (3)	26 (6)
šmw	I	II	III	IV	
No. examples	5 (2)	2 (1)	8 (1)	9 (3)[1]	24 (7)

The data supplied for the present study are shown in Table 7. This shows the distribution of the seventy-nine examples of basic ration (*diw*) deliveries which record a month, with the twenty-one records from the Journal shown in brackets. In both cases, the spread is fairly equal between the seasons, and it is probably coincidental that more Journal examples relate to a Month I than the other three. Granaries stored grain in the periods when it was not harvested, so since it is also logical that rations would have been delivered all year round, nothing should be read into this. However, when the month and day are both included, one day does stand out. Ten examples are known where day and month repeat twice[22], but more significant are four examples[23] of *prt* 13 being the date of delivery, all from different months with two being from the Journal. This observation appears to strengthen the suggestion that basic rations were delivered at least on a semi

21 Antoine (2010: 227); but keep in mind all the variances are calculated from the first of the month, with omissions included as a non-delivery. Many tests assume that the data presented here would be classed as "random" from the population.

22 Only once is the month and day the same. O. Cairo 25698 and O. DeM 276 both relate to I *ꜣḫt* 20. Two Journal entries three years apart (O. DeM 153 rt. and O. DeM 156) relate to *šmw* 5; and two further Journal records (O. DeM 45 and O. UC 39648) indicate *ꜣḫt* 19. It is unlikely that these are more than a coincidence.

23 O. DeM 34; O. DeM 43; O. DeM 177; and O. DeM 252.

regular basis, perhaps on or near the 13th of the month, and other distributions may have been given on a more random basis or whenever supplies permitted.

Examination of the Journal data for the nine-month period between Ramesses III Year 32 and Ramesses IV Year 1, which is almost continuous (see Appendix 1), also highlights this point. Here there are four examples in the nine months of basic ration deliveries which tool place in the middle decade of the month. Not only this, but it raises the question of where the records are for the corresponding journal entries for the remaining months[24]. As has been seen, it is clearly the case that material from the Journal did not always include ration deliveries, despite the standard entry being a short statement along the lines of O. DeM 42 vs. 7-8, which reads: *sw 15 ḥri dit diw n ꜣbd 3 ꜣḫt*, Day 15. Hori. The distribution of rations for Month 3 of Akhet. This would have required the minimum effort on the part of the scribe to record, and shortage of space on an ostracon was not an issue.

There seem to be two possible explanations for this absence of accounting. The first reason, albeit an unlikely one, is that there were other documents which have either been undated or lost. Undated material is obviously difficult to date, and the majority would therefore have not been matched by modern scholars. Similarly, there were occasions where documents may have been drafts or copies of the original with some differences[25], or where Journal documents overlapped. Initially on the position in Černý's publication of material written by the same scribe, and then upon examination of their layout, Donker van Heel has shown that the same scribe wrote the series of documents O. DeM 32 to O. DeM 47[26]. We would, therefore, expect that the same scribal practices to have been used by the same scribe, especially when writing out the same kind of record over time. However, the sequence of Journal documents strongly suggests that this is not the case.

A possible explanation is likely to be that the rations delivered and recorded in the Journal were either the minimum required or below the subsistence level[27], and that it was therefore not a major issue if the scribe omitted a delivery from his daily journal entry. This assumes, of course, that there was an arbitrary and unwritten value of minimum subsistence, although the standard ration payments may equate to this. Since the Journal entries did not have numerical amounts attached to them, we can only speculate that this value may have been fixed and well known to the village administration and, therefore, there was no need for any consistent records as what was recorded was considered to have been adequate. Far more likely is that the scribes only recorded what they needed to, and merely recording that rations were distributed sufficed.

However, it is implausible to accept that the same amount was paid each time, even if the

24 O. Berlin 12633 rt.; O. DeM 38; O. DeM 42; and O. DeM 43 vs.. Examples of Journal documents with no mention of rations are O. DeM 39, O. DeM 40, O. DeM 41, O. DeM 43 rt. and O. DeM 47, although the ostracon for IV *ꜣḫt* is lost.

25 Scribes did duplicate information, either wholly or in part. See Donker van Heel (2003: 39-82) for a detailed analysis on how this could have been carried out. A good, short, example (but not ration related) is O. DeM 44, rt. 2-3 (a Journal text) and O. DeM 161, 9-11 (not from the Journal).

26 See note 10. Černý (1935: 10-11) believed also that groups of these texts (O. DeM 38; O. DeM 39; O. DeM 40; O. DeM 41; and O. DeM 42) came from the same vessel.

27 A statement made by Janssen (1975: 470) in analysing ration amounts, but not as a reason for any irregularities in distribution patterns.

rations *due* were, and for this there seems to have been no fixed day[28]. Rations were paid in several portions, this being such common practice and was even the reason behind the use of the word *dni* to denote additional payments of the same monthly ration[29]. Additional payments, almost always smaller in amount than the initial payment and often causing the use of complex fractions in the records, were more important to the workmen themselves than to the administration, and any surplus grain could be traded with others for commodities including wood, luxuries and home-crafted items. This would explain the omission in amounts, but perhaps is not fully convincing in explaining the absence of any notification of any delivery to the village, as suggested by the relative numbers of examples surviving of the delivery of both categories of ration payments.

§4.2 Rations, festivals and the daily calendar

One possible line of investigation which will be followed through in the following paragraphs is the hypothesis that ration deliveries were in some way related to festival dates and also that they were not due on the first of the month. Interpretation of festival calendars and the dates of festivals is no easy matter for a number of reasons. Festivals were observed on a national level all over Egypt, or else they were regional[30] or local affairs, often depending on the god or gods primarily worshipped in any given area. Therefore it did not follow that a given festival in one locality took place in others. Similarly, even in smaller localities there were variations, for example, the festivals included on the festival lists, such as that of the temple of Medinet Habu, would undoubtedly have been on a larger scale and not the same as those celebrated at Deir el-Medina[31]. At Deir el-Medina, the majority of the festivals are only recorded once or twice in the source material, so that it can be difficult to prove one way or the other whether they were held annually[32]. The correlation between days of work inactivity and festivals is a strong one, and is crucial to Jauhiainen's reconstruction of the Deir el-Medina festival calendar[33]. In order to facilitate an approach based on festival dates, a detailed calendar has been drawn up on a daily basis, showing the dates of known festivals at Deir el-Medina and any definite ration deliveries known from the ostraca. The calendar is shown in Appendix 1, and details the ration deliveries and days of festivals during the

28 Černý (1954: 916).

29 Janssen (1991: 92).

30 Sadek (1988: 167-169) differentiates between the two, and follows up with a detailed survey (pp. 169-182) on the feasts of each. Feasts of a personal level will not be examined due to their large number and small-scale nature. These were carried out by very small groups of individuals, and almost never coincided with public holidays or festival dates (Sadek 1988: 192). Jauhiainen (2009: 66-196) provides a detailed, evidence-based, approach on feasts dedicated to national and local deities as well as to kings.

31 The Medinet Habu calendar was a copy of the festival calendar of Ramesses II at the Ramesseum. Even allowing for the additions at Medinet Habu, the festivals in the two places would undoubtedly have been different to the degree that occasionally festivals included on the Medinet Habu list were likely not celebrated at Thebes and even less at Deir el-Medina.

32 Wikgren (2005: 179).

33 Jauhiainen (2009: 222-223). Festivals such as the *w3g* on I *3ḫt* 17 are included since the focus here is not on days of inactivity. In contrast, references to four festivals within the period II *prt* 14 through to II *prt* 24 are omitted since the exact days may have been varied (Jauhiainen 2009: 205-206).

years from Year 25 of Ramesses III through to Year 2 of Ramesses IV[34].

In addition, the civil and lunar calendars in Ancient Egypt were not the same; the former being fixed in date (for example, Christmas in the modern western world) while the latter (such as Easter) changed from year to year depending on the cycles of the moon, so there can be problems hindering precise interpretation of the dates, with the Valley Festival being a good example. Highly important to the villagers, it was celebrated in II *šmw*, but the exact dates varied since it was a lunar festival and commenced with the new moon in II *šmw*[35]. Another important Theban festival was the Opet festival, which took place in II and III *3ḫt*, but probably only the first day was celebrated in Deir el-Medina itself[36], since it involved the king and his renewal of kingship and thus was not of significant interest to the workmen.

Table 8. Number of examples recording delivery of rations compared with festival dates

	During festival	Not during festival	Total
diw	4	21	25
dni	1	2	3
Total	5	23	28

During this period, there are twenty-eight examples of ration texts being fully datable (twenty-five relate to *diw* and three to *dni*). This means that they include the day and month, with the regnal year being either recorded or inferred with certainty. These are shown in the calendar in Appendix 1, and are summarised in Table 8, which indicates the number of documents with dates coinciding with known festivals together with those that do not. However, three of these dates are still doubtful in so far as it is not possible to assess whether the festivals held on these dates were annual events[37]. Deliveries whose dates coincided with festivals are only shown on a quarter of the documents, which can be interpreted perhaps as coincidence and we should not look into any significance. One possibility is that the rations were delivered at times just before the festivals, but given the number of festival days, and many of these were "public holidays" to the villagers, again it is unlikely to be significant. There are dates when possible festivals may have taken place[38], but often not the name. The majority of these were also recorded as holiday days or simply by a list of absences in the work lists. In addition, it must not be simply assumed from the numerous absence lists that it was because of a festival that work did not take place on a given day.

One feature which stands out upon examination of the calendar is the absence of ration de-

34 The information within Appendix 1 has been drawn from Helck (1964a), van Walsem (1982), Vleeming (1982), Sadek (1988) and Wikgren (2005), but follows primarily the recent work by Jauhiainen (2009).

35 Jauhiainen (2009: 150-511).

36 Sadek (1988: 168).

37 See notes 30, 31 and 32.

38 See Jauhiainen (2009: 199-233) for a survey and discussion of the evidence for festivals which were not included in her reconstruction of the festival calendar.

liveries over large periods of time during the years for which we have the most textual evidence. Twenty-five dated deliveries over a nine year period averages out at nearly three per year. This is low, and may reflect the accounting for what actually happened in the village. It is possible that the rations may not always have gone to the *ḫtm*, and therefore would not have been recorded by the scribes who worked from there. This strengthens the suggestion that there were no set days of delivery. Rations could only be delivered if there was grain available, in which case both the physical conditions in the *ḫtm* (and this includes the availability of the administrative personnel), and the practicality of both the delivery logistics and the accounting system had to properly maintained in order to facilitate a smooth administrative process. Undoubtedly there were periods when no deliveries were made, but apart from the strikes, there are no attestations of any failure to deliver. One of these periods was the primary reason behind the strike in Year 29, and this can facilitate investigation into how the strike fitted in with the known ration distribution immediately prior to the strike itself.

There are only a small handful of texts which record *diw* rations being delivered on a festival day, but even some of these are not conclusive. These are listed as follows, and interestingly there are no deliveries during the latter part of II *šmw*, the date of the Valley Festival in any of the years noted in Appendix 1.

Year 27, III *prt* 19	*ẖn mwt* [39]
Year 27, IV *prt* 13	Day 4 of an unknown festival[40]
Year 28, I *ꜣḫt* 2	Day 2 of the New Year festival (*wp rnpt*)
Year 28, I *ꜣḫt* 30	Day 2 of the *ḫꜥ n nsw imn-ḥtp*
Year 30, I *ꜣḫt* 3	*dni* delivered on Day 3 of the New Year festival
Year 32, I *šmw* 27	*ḥb nsw imn-ḥtp*[41]
Year 2, II *ꜣḫt* 19	*ḥb ipt* (Opet)

One month has two separate *diw* deliveries, I *ꜣḫt* in Year 28. Unfortunately neither O. DeM 427, nor O. Munich ÄS 397 rt., show the rations as relating to any given period, though the latter has an earlier delivery which was accounted for as an advance, so perhaps the verso is also an advance. It is possible that deliveries were adjusted to coincide with festivals, but it is obvious that one month is not enough to prove anything concrete about the relationship between festivals and ration payments. The sample of documents forming Table 8 may be large enough to prove one thing, namely that the expectation that the increased ration deliveries at the start of the month had something to do with the presence of festivals is undoubtedly a false one, even though the view that any festivals which fell during the weekend, such as the Festival of Thoth on I *ꜣḫt* 19, would not always show up in the textual record is probably correct[42]. Despite such occasions requiring a wide variety of food, the terminology *diw* and *dni* was rarely used. An isolated example,

39 It is impossible to ascertain whether this festival was held annually. See Jauhiainen (2009: 207).

40 This unknown festival may have had something to do with the birth of the gods. See Jauhiainen (2009: 211-212).

41 Not conclusive since the evidence suggests this was a working day. See Jauhiainen (2009: 215).

42 Spalinger (1994: 52), Jauhiainen (2009: 89).

O. DeM 739, 1-2, records *diw* for the foreman of the Left which was explicitly stated as being "for the festival", the terminology of which suggests that this was an exception. Grain was for making bread and beer, the staples of the Egyptian diet, whereas festival foods were prepared in advance, as the number of texts recording foodstuffs such as *psn*-loaves and *bit*-cakes indicate. It does appear that grain for rations and grain for festivals were for the most part kept completely separate, as we would have no reason to expect rations for workmen to have any relationship to festival days. But what can be categorically stated is that rations were delivered on festival days thus indicating that at least some work was being done on such days.

Further examination of the calendar in Appendix 1 reveals periods of time when ration deliveries clustered together. Although the amount of evidence is not great, we can make speculative observations about what may have happened and any possible links with the strike in Year 29. The material dating to Years 28 and 29 shows a marked prominence for deliveries in the first few days of the month or the very last day, but after the strikes the spread becomes more dispersed and at the start of Year 2 of Ramesses IV rations were being recorded in the last few days of the month. One possibility is that the workmen got used to getting their rations early in the month, or on the last day as in two successive months in *ꜣḫt* in Year 28. When this no longer happened, concern naturally spread amongst the workforce, which resulted in the strikes. It is unfortunate that we neither have the corresponding Journal entries for the Left side of the crew at this time, nor do we have more material detailing rations in the period immediately after the strike. We would expect a marked increase in the amount of *dni* payments, which would certainly reveal the effect the strike had, in reality, on rations.

Years 31 and 32 provide a good example of clustering, where three deliveries are made within four decades, and each was made in a different decade of the month. This would be further evidence suggesting that there was no fixed date when rations were due, although in an ideal situation it was more likely there was. In addition, rations were delivered in successive days, on III *šmw* days 4 and 5 in Year 29[43], so assuming the dates were correctly stated, this may indicate that there was some unrest in the months before the strikes. The first is broken and the second is a full record, so we may have two lengthy delivery lists.

One thing we do have is the complete Journal for the three seasons after the strikes, and apart from one payment seven days after the strike, there is nothing recorded until the *dni* of III *ꜣḫt* of Year 30. What this seems to imply is that there was a breakdown in the administration and especially in accounting, since the mere presence of delivery lists splitting the workforce up shows the importance of ration deliveries to the administration. The scribes may have had their attention drawn elsewhere and simply neglected recording the payments of rations, but given that Journal entries usually consisted of short entries, this would seem trivial. Even if the evidence is not conclusive, it is perhaps true that during periods when things were not going so well for the workmen, scribes do seem to have avoided keeping records. Apart from some records that mention action on the part of workmen due to non-delivery, nowhere is there any evidence explicitly stating that rations were not delivered, so perhaps the payments became more erratic and random in their amounts. As long as the rations were received then accountability for the rations was

43 O. DeM 738 and O. DeM 10033.

not important and the situation took on more of an oral aspect, at least in the short term, where things went as expected without the need to record ration payments in the Journal. The bottom line is we do not have everything that was recordable.

§4.3 Papyri from the late Ramesside period

Papyri have the potential to provide a greater amount of information than ostraca on a wide range of topics, especially since a papyrus roll could contain much more data. Furthermore, the changing social conditions within the village community itself[44], with the increased threat posed by Libyans, tomb robberies, and the subsequent move to Medinet Habu, resulted in the reporting of different subject matter. It should be expected that this statement would extend to provisions and supplies for the village. The number of surviving papyri which record details of ration deliveries is low[45], and using the methodology described in Chapter 2, these twelve documents provide twenty examples, which are shown above in Table 3. With one exception, the records refer to basic rather than additional rations, but an examination of the amounts recorded may indicate that by this time the two terms were sometimes used interchangeably. Note must be made of the first section of P. Turin 2013+2050+2061, which contains details of the periods to which the rations, including *dni*, related, but the other dates were recorded at the start of the lines; these are unfortunately lost, and are not included in the analysis.

Table 9: Late Ramesside papyri: days of delivery of rations (*diw* and *dni*)

Day (Decade 1)	1	2	3	4	5	6	7	8	9	10	Total
No. examples	0	0	0	2	0	0	1	0	1	0	4
Day (Decade 2)	**11**	**12**	**13**	**14**	**15**	**16**	**17**	**18**	**19**	**20**	
No. examples	0	0	0	0	0	1	1	0	0	0	2
Day (Decade 3)	**21**	**22**	**23**	**24**	**25**	**26**	**27**	**28**	**29**	**30**	
No. examples	0	0	0	0	1	3	0	3	1	2	10

The papyri are dated, with the date of delivery clearly shown in most cases, but it is impossible to show any variances between this date and the date to which the rations relate, since only on one document is the latter recorded. The individual days of delivery are shown in Table 9, and despite there being only sixteen examples where the day of delivery is recorded, the figures show a distinct pattern in that a larger proportion of deliveries were made in the last decade of the month, and not only this, but in the last half of any given decade. In the material examined, only three

44 Häggman (2002: 16). While this may be the case, except for the tomb robbery cases, which suggest an economic need to acquire capital, there seems to be very little direct proof of this being a direct cause of increased subject matter on papyri.

45 This is probably an archaeological issue, since the papyri came from a single find at Medinet Habu.

deliveries were made in the first half of any decade. If this is a representative sample of the period as a whole, then there was a strong tendency for deliveries to have been made near the end of the month, a contrast to the results in §4.1 as shown above in Table 5.

There must have been a reason why this was done. Looking at the papyri individually, the majority were lengthy documents with a wide range of subject matter. Four are from the Journal of the Necropolis[46], covering matters such as work and inactivity of the crew, lamp use, deliveries of various commodities and the delivery and distribution of rations. The content of four others is mainly accounts of grain and its distribution, with detailed amounts, though they do include other events such as a record of the making of a stela or the storage of grain. These accounts are not limited solely to grain. Only on three occasions, in P. Turin 2097+2105 and P. Turin 1898+1926+1937+2094 (rt. 2:12 and 2:27), are there what appears to be a notification of a ration delivery, so common in earlier material from the Journal,. However, on the recto of P. Turin 2097+2105 there are also lists of workmen with portions of grain. Detailed and lengthy ration lists form part of the main body of the text. The small number of examples renders the use of statistical tests inappropriate, but on the face of it, there does not seem to be any relationship between the day of delivery and the type of document, although there does seem to be a propensity for deliveries on the last few days of the month towards the end of the 20th Dynasty, but not because of the recording media.

Table 10. Late Ramesside papyri: month and season of ration delivery (*dìw* and *dni*)

Season	Month				Total
3ḫt	**I**	**II**	**III**	**IV**	
No. examples	1	3	4	1	9
prt	**I**	**II**	**III**	**IV**	
No. examples	0	0	0	1	1
šmw	**I**	**II**	**III**	**IV**	
No. examples	2	1	1	2	6

Looking at the same examples as before, the spread of months of delivery reveals a striking pattern, but certainly one which should not be taken as conclusive evidence that all material from the late 20th Dynasty would have followed the same distribution. There should be no reason why deliveries would have been concentrated on any particular month or season apart from the harvest season, which one would assume would contain a higher proportion of the material, since rations were needed for subsistence.

46 These are P. Turin 1884+2067+2071+2105, P. Turin 1898+1926+1937+2094, P. Turin 1960+2071 and P. Turin 2013+2050+2061.

The information is shown in Table 10, where nine out of fifteen[47] examples record a delivery as being made in the season of *ꜣḫt*, and in particular the middle two months. This may be explained by the harvest and also the subsequent absence of deliveries in *prt*, but with the storage facilities available in Thebes and the village itself, it is difficult to explain the differences in this respect between this later data and the earlier, more uniform, distribution exhibited in the earlier findings. The challenging social conditions that were becoming increasingly prevalent during the later years of the 20th Dynasty would have resulted in problems within the economic system, which itself would have caused the ration distribution to be more irregular. Logically, this would result in more frequent payments which consisted of smaller amounts and fewer individuals, but this is not necessarily the case[48].

§4.4 Days of delivery: a comparison

Perhaps the best method of a direct comparison between the two periods under examination is a simple scatter diagram, but even so it is necessary to clarify matters which may lead to ambiguities and result in an imperfect conclusion. Since there is far more material surviving from earlier than later periods (seventy-three from the earlier period against sixteen from the later), the following table (Table 11) shows the absolute values and not the proportions of documents which apply to each day.

Table 11. Days of delivery of rations: Ramesses II to Ramesses V (*diw*) and Ramesses IX to Ramesses XI

Day (Decade 1)	1	2	3	4	5	6	7	8	9	10	Total
R II-R V	2	4	5	2	6	4	0	0	2	3	28
R IX-R XI	0	0	0	2	0	0	1	0	1	0	4
Day (Decade 2)	**11**	**12**	**13**	**14**	**15**	**16**	**17**	**18**	**19**	**20**	
R II-R V	3	4	5	0	1	1	2	4	5	3	31
R IX-R XI	0	0	0	0	0	1	1	0	0	0	2
Day (Decade 3)	**21**	**22**	**23**	**24**	**25**	**26**	**27**	**28**	**29**	**30**	
R II-R V	3	1	0	1	2	2	2	1	0	2	14
R IX-R XI	0	0	0	0	1	3	0	3	1	2	10

47 The problem of differentiating between texts and examples is evident here, since the three examples in II *ꜣḫt* are all from one source, and those in III *ꜣḫt* are from three documents. This may project a bias in the analysis, skewed towards II *ꜣḫt* in particular. As long as a consistent method is used, and awareness of any potentially irregular results which may be based on methodology is noted, the analysis itself will be valid.
48 Ration amounts and the composition of ration lists are examined in detail in Chapter 8.

The data are taken directly from Tables 5 and 9, and two clarifications are needed[49]. Firstly, Figure 3 presents the same information contained in these tables in percentages as a scatter diagram, so the visual comparison is like with like rather than a disproportionate number of documents within each group. Secondly, the earlier period only includes the basic rations (*diw*), so the comparison is between the same categories of rations. The material for the later period includes all of the ration deliveries recorded, although there is only one instance of *dni* being explicitly stated. Overall, despite the lower amount of information on the later period, the diagram shows marked contrasts even if this may adversely affect the reliability of the results.

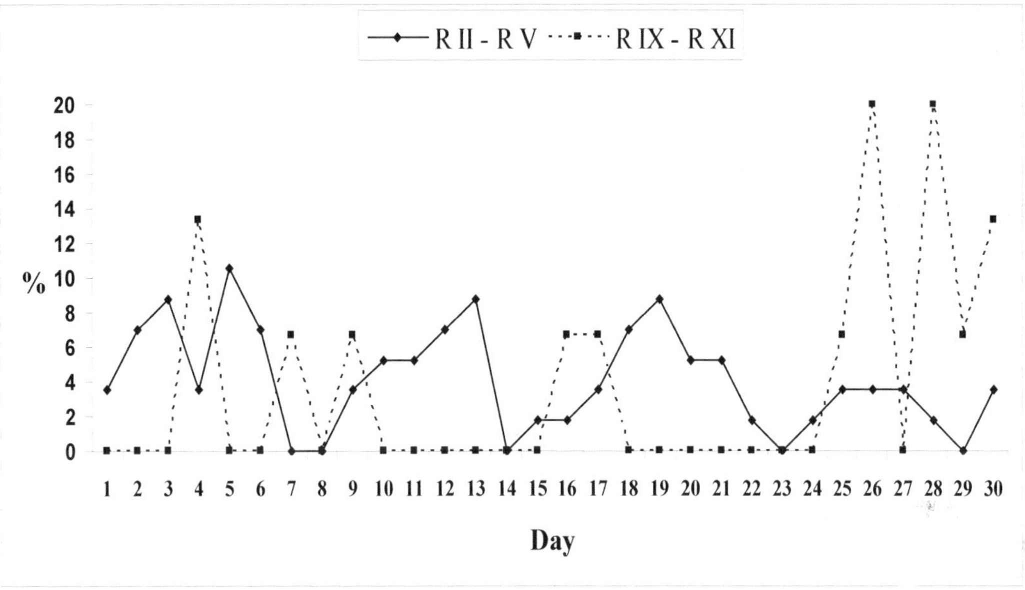

Figure 3. Days of delivery of rations: Ramesses II to Ramesses V (*diw*) and Ramesses IX to Ramesses XI

What stands out from Figure 3 are the differences in the third decade of the month, and in particular the second part of that decade, when a considerably higher percentage of recorded rations were distributed later in the Ramesside period, as well as the comparison between this and the middle decade, where there is almost a complete absence of surviving material. There may be reasons for this, but they are not clear. The reliability and amount of commodities to the community were dwindling[50] and several sources record workmen going to Thebes to complain about non-payment of rations[51] as the delivery system became ever more erratic. Factors such as tomb

49 Note that the dates of O. DeM 345, O. DeM 621 rt., and O. DeM 10165 are damaged. They are in the second decade, but the precise date is unclear. Therefore, they are included within the total of 31 in Table 11 (R II–R V), but not within the individual days. The Epagomenal Day delivery recorded on O. DeM 842 is not included in Table 11.

50 Antoine (2006: 32) has shown that there was a collapse in fish deliveries in the reign of Ramesses IX, and highlights the shortfalls with reference to the Turin Necropolis Journal (*KRI* VI, 581-590).

51 A good example of the non-payment of rations is O. DeM 571.

robberies and the status of those who participated in them show that there was a lower level of control by those in authority, and even these officials themselves were not adverse to transgression. It is possible that a change in practice may have been facilitated by the concentration of the administration in Medinet Habu and this included a change in the day the workmen received their rations, but the evidence is far from conclusive.

§4.5 Basic ration payment variances: arrears or advance

The relationship between the texts and the dates, of basic ration deliveries, and especially the time of delivery and the period covered, may reveal something about payment patterns, and in particular whether the rations were given in advance or as we would expect, in arrears. In addition, insights may be gleaned into how the ration system functioned with respect to accounting and recording. The texts and their associated variances are shown in Tables 12 and 13 for basic and additional rations respectively, with the last columns showing the variance between the two dates, in months and days. The variances can be grouped together into three groups: those which show a positive variance suggesting an advance payment where rations were paid prior to the period to which the rations related, a negative variance implying arrears where the rations were paid after the relevant ration period, or no variance, meaning the month of recording and ration delivery were both the same.

However, even a zero value may not show either the complete or the correct picture, since a delivery may have been made at the start or end of any given month, so the true variance in days could be anything between plus or minus twenty-nine. Antoine gets round this by taking the median value of any given delay in rations payment, in days, where the day is not stated in the month the rations related to, or the due month[52]. However, when it is not known if the delivery was during or after the due month, any corresponding figure taken for this is dubious, even if it is the only method by which a result can be obtained. For this section, the number of individual documents (as opposed to examples) in the entire ration corpus with dates for both issue and the related period is relatively low, thirty-four out of 104 (33%) basic ration texts (*diw*), whilst for *dni*, the figure is ten out of twenty-eight, slightly higher at 36%. This does not help us, but to get slightly more accurate results with the available data, a further exercise will be performed where variances are examined in terms of days rather than months. Even so, it has to be assumed that rations were due on the 1st of the month in order to facilitate this, for example the *diw* deliveries on O. Ashmol. 111 would be classed as being eight days in arrears.

52 Antoine (2010: 225-226). For the same month, the median is 16 days, for the following month 35 days.

Table 12. Basic rations: documents recording variances between the issue date of the document and the period to which the delivery relates

Ostracon	King	Date of issue	Period covered	Variance (months)	Variance (days)
O. Ashmol. 111	Seti II/Siptah	Yr 4 IV *šmw* 9	III *šmw*	-1	-8
O. Ashmol. 131 rt.	*20th Dynasty*	Yr 2 II *prt* 5	IV *ꜣḫt* - I *prt*	-2	-4/-34
O. Ashmol. 131 rt.	*20th Dynasty*	Yr 2 II *prt* 5	II prt	0	0
O. Ashmol. 262	-	Yr 4 II *ꜣḫt*	I *ꜣḫt* 5	-1	N/A
O. Berlin 12294	Ramesses II	IV *šmw* 21	IV *šmw*	0	0
O. Berlin 12294	Ramesses II	IV *šmw* 21	I *ꜣḫt* - II *ꜣḫt*	+1/+2	+10/+40
O. Berlin 14219	*20th Dynasty*	IV *prt* 2	I *šmw*	+1	+29
O. Berlin 14302 vs.	Ramesses IV	Yr 3 IV *ꜣḫt* 1	II *ꜣḫt*	-2	-30
O. Cairo 25608	*Mid 20th Dynasty*	I *šmw*	II *šmw*	+1	N/A
O. Cairo 25685 rt.	*Late 20th Dynasty*	IV *prt*	III *prt*	-1	N/A
O. Cairo 25685 rt.	*Late 20th Dynasty*	IV *prt*	IV *prt*	0	N/A
O. DeM 38	Ramesses III	Yr 32 II *šmw* 11	I *šmw*	-1	-10
O. DeM 42	Ramesses IV	Yr 1 III *ꜣḫt* 15	III *ꜣḫt*	0	0
O. DeM 43	Ramesses IV	Yr 1 I *prt* 13	I *prt*	0	0
O. DeM 44	Ramesses IV	Yr 2 III *šmw* 28	III *šmw*	0	0
O. DeM 44	Ramesses IV	Yr 2 III *šmw* 28	IV *šmw*	+1	+3
O. DeM 45	Ramesses IV	Yr 2 II *ꜣḫt* 19	II *ꜣḫt*	0	0
O. DeM 45	Ramesses IV	Yr 2 II *ꜣḫt* 19	III *ꜣḫt*	+1	+12
O. DeM 153 rt.	Ramesses III	Yr 31 I *šmw* 5	IV *prt*	-1	-4
O. DeM 153 vs.	Ramesses III	Yr 32 I *šmw* 27	I *šmw*	0	0
O. DeM 159	Ramesses III	Yr 31 I *prt* 6	IV *ꜣḫt*	-1	-5
O. DeM 177	*Amenmesse*	Yr 1 II *prt* 13	I *prt*	-1	-12
O. DeM 177	*Amenmesse*	Yr 1 II *prt* 13	II *prt*	0	0
O. DeM 177	*Amenmesse*	Yr 1 II *prt* 13	III *prt* - IV *prt*	+1/+2	+18/+48
O. DeM 184	*20th Dynasty*	Yr 4 II *prt* 10	III *prt* - IV *prt*	+1/+2	+21/+51
O. DeM 186	*20th Dynasty*	? *šmw*	IV *prt*	-1	N/A
O. DeM 345	*20th Dynasty*	IV *ꜣḫt* 10 (+?)	IV *ꜣḫt*	0	N/A
O. DeM 379	*20th Dynasty*	IV *prt* 25	IV *prt*	0	0
O. DeM 380	Ramesses IV	Yr 2 IV *šmw* 17	III *šmw*	-1	-16
O. DeM 386	*20th Dynasty*	III *prt* 6	III *prt*	0	0
O. DeM 611	Siptah	Yr 1 III *šmw* 19	I *prt*	+6	>+100
O. DeM 621 rt.	Ramesses II	I *šmw* 12 (+?)	I *šmw*	0	N/A
O. DeM 621 rt.	Ramesses II	I *šmw* 12 (+?)	II *šmw*	+1	N/A

Ostracon	King	Date of issue	Period covered	Variance (months)	Variance (days)
O. DeM 739	-	I *ꜣḫt* 3	I *ꜣḫt*	0	0
O. DeM 852	Ramesses II	I *ꜣḫt* 5	I *ꜣḫt*	0	0
O. DeM 10039 rt.	-	Yr 2 III *šmw* 13	IV *ꜣḫt* - I *prt*	+5/+6	>+100
O. DeM 10164	Siptah	Yr 1 III *prt* 20	II *prt*	-1	-19
O. DeM 10165	Siptah	III *ꜣḫt* 10(+?)	III *ꜣḫt*	0	0
O. Michaelides 73	Ramesses III	Yr 31 III *prt* 26	III *prt*	0	0
O. Munich ÄS 397	Ramesses III	Yr 28 I *ꜣḫt* 30	II *ꜣḫt*	+1	+1
O. Strasbourg H110 rt.	*Late 19th Dynasty*	IV *ꜣḫt* 8	III *ꜣḫt*	-1	-7
O. Strasbourg H110 rt.	*Late 19th Dynasty*	IV *ꜣḫt* 8	I *prt*	+1	+23
O. Strasbourg H110 vs.	*Late 19th Dynasty*	IV *ꜣḫt* 18	I *prt*	+1	+13
P. Turin 1880	Ramesses III	II *prt* 17	II *prt*	0	0
P. Turin 2081+2095	*Ramesses V*	II *ꜣḫt* 16	II *ꜣḫt*	0	0

Table 13. Additional rations: ostraca recording variances between the issue date of the document and the period to which the delivery relates

Ostracon	King	Date of issue	Period covered	Variance (months)	Variance (days)
O. Ashmol. 111	Seti II/Siptah	Yr 4 IV *šmw* 9	III *šmw*	-1	-8
O. Ashmol. 262	-	Yr 4 II *ꜣḫt*	I *ꜣḫt*	-1	N/A
O. Cairo 25517γ	Siptah	IV *šmw* 9	I *prt*	-7	>-100
O. Cairo 25685 rt.	*Late 20th Dynasty*	IV *prt* 28	III *prt*	-1	-27
O. Cairo 25685 rt.	*Late 20th Dynasty*	IV *prt* 28	IV *prt*	0	0
O. Cairo 25685 vs.	*Late 20th Dynasty*	I *šmw* 7	IV *prt*	-1	-6
O. DeM 184	*20th Dynasty*	Yr 4 II *prt* 10	III *prt* - IV *prt*	+1/+2	+21/+51
O. DeM 712	-	IV *šmw* 30	I *ꜣḫt*	+1	+1
O. DeM 737	-	I *ꜣḫt* 12	I *ꜣḫt* 21	0	0
O. Strasbourg H110 rt.	*Late 19th Dynasty*	IV *ꜣḫt* 8	III *ꜣḫt*	-1	-7
O. Strasbourg H110 rt.	*Late 19th Dynasty*	IV *ꜣḫt* 8	IV *ꜣḫt*	0	0
O. Strasbourg H110 rt.	*Late 19th Dynasty*	IV *ꜣḫt* 8	I *prt* – II *prt*	+1/+2	+23/+53
O. Strasbourg H110 vs.	*Late 19th Dynasty*	IV *ꜣḫt* 18	IV *ꜣḫt*	0	0
O. Strasbourg H110 vs.	*Late 19th Dynasty*	IV *ꜣḫt* 18	I *prt* – II *prt*	+1/+2	+13/+43
O. UC 39661	*20th Dynasty*	II *ꜣḫt* 5	I *ꜣḫt*	-1	-4
P. Bib. Nat. 237 Cart.1	*Ramesses VI*	II *ꜣḫt* 20	II *ꜣḫt*	0	0

In order to examine any recording techniques, and to attempt to quantify the proportion of deliveries which were late, the variances have to be examined more closely in terms of date, season and the number of months specified on a given record, as well as looking at any aberrant results. Only on five occasions is there evidence of a variance of more than one month, and with one exception, O. Berlin 14302 vs., the variance appears to indicate an advance payment. One of these, O. DeM 177, appears to be a schedule of payments made for four successive months, including both payments of arrears and advance, but it is not clear whether these deliveries were actually carried out, since the delivery patterns were not constant in terms of timing. It is equally possible that, in cases such as O. DeM 177, the scribe has recorded a delivery relating to arrears, but it is also a statement of intention that rations were to be delivered for the next months.

Casual observation of the monthly variance columns in Table 12 shows that there appears to have been very little difference between the issue date and the period covered by the delivery, with two exceptions. These are O. DeM 611, a distribution record showing payment to individuals six months in advance, and O. DeM 10039 rt.; O. DeM 611 dates from the reign of Siptaḥ, as does O. Cairo 25517γ; the latter text appears to show a seven month arrears for additional rations. The extreme variances of both would either suggest that recording techniques may have differed significantly at this earlier time, or one record, perhaps the first, contains a date error. Similarly, O. DeM 10039 rt. is dated to III *šmw* 13, but the left side is lost. It consists of at least two ration lists; one of these either includes or is solely a payment to the women servants for the two months IV *3ḫt* and I *prt*, or several months in advance. Surely this is not plausible, especially regarding servants, so the only alternative is that this was indeed a ration payment in arrears of about ten months, this may also hold for O. Cairo 25517γ, assuming the dates are all correct.

The variances can be broken down further by using days rather than months, as indicated in the final column in Table 12. However, out of the forty-five examples, sixteen have a zero variance and another eight do not indicate a day, leaving only seventeen examples of differences in due date and actual delivery date. The data pool would be too diluted to make any meaningful observations on this basis, without making excessive assumptions such as choosing a specific due date and inserting variances in the event of missing information due to lacunae or non-recording. Where a variance is shown as zero, this classes as "on time", whether or not the rations were paid on the first or last day of the month, so any fabrication of this sort could produce more inaccurate results than those we presently have.

The use of *dni* to denote additional rations is itself a specification about the rations being delivered late[53] so there would be an expectation that the variances would be more marked than before. However, this does not appear to be totally supported by the evidence, as it is presented in Table 14, which shows percentages for the distributions for basic and additional ration deliveries, where *n* is the number of examples, and the variances are in months. For *diw*, just under half (42%) of the documents indicate the rations being delivered on time, while the remainder is split equally, which is not what we would expect. For *dni*, there is a skew towards payments being made in arrears, but even here there are still four out of sixteen examples indicating advance payments, which is surely by definition incorrect. On the face of it, this suggests that there was

53 Haring (2003: 138) states that the month stated is the month before the date of the document, but occasionally an even earlier month is noted.

no real pattern to delivery schedules, assuming that the sample of documents examined in the present study is representative of the whole picture.

Table 14. Period variances of basic and additional rations

	Arrears	Same month	Advance
diw (n=45)	13 (29%)	19 (42%)	13 (29%)
dni (n=16)	7 (44%)	5 (31%)	4 (25%)

The corresponding information from the Journal is no more forthcoming, with only nine known examples with both dates recorded. When the number of days from all these documents is taken as a total, they cover only about six months out of the whole period of 104 months. In other words, it can hardly be expected to yield detailed findings. Only twice does a Journal indicate an advance basic ration payment; both of these record single payments of rations for the current month and the next, but given the small sample we should not take this as being significant.

However, the mere suggestion that the ancient Egyptians paid their rations in advance[54] seems to be a fallacy, so what is the meaning behind the frequency of "advance" payments revealed in both these tables? One possibility is that the scribes did show a tendency to record ration payments in a logical order, but more in the manner in which they would compose a journal, in sequential order. This does not explain Journal documents such as O. DeM 45, covering just over a month from Year 2 II *ꜣḫt* 1 through to III *ꜣḫt* 5, and where rations are clearly shown (rt. 19) as being given (*dit*) for II *ꜣḫt* and III *ꜣḫt*[55]. A document may be incorrectly dated to a given month[56], which would give the impression of advance payments and would seem like the least plausible explanation; in addition date errors in documents which were not from the Journal and had no other dating criteria would be impossible to spot. A document may have an initial date with entries in the format of a journal but without dating each entry; this kind of incomplete record was not uncommon in the modern age before the advent of computerised accounting systems[57].

The instances where advance payments appear to be recorded are worth examining in detail. The first query is in the date of O. DeM 184, which Černý marked as an error; if this is the case a date of IV *prt* might be expected, which would be more in line with a payment a month in arrears. The year may also be incorrectly stated as 4 instead of 2, possibly an early example similar to the modern accountant's bane, and one which the ancient Egyptian scribe surely suffered, a complete misreading of numbers or a transposition error—but Year 2 Month 4 would make more

54 A suggestion put forward by Häggman (2002: 81). Despite accepting that wages were almost always "late" this itself seems to be contradictory to this proposition.

55 Also but not from the Journal, O. Cairo 25608, 2; O. DeM 177, 6 (*rdit n* III *prt*), and 8 (*rdit n* IV *prt*); O. DeM 621, rt. 5; O. Munich ÄS 397, 2.

56 According to Černý, scribal errors [*sic*] are present in the dates of O. DeM 44, rt. 1, and O. DeM 184, 1.

57 Probably the case on O. Strasbourg H110, where apart from the initial line there are no dates to go with the corresponding deliveries.

sense. The opening line on O. DeM 712 is clear, reading "IV *šmw*, last day: ¾ *khar* which is for I *3ḫt*", so there can be no doubt about this being correct and therefore a small amount paid in advance. Similarly, O. Berlin 14219, 1-2, reads *3bd 4 prt sw 2 dit diw n 3bd 1 šmw*, "IV Peret, day 2, giving/distribution of rations for I Shemu", a clear example of an advance ration payment.

Line 3 of O. Berlin 12294 records a date of IV *šmw* 21, and continues with a list of *diw n 3bd 4 šmw r 3bd 2 3ḫt*, "rations for IV Shemu until II Akhet", implying the period is for three successive months. However, the hieratic sign *r* is not clear as the beginning of the line is badly abraded on the ostracon. Although it is treated as an advance payment, this example must be treated with some circumspection.

O. DeM 177 is an issue of interpretation, and centres on the date of the complete document as being II *prt* 13. Lines 6 to 7 record a long delivery list for III *prt*, followed by payments to twelve men and the guardsman, the latter being for III and IV *prt*. Assuming the initial date is correct, what seems most likely here is that the scribe continued his records on the same text, but at different times, without inserting further dates in the document. An incorrect date would conveniently sort the problem out for us, but it is an issue which can not be conclusively resolved without physically examining the writing.

O. Strasbourg H110 is more problematic in that it can be interpreted in two ways. The recto is dated to IV *3ḫt* 8, and records *dnỉ* deliveries for the same month as well as *diw* deliveries for I and II *prt*. Taking this at face value, it would indicate an advance payment, which does not seem plausible in an ancient barter society. The verso, dated the same day, is very similar: *dnỉ* for the same month and both types of rations for I *prt*. This question could be answered by examination of the writing on the ostracon itself; only then would we know whether or not it is the date on the first line of either side which is confusing. The text was not written in entirety on IV *3ḫt* 8 but the records were drawn up at some time during each month. Therefore, the day was not recorded, since the payments to groups such as women servants were for more than one month.

The statistical distribution of *dnỉ* payments shows a slight tendency towards deliveries in arrears (seven out of sixteen examples, or 44%), while there are four and five examples of the same month and advance payments respectively, but this is far too small a sample to be significant. Since additional payments were exactly that, it is easy to suggest that the likelihood of arrears is higher than that for basic ration payments. There are still five examples in which it appears that advances payments were given, so perhaps there were cases of an advance in rations, although it was not the normal practice. A further possibility, albeit one which is impossible to substantiate with any evidence, is that in many instances the calculations of rations were made outside the regular delivery system and these documents were drawn up in advance and may not have reflected actual deliveries. If this were true, the implications of this could render much of the preceding discussion invalid, but even so, the uncertainty as to the reasons behind the advance payments is unavoidable.

With the occasional exception, it was highly unlikely that basic ration payments were made in advance, but not because of the administration. The reason for this was not idleness or neglect on the part of the scribe, but that the workmen knew what was going on, primarily because society was at that time mainly based on oral tradition[58], that the basic rations were known and the workmen could expect them every month. The evidence presented above on the day and month of issue strengthens this argument[59]. Once things began to get out of hand, and rations were in serious arrears, then the workmen would take action, as happened with the strikes in Year 29 of Ramesses III[60].

One question, which must be addressed, is what would be classed as a late delivery, if it is possible to define what is meant by "late". Furthermore, based on the evidence available, is it possible to ascertain if a significant proportion of deliveries were late. In order to do this, both the variances and the days of issue would have to be examined, but even so we have to make assumptions based on definitions of "late". In today's western society, it is the norm for wages to be paid in the last week of the month, and this would be classed as a nil variance in the analysis used in the present study. It is difficult, if it is indeed possible, to prove that there was what could be assigned a "normal" date of payment of rations partly because of the irregular patterns of ration deliveries which have been recorded, and partly due to the incomplete picture given by the surviving material. In addition to this, as modern scholars we must be careful not to impose modern viewpoints on the ancient data and look at terminology issues contextually, and provide interpretations not influenced by modern equivalents. The notion of what was "late" to the Egyptians may be different to our own views; society today has a very low tolerance level for anything being overdue, and although this can not be substantiated by evidence, the ancient view of what was late was almost certainly considerably different to our own. Unless there is any direct and specific recording to the contrary, such as the Year 29 strike papyri, it would be almost impossible to show what was "late" in the eyes of the villagers.

It may be expected that the season of the year affected recording procedures, but even allowing for poor harvests, the workmen and the central administration of Thebes would have built up some surplus to be used in an emergency or when the harvest failed. On a seasonal level, the supply chain was variable according to the state of the Nile, but once the grain had arrived at the village, the distribution of rations to the workmen should not, in theory at least, have been noticeably affected because of the available storage facilities. For documents indicating variances, although the split of dates of issue of *diw* is 11 in *šmw*, 12 in *prt* and 11 in *3ḫt*, the number of texts examined, at thirty-four, is too small to make any sort of conclusion which would be statistically significant, as twelve available texts during a given season over several decades is a very low number. The only conclusions which can be made on this basis may be stating the obvious; that there are either lost documents or that they were never written in the first place.

§4.6 Conclusion

Perhaps the main point raised on close scrutiny of delivery patterns, and in particular those from the Journal, is that the scribes did not record everything on a daily basis, and also the patterns of delivery reveal many periods where no rations were recorded. Despite the large number of ostraca

58 Janssen (2005: 147).

59 This is presented and discussed above in §§4.1-4.3.

60 See Gardiner (1948a: 45-58) for the text of Turin Strike Papyrus (P. Turin 1880 rt). Rations are included as part of the discussion by Eyre (1980: 191 ff.) on labour relations at the time of the Year 29 strikes.

found at Deir el-Medina, the size of the population recording rations is small, so any conclusions as to results found in the data must be treated with a little circumspection. It can hardly be imagined that nothing was delivered. Despite this, there are distinct instances of clustering, perhaps as a result of economic conditions but more likely as a result of continual recording during these periods rather than a complete absence.

The relationship between the first payment of a given month (*diw*) and subsequent payments (*dni*) is not evident in the results, partly due to the small sample size of surviving material and partly due to our inability to relate an additional delivery to a corresponding basic ration payment based on the evidence that we do have. Analysis of the days of payment on ostraca reveals that there was a broad tendency for payments of *diw* to be in the middle decade and *dni* in the first - a contrast to what might be expected even if we accept the 1st of the month as the day from which payments were calculated. For papyri, the results are different, with many *diw* payments being made during the last five days of the month, so whether accounting practices changed over the course of the 20th Dynasty, we can only speculate. This is highlighted by both the lack of available evidence from the earlier periods and the low impact on the distribution of days of delivery when these are removed from the analysis. The impact of festivals on the day of distribution was not great, partly due to the lunar nature of some festivals such as the Opet festival, and also many festivals were held at weekends. In addition, there was a man on watch every day, as recorded in the Journal, and this included festival days, so all that this does is to disprove the notion that no work was ever done on festival days; the opposite holds and things often carried on as normal.

Examination of the variances between the date of the document and that to which the deliveries relate reveals that there appear to be instances where rations were paid in advance and in arrears. The problem we have here is that it is not known when during the month rations were due, so a document dated to a specified month would not be able to differentiate any variance between a delivery on the first or last days of the month, and in either case, the variance would be treated as zero despite there being a month between the delivery dates. As we would expect, rations being paid in advance was highly unusual, and there tends to be a reason for such differences, either an error in the date or in the case of *dni*, where the scribe has entered multiple deliveries with different dates in a single document.

The vast majority of ration deliveries were, as expected, delivered either in the same month or in arrears by one or two months, with consequences for the workforce and the state officials in the event of non-delivery. The variance in additional payments appears to be greater than those for basic rations, but even this must be treated with caution as it is impossible to know the due date for the former, more so since there is no indication of any additional payments being part of a specified month's rations. More extreme results such as those on O. Cairo 25517γ and O. DeM 10039 rt. can be explained not as advance payments, but as payments long overdue and either not initially recorded or only subsequently recorded when those receiving the rations complained about their previous omission.

The month and season of payments on the rations ostraca do not reveal any significant pattern, primarily because the granaries stored grain when it was not being harvested, so deliveries could continue during these months. The papyri reveal a marked preference for the season of *ꜣḫt* but this is undoubtedly due to the very small number of examples which survive. Grain was delivered and distributed when it was needed, and since society had a significant oral component, many movements were not recorded by the scribes.

Further research is needed in order to clarify the areas where there is doubt, but until more information comes to light in the form of additional evidence from new finds, this is not possible. The number of papyri for which we have dated ration distribution lists is small, and there is little chance for a sequence of dates long enough to allow a comparison with the earlier periods. Thus, if there were any real changes in the frequency and pattern of recording over the course of the Ramesside period they can not be tracked and the timing of any technical shifts can not be followed.

CHAPTER 5

RATION RECIPIENTS & QUANTITIES

The data analysis is continued as the emphasis moves away from dates towards the detailed content of the documents, highlighting some of the issues raised in relation to the recipients of the rations and the amounts recorded. What is accepted as the standard ration payments given to the classes of workmen will not be given much detail since much work has already been done on this topic[1]. Instead this information will be provided for reference in a highly generalised form for completeness and examined as a motive for consistency. For those documents contained within this particular research, it will also be natural to check the mathematics for errors and correct them wherever possible, but obtaining a broad idea of how often and why such mistakes were made is an area dealt with comprehensively in Chapter 7 and does not enter into the present discussion. Although here would be appropriate, one question which is better answered in due course is the inclination to include barley and emmer as separate rations or together in one total.

Detailed analysis of the amounts of rations paid, and the various categories of workmen receiving the rations, is performed in a similar manner to the variances looked at in the previous chapter and allows detailed investigation into a number of issues. Much of the discussion is concentrated on the tabulation of data and accompanying scatter diagrams and graphs in an attempt to show whether there were any significant differences between the early and later Ramesside periods, and by splitting the ostraca up into two distinct periods, to dissect the data for the 19th and early 20th Dynasties in much the same way. With the exception of individual ration amounts, previous studies including a component on rations and rations in any degree of detail have not explored the arrangement and composition of the ration list in depth, either in entirety or in part. Therefore the present study can branch out from the standard approach and look for absent or incomplete information such as what a complete ration list was and the reasons behind why certain designations of workmen were not on the ration lists at given points of time during the Ramesside period. The frequency of recording specified members of the workforce, not by name but by rank or title,

1 See especially Černý (1954) and Janssen (1997), also Černý (1973), Janssen (1975a) and Janssen (1991). It is also important to note that the material relates to the Right side of the workforce; that for the Left side is very scant indeed.

may have connotations in their organisation at any given time, and furthermore, may be reflected in different practices of accounting.

It is necessary to ascertain the order in which the recipients of rations were written down, and whether there was any consistency in the recording between documents which were lists, partial lists or more lengthy compositions. It may be possible to show that there were differences in the order of workmen receiving rations between the records on ostraca and those on papyrus, and therefore indicating any changes which resulted throughout the Ramesside period as far as is possible, given the gaps in the material. In addition, the manner in which the associated ration payments were dealt with will also be examined, such as the way any fractions were calculated and recorded with specific reference to as complete an example as we have, namely O. DeM 381.

§5.1 The source material

Much of the following sections are drawn from the relevant source documents, which consist of material recording a list of one or more members of the Deir el-Medina society, whether or not individual ration amounts were included. There are many instances of a document having multiple lists of recipients; it is counted as one example unless the recto and verso show different lists, in which case the recto and verso of an ostracon are taken to be two examples. As in previous sections, as many documents as possible will be tested against the most complete lists in order to demonstrate rations, recipients and ration patterns. The corpus for this section consists of 124 examples: 113 examples from 106 ostraca, three papyri from the middle Ramesside period adding a further five (the recto of P. Turin 2081+2095 consists of two columns and has twelve lists in total, plus the verso, therefore three examples), and finally six late Ramesside papyri.

This material is shown in the table in Appendix 2. The key to the table is very straightforward. The members of the village listed are: captains (C), foremen (F), scribes (S), guardsmen (G), youths (Y), women servants (W), doorkeepers (D) and old men (O). There is the occasional reference to a scorpion charmer (SC), doctor (DR) and deputy (DP). There is also one reference to a sculptor[2] being on the ration list. On many occasions there are one or more references to "men", and these are kept separate, hence the multiple columns headed "M". Also shown are references to a specific side of the workforce, the date of the document, whether there is more than one list of workmen on the same ostracon or papyrus, and notes relating to named (N) individuals and other points of interest.

In order to allow intra-period comparisons and analysis, there is the need to split the material into a small number of distinct time periods, therefore the approach used by Haring is used, where the dates of the texts are split into the following time brackets[3] and allocated group numbers. This is as follows:

1st half 19th Dynasty	Ramesses I–Year 38 Ramesses II	*c.*1295–1239 BC	Group I
2nd half 19th Dynasty	Year 38 Ramesses II–Tausret	*c.*1239–1186 BC	Group II

2 O. DeM 621, rt. 7.

3 Haring (2003: 126). Note 5 gives a breakdown of all presently known texts, in percentages, attributed to each period, with the majority of the dated texts being from the late 19th Dynasty or early 20th. 42% are undated.

1st half 20th Dynasty	Setnakht–Ramesses VIII	*c.*1186–1127 BC	Group III
2nd half 20th Dynasty	Ramesses IX–Ramesses XI	*c.*1127–1070 BC	Group IV

§5.2 Ration amounts and mathematics

Calculations were performed in a simple manner, either as straightforward addition, or where multiplication was carried out, using the standard formula:

s x, *wꜥ nb ẖꜣr* y *ir.n ẖꜣr* z   x men, each y *khar*, making z *khar*.

Complete ration documents are presented with translations of O. Cairo 25608 rt. and O. DeM 376[4], but to fully understand the accounting a more lengthy example will be discussed, showing multiple calculations and highlighting the layout of the text, including the divisions and sub-divisions and writing of totals. The important part of the process was that of distribution rather than production, so the scribes recorded the inflow and outflow of commodities, or rations in this case. O. DeM 381 rt. is a ration distribution list which is almost complete and showing a variety of recipients, and is translated in its original format as follows:

1 *rnpt sp 4 ꜣbd 2 prt sw 22 dit diw* [...]	Regnal year 4, II Peret 22. Distribution of rations [...]
2 *m-drt pꜣ* [...]	Through the hand of [...]
3 *ḥwtyw 4 wꜥ nb ẖꜣr 2 ir.n ẖꜣr 8*	4 captains, each 2 *khar*, making 8 *khar*
4 *s 62 wꜥ nb ẖꜣr 1¼ ir.n ẖꜣr 77½*	62 men, each 1¼ *khar*, making 77½ *khar*
5 *nꜣ ḥmwt ẖꜣr 2¼*	The women servants 2¼ *khar*
6 *imn-ms ẖꜣr ¾*	Amenmose ¾ *khar*
7 *nꜣ iry-ꜥꜣ* [...] *ẖꜣr 3*	The doorkeepers 3 *khar*
8 *s 29 wꜥ nb ẖꜣr ¼ ir.n ẖꜣr 7¼*	29 men, each ¼ *khar*, making 7¼ *khar*
9 *dmḏ ẖꜣr 92 wḏꜣt ẖꜣr 1*	Total 92[5] *khar*. Remainder 1 *khar*.

The precise meanings of individual words have been discussed in Chapter 3, but there are a couple of examples which need further clarification at this point. Where there is more than one individual in a category of workmen, and this number matters, the total is recorded by the use of *ir.n* "making". With doorkeepers or servant women, the rations were given to them as a group, rendering the number in the group unimportant so one ration value was written. At the end of the list is the total, denoted by the word *dmḏ*, occasionally with a remainder or balance (*wḏꜣt*). In this example, the list and amounts are clearly listed, albeit erroneously, even though we do not know what the remainder in line 9 relates to. There are occasions where there is more than one total within the document, and examination of these can test whether Ezzamel is correct in his assertion that the "terminology such as sub-total, total, grand total, balance due ... was both technically precise and specific to accounting"[6]. O. Ashmol. 1139 is a short ration list, in much the same style, but with the use of *dmḏ* in lines 2 and 4. The first use merely adds Amenwia's ration to that of the scribe, which was inexplicably left blank, while omitting that of the foreman in line 1. The same word is used for what we would class as the "grand total" at the end of the document,

4 See §5.3.

5 The total seems to be within a damaged part of the ostracon, so Černý notes *sic* on his transcription.

6 Ezzamel (1994: 236).

adding the previous *dmḏ* to the rations of the foreman, Hori and the twenty men, thus suggesting that the scribes were not precise in their terminology, and it is a modern concept whereby we use the terms "sub-total", "running total" and "grand total" as anything different than a sum of a set of amounts.

[1] *diw ꜣbd 2 šmw pꜣ ꜥꜣ n i͗st ḫꜣr 5½*	Rations. II Shemu. The foreman 5½ *khar*
[2] *pꜣ sš ḫꜣr <> i͗mn-wiꜣ ḫꜣr 1¼*	The scribe, <blank space> *khar*. Amenwia 1¼ *khar*.
dmḏ ḫꜣr 2¾	Total 2¾ *khar*.
[3] *ḥri ḫꜣr 3 s 20 wꜥ nb ḫꜣr 4 i͗r.n ḫꜣr 80*	Hori, 3 *khar*; 20 men, each 4 *khar* making 80 *khar*
[4] *pꜣ i͗ꜣw 1½ dmḏ ḫꜣr 94*	The old man, 1½ *khar*. Total 94 *khar*

The example discussed previously[7] and reproduced in part below, O. DeM 379, uses *dmḏ* three times. On the first occasion it is used to total the previous two amounts, consisting of rations for one side of the workforce and an associated doorkeeper. The next use must bring in information which we can not account for, while the final use erroneously totals two of the previous amounts. In modern accounting, these figures would be laid out in columns and highlighted as totals, but the Egyptian scribes merely used the same term each time in what could be termed as a continual list in a semi narrative form, with little attempt in this example to construct an organised presentation. The terminology used in the original records covers a range of modern day divisions so can hardly be precise, which in turn may indicate that we do not really understand the true importance of the word *dmḏ* or its significance to the Egyptians.

§5.3 The workmen: hierarchy and rations

Since many scholars have produced publications[8] on the rations aspect of village life, this section will provide a summary, partly for reference purposes, on the functions of some of the less obvious class of workmen, and an examination of how often each appears in the ration records. More importantly, the two "master lists" O. DeM 376 and O. Cairo 25608 rt. will be checked to see if they are the most complete lists available for the village. At Deir el-Medina, workmen (*rmṯ-i͗st*) were divided into two sides of the institution (the Tomb, or *pꜣ ḫr*); Right (*wnmy*) and Left (*smḥy*), although it is improbable that they worked down each side of the tombs. Each side was supervised by a foreman (*ꜥꜣ-n-i͗st*) who was supported by a scribe (*sš*). The two foremen and the administrative scribe of Right were collectively referred to as the captains (*ḥwtyw*), and one member of each side was assigned as the deputy (*i͗dnw*). Also included in the ration texts were youths (*mnḥ*), old men (*i͗ꜣw*), workmen with specific tasks such as doctors (*swnw*) and scorpion charmers (*ḫrp srḳt*), and those individuals who were closely connected to the crew such as guards (*sꜣw*), doorkeepers (*i͗ry-ꜥꜣ*), and female servants (*ḥmwt*). Where there are four captains in the ration lists, the fourth is the chief draughtsman (*ḥry sš-ḳd*) of the Left[9] side, an individual who may have been a scribe but one who was not involved with administrative duties. The support staff "from outside" (*smdt n bnr*) who delivered commodities such as water, wood, fish and vegetables were not part of the

7 See §1.5.

8 See §1.2, also Junge (2001: 298-301).

9 Černý (1973: 236-237).

village proper and subsequently were generally not included in the ration lists[10].

Despite the fact that rations have been discussed in earlier studies[11], it is still necessary to include the general amounts in the present study since the accounting for rations naturally forms an important component of the distribution process, and also the material examined will be comprehensive. The recording of any deviations in amounts and the order of recipients and notable omissions have to be noted and explanations attempted wherever possible, including the question why some ration lists were short and incomplete. Two documents can be reproduced in order to highlight the differences in content for what was in essence the same concept, whilst accentuating the problems we have relating to what can be stated to be the full ration of workmen and scribe errors in the calculations. With a number of different recipients and associated payments, O. Cairo 25608 rt. and O. DeM 376[12] are perhaps the best sources for ration lists for an individual month, for two distinct time periods. They read as follows:

O. DeM 376 (Group I: Siptah)

[1] *pꜣ dit diw n ꜣbd 2 šmw*	The distribution of rations for II Shemu
m-drt sš pn-tꜣ-wrt	through the scribe Pentaweret.
[2] *pꜣ ꜥꜣ n ist ḫꜣr 1½, 5¾*	The foreman 1½, 5¾ *khar.*
ḏꜣt ipt 1 m-di mr-sḫmt	Balance 1 *oipe*, with Merysekhmet.
[3] *pꜣ sš ḫꜣr 1, 2¾*	The scribe 1, 2¾ *khar*
[4] *s 17 wꜥ nb ḫꜣr 1, 4½*	17 men, each 1, 4½ *khar*,
ir.n ḫꜣr 17, 76½	making 17, 76½ *khar*
[5] *pꜣ sꜣw ḫꜣr ½, 2¼*	The guardsman ½, 2¼ *khar*
[6] *mnḥw 2 wꜥ nb ḫꜣr 1½* [...]	2 youths, each 1½ [...] *khar*,
ir.n ḫꜣr 3, 1	making 3, 1 *khar*
[7] *ḥmwt ḫꜣr 3*	Women servants 3 *khar*
[8] *nꜣ iry-ꜥꜣ ḫꜣr 1*	The doorkeepers 1 *khar*
[9] *pꜣ swnw ḫꜣr ¼, 1*	The doctor ¼, 1 *khar*
[10] *dmḏ ḫꜣr 23½, 93¼ dmḏ ḫꜣr* [...]	Total: 23½, 93¼ *khar*. Total *khar* [...]

O. Cairo 25608 rt. (Group III: Mid 20th Dynasty)

[1] *ꜣbd 1 šmw ḥr wnmy*	I Shemu For the Right.
[2] *pꜣ dit diw n ꜣbd 2 šmw*	The distribution of rations for II Shemu.
[3] *pꜣ ꜥꜣ n ist ḫꜣr 2, 5½*	The foreman 2, 5½ *khar.*
[4] *pꜣ sš ḫꜣr 2, 5½*	The scribe 2, 5½ *khar*
[5] *s 17 wꜥ nb ḫꜣr 1½, 4*	17 men, each 1½, 4 *khar*,

10 There are exceptions; for example O. DeM 10161, 1, records the water-carriers as receiving 2¾ *khar*, and interestingly they are listed before the foreman. By the end of the Ramesside period the presence of support staff on ration lists became greater; this will be discussed in Section §5.6.

11 Especially Janssen (1997: 13-35).

12 The figures are split into emmer and barley, the underlined amounts are emmer, and were written in red ink on the original. The list refers to the first half of the document, the second half consists of another rations list.

ỉr.n ẖꜣr 25½, 68	making 25½, 68 *khar*
6 *mnḥw 2 wꜥ nb ẖꜣr ½, 1½*	2 youths, each ½, 1½ *khar*,
ỉr.n ẖꜣr 1, 3	making 1, 3 *khar*
7 *pꜣ sꜣw ẖꜣr 1¼, 3¼*	The guardsman 1¼, 3¼ *khar*
8 *nꜣ ḥmt ẖꜣr 1½, 1½*	The women servants 1½, 1½ *khar*
9 *pꜣ ỉry-ꜥꜣ ẖꜣr ½, 1*	The doorkeeper ½, 1 *khar*
10 *pꜣ swnw ẖꜣr ¼, 1*	The doctor ¼, 1 *khar*
11 *dmḏ ẖꜣr 32½*	Total 32½ *khar*,
12 *84¾*	84¾

O. Ashmol. 184 records the same ration distribution as O. DeM 376, but they exhibit differences and indicate that the scribes often made mistakes, a subject discussed in more detail in Chapter 7. O. DeM 376 omits the youths' ½ *khar* of emmer each whereas the emmer total for the men recorded on O. Ashmol. 184 is shown as 68 *khar* and may be incorrect, although ½ *khar* may have been paid in barley and not emmer on this occasion. The scribe may have lost concentration by automatically writing the emmer ration as 4½ *khar*, but using 4 *khar* in his calculations, which appears to be the standard monthly ration along with 1½ *khar* of barley, as shown on the recto of O. Cairo 25608. The barley portion of their ration is also omitted on the same ostracon. Similarly, O. Cairo 25608 rt. misses one man's ration in the total at the end, so no matter how complete a document is, there is a high probability that the scribe was careless, and the number of errors indicates that there was no check on the calculations. It was highly unlikely that the ration payment records were ever checked and audited by the central administration. Instead, it was more likely that they were either stored in an archive (although the presence of archives is another matter of uncertainty[13]) or storage area, removed by the scribe to his own office or residence, or perhaps merely discarded.

The two texts above give slightly conflicting values as to what the standard ration of the workmen was. The barley ration is different, the balance (*wḏꜣt*) or arrears of 1 *oipe* (or ¼ *khar*) mentioned in O. DeM 376, 1, a small amount said to be *m-di* "with" Merysekhmet and which may have been owed from the previous month, but without the corresponding document this is speculation. Based on a considerable number of texts, the standard ration for the foremen and scribes was 5½ *khar* of emmer and 2 *khar* of barley, with the latter being paid half from each side[14], and the standard ration for a workman was 4 *khar* of emmer and 1½ *khar* of barley. The youths were members of the crew who did not have a family to support[15], and consequently received a lower ration payment of 1½ *khar* of emmer and ½ *khar* of barley, which was just above the subsistence rate. They may have served as apprentices or sons of workmen who might inherit the positions of their fathers. The old men were elderly men who were retired, and perhaps were given the equivalent of a pension in today's society, but since they only appear in a dozen or so ostraca, this

13 Discussed by Donker van Heel (2003: 7-18).

14 The scribe's ration was originally and incorrectly stated by Černý (1954: 917) to have been half this figure, based on the material tending to record the rations to only one side. O. DeM 376 is the only example of a foreman's emmer ration being 5¾ *khar*, but that includes a small balancing amount.

15 Černý (1973: 113 and note 7).

is speculation. Their ration was relatively low and variable, between ½ and 1½ *khar* of emmer per month, but barley was only recorded as *dni*.[16] The women slaves, who were property of the state, were given a small ration which varied in amount depending on whether or not a number of individuals were recorded, or they were treated as a group. Their ration would have served as subsistence. The guards' role was to guard and issue the materials such as copper tools, lamp wicks and pigments used in the course of tomb building, and the doorkeepers' job was possibly to man the doors in an unknown location, whist also performing many *smdt* activities and provide physical support in relation to tax collecting. The members of these two classes were not workmen, but closely associated with the crew and therefore they often appear in the ration lists. Generally the standard ration for the guardsmen was 3¼ *khar* of emmer and 1¼ *khar* of barley, and for the doorkeepers a lower subsistence of 1 *khar* of emmer and ½ *khar* of barley[17]. Incidentally, the scribe has become confused with his writing of the definite articles *pꜣ* and *nꜣ* when referring to the doorman and the women servants; the errors are in line 8 of both documents.

As a postscript to the amount of rations paid to the workmen, an interesting set of calculations has been put forward by Janssen[18] relating to the temple's role in the economy and in particular, the possible effect of offerings in the ration cycle. The lists of daily offerings were copied from the Ramesseum, amounting to some thirty sacks (*khar*), to which Ramesses III added another eighty per day, making 110 sacks per day. According to Janssen, the amount of daily offerings equates roughly to the monthly rations of approximately 600 families, and given the impossibility of being able to physically pile such a volume of food and jars of beer made from the grain on the offering tables, the figures quoted appear perfectly plausible. What this suggests is twofold. Firstly there was another supply of grain which fed the workmen and their families, coming from the reversion of offerings. Whether the offerings placed in the necropolis area north west of the village were used in the same way is unclear, but it would certainly account for the relatively large number of silos present in the area of the necropolis in this part of the settlement (see §9.1). Secondly, and perhaps more importantly, this may be the reason behind both the lack of Journal entries recording ration deliveries and the relatively small average ration amounts distributed, a subject which will be explored in detail in §5.4.2.

§5.4 Recipients of rations

If O. DeM 376 and O. Cairo 25608 rt. were the complete ration lists, there must have been reasons why the rest of the material was not detailed in full. This question has several possible answers, but getting to the core of the problem is not easy since we do not know what happened in reality during the distribution process. It is easy to put the blame onto archaeological survival issues; this is part of the answer, but does not explain the relatively large number of documents which record a small amount of ration recipients. It would make sense to copy texts over and repeat them, but this does not appear to have been done[19]. It is also plausible that workmen carried

16 Janssen (1997: 22) has also listed these four texts (n. 55).

17 Janssen (1997:30-31), based on O. Cairo 25608, a ration list including the full range of classes of workman, however this ostracon is one of only two examples indicating the *guardsmen's* ration.

18 Janssen (1979:512-3).

19 Further research may yield results upon an examination of the hieratic for evidence of the use of

out tasks in smaller groups and perhaps in different locations, such as the Valley of the Queens, so rations could have been given on the basis of tasks performed. This is logically sound and is a possible explanation of short ration lists; indeed some of the ostraca found by the Basel expedition show that some rations were distributed in the Valley of the Kings[20].

Until now, nobody has tested the weight of rations recorded in the material as a whole, taking texts as percentages of the full corpus, assuming that O. DeM 376 can be taken as a complete example. This is then examined as a comparison between the times of Groups I and III to see if there are any changes in accounting in this respect, and can be done in two ways. The complete ration amounts, although unknown, could have to be assumed to be the sum of those on O. DeM 376. However, this would not be quite correct, because of the numbers of men known to have been in the workforce at this time, it is clear that some of these were omitted from both the "master" texts. The only way round this would be to create a theoretical ration list, assuming the whole workforce was paid at a single time. By doing this, there should be enough comparisons to obtain an accurate result as a conclusion showing the detail in ration texts as percentages of the theoretical ideal. The second method brings the recipients into the equation rather than the amounts. By performing both exercises, comparisons can be made between both methodology and time periods, and therefore some of the accounting techniques.

Both O. DeM 376 and O. Cairo 25608 rt. have twenty-four individuals receiving their rations, and despite there being no alternative for this methodology, taking this as the "full" ration list has its problems. The women servants[21] are included on both ostraca, but are not included in the twenty-four since the number of women is not known, also the scribe's rations are considerably different. There are seventeen men grouped as "men", and as will be seen in §5.5, there are many examples where there are either more men in this group, or else there are several groups consisting of separate numbers of men often resulting in a number greater than twenty-four. This in itself would not be surprising with some of the Group III ostraca, since Ramesses IV increased the size of the workforce early in his reign[22] so any analysis using this criterion would show a higher bias. Splitting the Group III texts into groups dated before and after the date of the workforce increase would dilute the results significantly, since many ostraca are dated less precisely to the early to mid 20th Dynasty, which could be either side of the aforementioned date.

The approach which will be taken is to treat each group of individuals as a single entry, in which case these ostraca would have a "score" of 8, but the problem of "men", and particularly named individuals, remains. In these cases, no matter how many groups of unspecified workmen there are in a list, they will be treated as a single category. The same problem exists with named individuals where we do not always know who these men were; here also they will be treated as part of the above group of men. Due to some preliminary fiddling around with subset descriptions, which is unavoidable, the conclusions reached would not therefore be totally correct, but should be close enough to provide accurate enough statistics. Many ostraca have been dated to Ramesses II or the 19th Dynasty in general; for this reason Groups I and II will be treated as one

pro-forma ration documentation; this is covered in Chapter 6.

20 Dorn (2011).

21 The rations of the *ḥmwt* are discussed by Hofmann, in Dorn & Hofmann (eds.) (2006).

22 Explicitly stated in P. Turin 1891, rt. 1-5, dated to Year 2.

subset. In Appendix 2, where there is a question mark in an entry, this denotes uncertainty as to whether or not the class was included in the distribution list; such entries are not included in the analysis which follows.

The analysis will be performed using each criterion in turn. Taking O. DeM 376 (Group II) and O. Cairo 25608 rt. (Group III) as benchmarks, the breakdown of the data for each time period is shown in the following tables and line charts. One exercise takes each record as a proportion of eight (§5.4.1), the number of individual groups of recipients in both examples; the other takes each record as a proportion of the sum of the theoretical ideal ration delivery. Statistical tests will be performed on both sets of data, and in both exercises, *diw* and *dni* will not be separated. It must be borne in mind that the sample sizes are smaller than the tests would ideally require, but the results are still important and warrant discussion.

§5.4.1 Individual groups of recipients

By examining the proportions of documents which record different groups of individuals receiving their ration payments, it is possible to visualise the completeness of recording and furthermore attempt to explain why the majority of ration lists are relatively short. Table 15 shows the frequencies of groups of workmen being represented in the ration lists as a comparison with the "master" ostraca O. DeM 376 and O. Cairo 25608 rt. from the late 19th and mid 20th Dynasties respectively. The information is then shown in Figure 4 as a line graph for ease of visual comparison.

Table 15. Late 19th and mid 20th Dynasty: number and percentages of examples recording different individual groups as receiving rations

	Group I/II O. DeM 376		Group III O. Cairo 25608 rt.	
	No.	%	No.	%
1	12	26.09	13	16.25
2	11	23.91	17	21.25
3	13	28.27	28	35.00
4	7	15.22	9	11.25
5	1	2.17	9	11.25
6	0	0.00	4	5.00
7	1	2.17	0	0.00
8	1	2.17	0	0.00
Total	46	100	80	100

In both cases, ration lists document three groups as recipients more than any other, although during the 19th Dynasty there was a greater tendency to record fewer. Calculations show a mean value of 2.63 groups per example for the 19th Dynasty and 2.95 for the middle of the 20th, which brings into question whether the period of time had any effect on the manner of recording. The difference appears to be considerable, so as a consequence, the hypothesis that the two sets of data come from the same population can be tested statistically using the Mann-Whitney test, thereby investigating the significance of the difference between the means. The Mann-Whitney U-statistic is 0.138 and is not significant, therefore a negative result in that the two data sets are not significantly different using a 95% confidence interval, and that the recording of ration recipients in the 19th and 20th Dynasties was not noticeably different. The result may not be foolproof, but it does highlight caution in firmly concluding there are deviations when there are not, and any statistical differences must, given the sample size, be treated with circumspection.

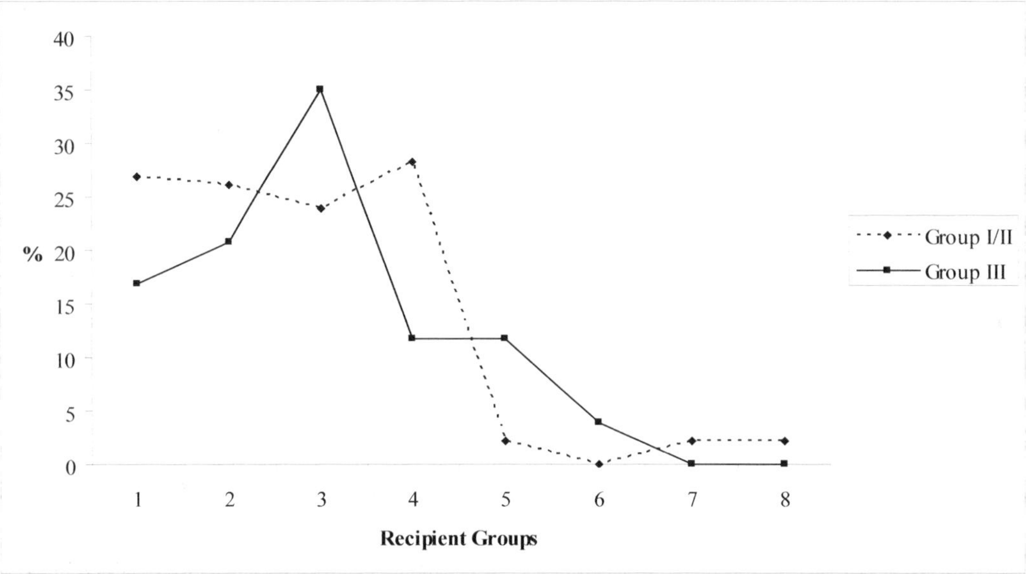

Figure 4. Percentages of texts recording different groups of workmen as receiving rations

It is easy to state that there were differences in accounting techniques, but getting behind the results is an entirely different matter. One factor which may have skewed the value of the later period slightly was the increase in the number of workmen in Year 2 of Ramesses IV, but even so it should affect the number of workmen who got their rations but not have that great an effect, if any, on the number of groups. It is plausible that recording techniques changed over time as the accounting system evolved into one which was more complete, but the absence of material from the first half of the reign of Ramesses III makes this impossible to prove to any degree. Groups such as doorkeepers and women servants, who were not workmen, but still connected to the crew, tended not to have been included as often in the earlier period[23] and neither were the captains (*ḥwtyw*) who were included in their positions of foreman and scribe within the gang. This may suggest that the position of captain had increased in importance by the middle of the 20th Dynasty, but equally it could also have been a title used more for convenience in the administration.

23 The composition and order of recipients as recorded in the ration documentation are analysed in §5.5.

If we have an example of a complete ration list, one matter which stands out is why there are so few examples which record more lengthy lists as opposed to the bulk of the material recording significantly fewer. Archaeological survival is undoubtedly one reason, but the difference over time in recording techniques can be highlighted both with reference to the texts themselves and to the results produced here. Based on the increased numbers of private and judicial texts being written from the late 19th Dynasty onwards, it is highly probable that there was less writing during the early part of the 19th Dynasty[24] and this is not down to survival. It may well follow that the similar distribution of ration texts through the late Ramesside period follows the same pattern and for the same reason, but the evidence does not prove this conclusively. Therefore, one important matter which this exercise does prove is that we can not transfer 19th Dynasty material to the 20th Dynasty and vice versa, and despite there being only some forty years between the respective periods there is a distinction between them. In the event that the material from the first half of the reign of Ramesses III becomes available then that data can be tested, and filling in the period when the change may have taken place.

§5.4.2 Total amount of rations delivered

Calculating what a complete ration list was is an impossible task for reasons other than archaeological survival. The notion of what a "complete" ration list was may itself have a different meaning today than in an ancient context in so far that what would be regarded as "complete" may well be about only what was required for the delivery itself, and not what we would think of as complete for our own convenience.

Table 16. Frequencies of total rations (*diw* and *dni*) distributed as a percentage of a complete delivery

Rations %	Group I/II No. of examples	Group III No. of examples	Group IV No. of examples
1-10	14	3	2
10-20	6	2	1
20-30	6	7	2
30-40	1	5	4
40-50	3	4	0
50-60	2	1	1
60-70	3	2	1
70-80	3	3	1
80-90	0	2	1
90-100	1	1	0
>100	2	10	1
Total	41	41	14

24 Haring (2003a: 255).

The surviving material exhibits a wide range of content, ranging from those with either small amounts of grain or a single recipient to those which record a large amount of grain being given to a group of men. There are many texts which are either broken or damaged so as to result in uncertainty as to who was paid what, and whether any totals recorded are exactly that or are actually sub totals, since the vocabulary used has been shown to be not specific. Mathematical errors have been corrected where possible, and any uncertain examples are not included in the following analysis. Mention has already been made to the increase in the workforce in Year 2 of Ramesses IV, this would have a slight positive effect on the totals delivered since some of the Group III ostraca have been dated roughly to the 20th Dynasty, covering the period either side of the aforementioned date. Importantly, any excessively high ration totals, which may distort the analysis, will be highlighted and examined individually.

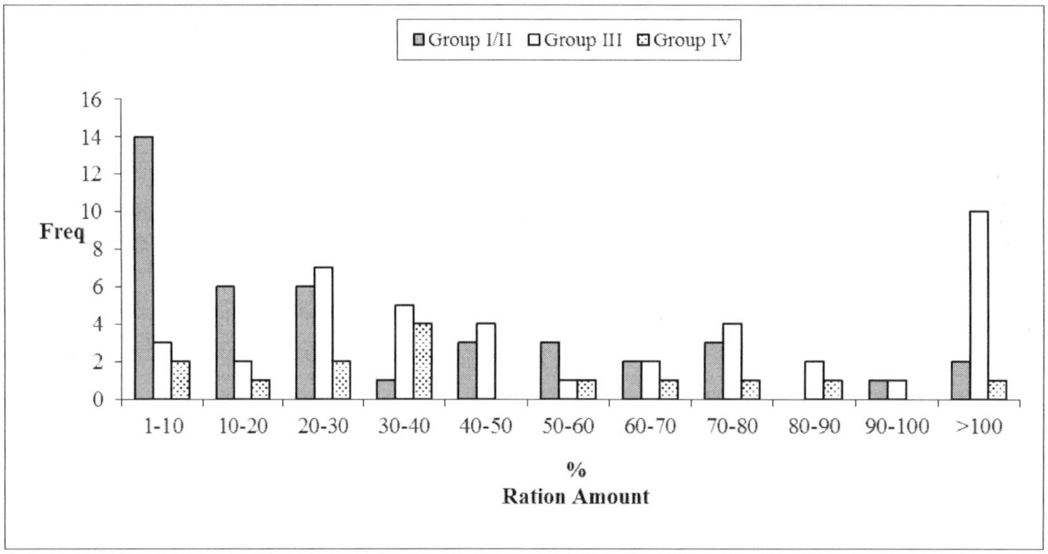

Figure 5. Total rations distributed as a percentage of a complete delivery

The only way to really test this data and determine whether ration lists were significantly incomplete, is to create an arbitrary ration distribution record, where all the men are assumed to be paid their allocated monthly amount. Individuals such as doorkeepers and women servants were not part of the workforce so are not included in this record.

It is also assumed that there were forty men in total, including the foremen and scribes, although the workforce size was certainly not constant throughout the Ramesside period[25]. Since deliveries were made to one side of the workforce, care must be taken to ensure that any comparisons are made on the same basis. The arbitrary ration list will, therefore, consist of twenty men

25 Collier (2004: 41) suggests the size of the workforce at Year 6 of Seti II was approximately 50, rising to slightly over 60 by the time of O. Ashmol. 57 (about Year 2 of Siptah). The workforce size increased from 60 to 120 in Year 2 of Ramesses IV (see P. Turin 1891, rt. 1-5), and was reduced to 60 under Ramesses V.

for one side of the crew. The deliveries will then be recalculated so each one is treated not as an absolute value, but as a percentage of the arbitrary value of 114, which may represent an "ideal" ration value based on an "ideal" list of recipients. Therefore, for example, O. DeM 384 records rations totalling 48½ *khar*, so the reworked value is 42.76%. Table 16 shows both actual and percentage values as a frequency distribution, these percentages form the basis of the bar chart shown as Figure 5.

The exercise can be expanded to incorporate the results from the papyri from Group IV. However, the results are not so sound primarily since there are many instances of ration distribution lists which are fragmentary, and also because of the small number of examples with which to work. One document, P. Turin 2013+2050+2061, has several such broken lists but four instances where the recipients and amounts are still clear. Therefore only where it is certain that we have a complete list are they examined. Another problem is the size of the workforce during this period, which appears to have been variable[26]; for this exercise the most frequently recorded number of sixty-six, or thirty-one plus a foreman and scribe (or chief draughtsman) for one side, will be used, therefore the calculations for Group IV are based on a figure of 189½ *khar* and not 114.

Groups I/II & III	Group IV
The foreman, 2, 5½ *khar*.	The foreman, 2, 5½ *khar*.
The scribe, 2, 5½ *khar*	The scribe, 2, 5½ *khar*
18 men, each 1½, 4 *khar*, making 27, 72 *khar*	31 men, each 1½, 4 *khar*, making 46½, 124 *khar*
Total: 31, 83 *khar*.	Total: 50½, 139 *khar*.
Total: 114 *khar*.	Total: 189½ *khar*.

The sample size for the earlier periods is almost the same, but there are noticeable differences in the ration amounts recorded at both ends of the spectrum resulting in mean values which differ considerably. The mean ration amount for the 19th Dynasty material is 31.70% of the arbitrary complete ration delivery of 114 *khar*, for the late 20th Dynasty 44.69%, and the corresponding figure for the mid 20th Dynasty is higher, at 89.57%. Even discounting O. Turin 57072, which records deliveries of 630 and 665 *khar*, the average is still 70.55%. The last two lines of this ostracon records deliveries to each side; eighteen men receiving 35 *khar* each (total 630) and nineteen men getting 35 *khar* each (total 665) along with values of 3¼ *khar* and 3 respectively. In addition, the three captains received 22 *khar* each (total 66) so the combined ration drop for the whole workforce of forty men of both sides was 1,317 *khar*. It is likely that this was a combined delivery for four months, which indicates that the accounts were not kept every month but suggests once again that rations were delivered when they were available, and this was not always the case.

O. Turin 57072[27] may not be as abnormal in its content as one might presume, since during the last years of Ramesses III we know that workmen were not being paid their rations when they

26 Valbelle (1985: 102-105) provides, in table form, a summary of the material which indicates the size of the crew throughout the Ramesside period. During the reign of Ramesses IX, the numbers varied from 44 (*Giornale*, pl. 11, 11-13) to 73 (P. Turin 2002 vs.), with the most frequent being 6.

27 For O. Turin 57072, see Section §3.2.4.

were expected, which resulted in a series of strikes. The higher mean value may be a reflection of this social situation, with higher total deliveries, but even so it is unusual for a distribution list to refer to more than one month, as this ostracon does. On the contrary, it may be expected that more payments were made, these being smaller and given when available. As with much of the documentary evidence in an administrative context, it is unclear what is implied, and we can only speculate as to what might have been done.

The high number of examples in Group III where a figure greater than 100% is shown in Figure 5 should be investigated more closely. Out of ten examples, four include the presence of captains in the list, which indicates that on these occasions rations were paid to both sides of the workforce at the same time. Despite journals being recorded for one side only, it was not always the case for rations, so one scribe was at least on some occasions responsible for recording for the whole crew. Perhaps the strikes had an effect on this and recording was sometimes hurried through rather than being performed for each side individually. The inclusion of individuals who were not workmen accounted for additional rations over the "ideal" amount, including O. Cairo 25608 rt., in addition to those occasions where the total is considerably smaller. Where the ration amounts are higher, as in O. DeM 10033 and O. DeM 386, the rations were for more than one month. It must be noted that three ostraca, O. Berlin 12294 and O. Berlin 14842 (from Group II) and O. Berlin 14210 (Group III) are not included. In each case we have a sub-total and the lists continue with the delivery lists being greater than 67½, 98¼ and 190 *khar* respectively.

It has been stated that the mean ration amount for the 19th Dynasty material is 31.70% of the arbitrary complete ration delivery of 114 *khar*, and 68.45%[28] for the mid 20th Dynasty. Using the same criteria as before, the Mann-Whitney test has only been performed on Groups I/II and III since the number of examples in Group IV is far too small, but the result is not surprising given the difference in their respective means. The test produces a significant result (U=0.001), therefore the data sets from the two earlier groups are not from the same population. In other words, there are significant differences between them, some of which may be explained with the aid of Figure 5, which shows the comparative ration distribution for all three periods as percentages of the complete delivery.

The smallest deliveries were considerably more frequent in the 19th Dynasty and a number of reasons can be proposed for this. The long reign of Ramesses II ensured that there was ample time for his tomb to be completed, so the workmen could perform other tasks such as work on commissioned tombs in the Valley of the Queens, the magnificent mausoleum for the sons of the king (KV 5), or tombs for themselves, or even individual tasks possibly with fewer men so the type of work itself was probably a factor. In all such cases the whole workforce was not needed so several projects could be initiated at once. The smaller ration amounts are reflected in the smaller group numbers, and the evidence presented in Table 15 and Figure 4 appears to support this assertion. The short reigns of Amenmesse, Seti II, Siptah and Tausret would have worked in the opposite manner; although material from these reigns are included in the first set of data (Group I/II), the overall effect of Ramesses II on the accounting for the volume of ration amounts was considerable.

28 O. Turin 57072 contains two examples which significantly distort this figure; these are left out. With this text included, the figure is 89.57%.

Since the number of examples from the late 20th Dynasty is low, and because any erratic texts such as O. Turin 57072 can noticeably skew the results, any conclusions garnered from the data are not as reliable as we would hope. The evidence suggests that ration deliveries were smaller, very similar to those in the 19th Dynasty, but since there is no indication of any patterns in delivery it is impossible to determine whether this was normal. Given the social problems towards the end of the Ramesside period, it would seem logical that rations were erratic in their supply and the recording was equally sporadic, though the evidence does not confirm or deny this.

There is evidence in the form of lists showing absence from work during the reigns of Seti II and Siptah,[29] from which the number of men who were working on a given day can be worked out. Not confined to this period, one possibility is that the differences in rations paid could be due to fines because of their absence for a multitude of reasons. More men would therefore be given a lower level of rations and this would not show up in the data shown in Figure 5.

Clearly many smaller amounts were given, perhaps on an ad hoc basis or for shorter tasks in a variety of locations, or when rations became available to distribute. These were recorded, as Figure 5 shows, and despite their small amounts several of these lists were complete lists. Even if the administration itself was standardised in character[30], the scribes had considerable freedom in what they recorded in respect to the terminology and amount of detail. It is impossible to tell how consistent the scribes were in their recording over a period of time; all we can say with certainty is that even the smallest deliveries were accountable on occasions but whether this was the norm is unknown.

Table 17. Late 19th and mid 20th Dynasty: mean distribution of rations per delivery

		Group I/II	Group III	Group IV
	diw	39.89	102.11 (78.03)	80.78
Total Amount	*dni*	17.95	42.50	81.50
	diw/dni	36.14	96.29 (77.71)	80.83
	diw	34.99	89.57 (68.45)	42.63
% of Total Amount	*dni*	15.74	37.28	71.49
	diw/dni	31.70	84.47 (64.06)	44.69

Since there are a number of examples where *dni* are stated[31], one final exercise would be to take the *dni* out and recalculate the figures to establish if these additional payments had any effect on the population as a whole. Group I/II and Group III data are shown as a comparison of three mean values (in *khar* and as a percentage of the arbitrary figure of 114 *khar*) in Table 17. The sep-

29 These are discussed at length by Collier (2004: 30–41).

30 A theme discussed by Haring (2003a: 251) following the assumption that the administration of Deir el-Medina was non-bureaucratic.

31 Group I/II: Ashmol. 111; O. Cairo 25517γ; O. DeM 844; O. Strasbourg H110 (5 instances). Group III: O. Cairo 25592; O. Cairo 25620; O. DeM 382; O. UC 39626 vs.; P. Turin PN109. In addition, the undated O. DeM 10162 rt. has a total, but the beginning lines are lost.

arate deliveries of *diw* and *dni* and those of the entire available corpus are all examined to provide six averages for each data group, as well as the figures in brackets, which do not include O. Turin 57072. The analysis will concentrate on the percentages in the lower part of the table.

Two two main trends emerge from Table 17. Firstly, the average *diw* payment was greater than the average *dni* payment and secondly, the later data set from the mid 20th Dynasty records higher ration totals than the earlier 19th Dynasty data. The first observation is not surprising, since it has been established that *dni* were additional ration payments over and above the first in any given period. Comparing the two ration categories directly, the ratio of the average delivery of *dni* to *diw* was 40% for the Group I/II material and 44% for that of Group III; in other words between a third and a half. The second observation that ration amounts were smaller during the earlier period does not appear particularly unusual, but the magnitude of the difference must surely indicate a change in the manner in which rations were delivered and recorded. The increase in *diw* from 34.99% to 89.57% of a "complete" ration list is considerable, as is the corresponding value of *dni* from 15.74% to 37.28%. Even allowing for O. Turin 57072, the average combined delivery is still significant at 64.06% of the arbitrary figure, and for *diw* only this figure is 77.71%. In this example, one single ostracon containing two examples can noticeably distort the results.

The information contained in Table 17 shows that there were undoubtedly differences in accounting, but gaps in the evidence at the start of the 20th Dynasty do not allow us to determine the pace or chronicle the course of the change over time. The only way to attempt to examine if there was a distinct period of change during the periods where evidence is available is to try and split the material from Group I/II into two distinct groups (I and II), and the Group III material into two groups based on the date when Ramesses IV increased the size of the workforce in Year 2 of his reign. By doing this, it may also reveal whether ration levels were in any way related to the size of the crew, as would be expected. Unfortunately, there are only two documents detailing rations distribution (O. DeM 380 and O. DeM 381), which can be dated to Year 2 or later of Ramesses IV, so unless more material is forthcoming, this avenue is not possible.

It is probable that a full delivery list, or at least one which was recorded by the scribes, did not exist. The relatively low amounts in the 19th Dynasty may have been a result of an administrative system which was not yet developed at this point, but this is speculation based on the need for recording rather than any particular conventions used at the time. The scribes may have been more selective with what they recorded; and there was certainly scope for variation. On the basis that the scribes and not the parties involved recorded barter transactions, it has been suggested that the scribes were paid extra for recording such trades[32]. Whether or not this assertion extends into ration accounting, the proposition seems highly dubious since the scribes within the village received rations in the same manner as the workmen.

It has been stated on several occasions that the pattern of deliveries of grain from the granaries of Thebes, for which there are no records, must have been irregular, and as a result rations were distributed as they became available. This was evident throughout the life of the village, but does not itself explain the significant increase in the amounts during the mid 20th Dynasty. The presence of strikes may have had an effect, but why there were not a greater number of smaller

32 Ezzamel (1994: 242).

amounts recorded in the surviving ostraca is baffling, since logically this would seem to have a reverse effect on total ration payments. Perhaps there were unknown events during the early 20th Dynasty and during the future we may uncover records for this period and the mystery may finally be solved.

§5.5 The class and order of the workmen in the recording

It is simple to state what the level of the rations of each class of workmen was, and the hierarchy of the crew is also relatively clear and well known. We must now turn to the material itself, and get behind the accounting by extracting information from it concerning the presence, or otherwise, of each class of workman in the ration documents, and whether there was a consistent order in which they were recorded. At the same time it is necessary to realise that the evidence comes from delivery lists, journals and memoranda, from different times during the Ramesside period, and consisted of *diw* and *dni*, thus an examination can be made into whether there are any distinct patterns or changes in the data.

Taken from the whole pool of material available as shown in Appendix 2, in general, the most frequent order in which the categories of workmen were written down was as follows: foreman, scribe, one or more groups of "men", guardsmen, youths, women servants, doorkeepers and old men. Included in many of the texts were named individuals, who appear in many positions within the lists. Since the crew was split into two sides, many of the texts were labelled as Left or Right, but even where two or more lists were recorded on the same document, a larger number seem to have omitted this heading. Twenty-eight (approximately a fifth) of the 127 documents are labelled as such, with only ten specifically stating Right and Left[33]. In a society where there is the impression that the scribes recorded as much as they could, this would seem to be a surprising shortage of a simple piece of information which could be recorded with little effort. Broken texts where information is lost would be one factor, but a more likely reason may well be the lack of necessity to actually record everything when it would have been known by the recipients and the administration alike, if in reality the latter were really concerned. Once the grain left the administration's granaries it would have been more important to the workmen than the state that rations were paid.

The details of each document which records a class of workman is shown in Appendix 2, with an asterisk indicating confirmation of a known class of recipient. There are occasions where there is more than one list on a given ostracon or papyrus; these are indicated by a slash. When dealing with statistics concerning material of often incomplete preservation, there is the natural problem of what would be included and classed as a list, but for this study a "list" would be composed of more than one ration recipient. Where the presence of a given class is likely, but uncertain, a question mark is included in the table, but this is not included in any analysis.

33 O. Berlin 12294; O. Berlin 14842 rt.; O. BM EA 50726; O. DeM 179; O. DeM 621; O. DeM 737; O. DeM 739; O. Turin 57072; P. Turin 1884+2067+2071+2105; and P. Turin 2081+2095, rt. II.

Table 18. Workmen categories: number of documents by period

	Total	C	F	S	G	Y	W	D	O	DR	SC
19th Dynasty	31	0	20	18	3	3	10	3	3	1	0
Ramesses III–V	55	10	30	28	5	6	25	11	4	4	5
Ramesses IX–XI	7	4	3	3	0	2	1	6	0	1	0
Undated	31	1	15	12	0	6	14	7	4	0	1
Total	**127**	**15**	**68**	**61**	**8**	**17**	**50**	**27**	**11**	**6**	**6**
Average (%)		**11.8**	**53.5**	**48.0**	**6.3**	**13.4**	**39.4**	**21.3**	**8.7**	**4.7**	**4.7**

The frequency of inclusion of each class of workmen recorded in the texts of Deir el-Medina is presented in Table 18 together with the relative percentages for each category[34]. Not including their inclusion as a captain, sixty-eight documents, or over half, record the presence of one or more foremen in the ration lists, and with very few exceptions[35], they are the first on the ration documents. A scribe is recorded sixty-one times in the ration distribution lists, and in all but six lists he is listed with the foreman[36]. Further to this, on three papyri from the reign of Ramesses IX, there is a chief draughtsman listed instead of the scribe, two relating to the Left and one to the Right. In each case, there is another list which does include the scribe, so perhaps the chief draughtsman was by this time a slightly more elevated position, belonging to the administration of the Tomb[37]. With no evidence from the earlier period this is merely speculation, and there is no evidence from the ration lists that this was the case. However, the absence from the ration lists of any draughtsmen is likely to be because the title of scribe was sometimes an abbreviation of that of draughtsman[38], so the title of "chief draughtsman" would undoubtedly have been more specific. There are eighteen examples of captains being included on the ration lists, always at the front, which befitted their status. Not surprisingly they are never mentioned in the same list as

34 The percentages for each period are discussed in detail in §5.7. The breakdown is shown here more for reference purposes; what is more important at this stage are the percentages of the total pool of material and the ordering of workmen in the lists.

35 O. DeM 182 (second list) records the scribe before the foreman.

36 This does not include instances where the presence of an individual is doubtful, such as O. Cairo 25698 and O. DeM 186. Only where individuals are clearly recorded is the text taken into account.

37 The chief draughtsman may well have been part of the administration, but the draughtsmen were scribes and were classed amongst the ordinary workmen (Černý 1973: 191). It was their job to outline and draw the hieroglyphs and the figural representations on the walls of the royal tombs.

38 Eyre (1987a: 173). The exception is O. DeM 847 rt., which reads "The draughtsmen. Total of their rations: 2,340", though nothing can be read into this.

either the foremen or the scribes, instead they are almost certainly included within their official groups since they were foremen or scribes.

The increased presence of the higher ranked personnel of the crew on the ration lists proves very little, except perhaps that if there were rations then in theory at least, they would be the first to receive them; this would be as expected. It may also have been possible that scribes[39] did not feel it was always necessary to record ration distribution if there was no superior included in the payments; the scribe would have then given himself prestige, associating himself with the foremen when the scribe of the Tomb wrote their ration documents out. Based on the dynasty of the scribe Amennakht, it can be speculated that the perceived increase in trivial texts towards the end of the reign of Ramesses III was due to the scribes wanting prestige for their writing.

Where the accounting system gets interesting is when there are groups of "men", and this occurs in many documents. These groups always come after the scribe, and occasionally a named individual follows them. This is always written in full and takes the form *s* (number) *wˁ nb ẖ3r* (amount) *ỉr n ẖ3r* (amount), or "x men, each y *khar*, making z *khar*". A possible suggestion has been put forward that the differences in rations within the group of men was attributable to absences, after all it did not take much for workmen to be absent[40] from their duties. Another possibility is that one of these groups may have been the *mnḥw*, or striplings, themselves rarely recorded as such and who may have done some of the more menial tasks for a lower ration.

The number of groups in examples such as O. BM EA 50726, a lengthy example detailing one list for each side of the workforce, would indicate that this may not have been the case, at least in part, since the groups of men are shown as 31, 8, 4, 7 and 5 for the Right 32, 8, 5, 5, and 5 for the Left. O. Cairo 25698 shows thirty-two men receiving full rations, with groups of 18, 2 and 4 receiving less; both these examples would seem to be excessive in terms of inactivity. On the other hand, O. Cairo 25689 shows thirty-one men receiving their full ration, and four unnamed men shown separately receiving less, which would certainly support the assertion that this reflected absences, and that such inactivity was accounted for in this straightforward manner. One possible explanation is that the workmen were unofficially ranked in terms of factors such as length of service, seniority or additional tasks carried out, but there is no evidence to support this. More likely is that since the external administration was more concerned with the project as a whole and not what was done each day[41], it did not matter what the workmen did with their time, as long as the main task was achieved, and therefore there were ration payment differentials.

It is clear that every man's monthly quota was not completed by a single delivery, so perhaps some of the "men" listed in the records had previously received a part of their allowance while others had not, but again, this is only a suggestion since the evidence is not conclusive. Despite many texts recording evidence of guardsmen, they were only recorded on eight ration lists, where they almost always followed the groups of men[42]. Interestingly, not once do they show up on pa-

39 There is a difference between the "scribe of the Tomb" and the "scribe", since the latter designation could be used to describe one of the draughtsmen (*sš-ḳd*) of the workforce, as opposed to members of the administration (Černý 1973: 191).

40 See Janssen (1980) for a discussion on absences from work; cf. also idem (1997), 87-98.

41 Eyre (1987a: 178).

42 See Černý (1973: 149-160) for a detailed chapter on the guardsmen, many of whom are known by

pyri, but since it is unlikely that they were treated any differently from the earlier period, it may well be down to misfortune that the evidence does not survive. Seventeen texts record youths[43] receiving rations; usually they follow the guardsmen in the order; and one of these, P. Turin 1884+2067+2071+2105, records "striplings" as receiving rations.

A surprisingly high number, at fifty, of texts record the women servants[44] among the recipients of rations, and this group did not seem to appear in a fixed position in the records, perhaps suggesting that unlike other members of the community, and given that they were property of the state, the scribe was unsure of their rank in relation to the doorkeepers and old men. More likely, and perhaps because of the same reason, is that there was no strict order when it came to the women slaves, the doorkeeper, old men and those with additional duties such as the doctor and scorpion charmer[45]. Doorkeepers are present twenty-seven times on the ration distribution lists, positioned close to the end because of their lowly position[46] and possible connection to the *smdt*. The doorkeepers served as "henchmen" in defence of officials in their collection duties as recorded on the Turin Taxation Papyrus, and it is also likely that they watched the deliveries into the village. Even so, their precise position is not standard since they are sometimes recorded after the women servants and the old men; the latter are present on ten texts and almost always right at the end.

The doctor is present in six of the ration lists, and almost always at the end, and the scorpion charmer is recorded six times[47], also near the end. Both these classes would likely have been included in the "men" so the rations given over and above this may well have been added at the end of the list as a course of standard accounting procedure. There were occasions such as O. DeM 149, where the doorkeepers, doctor and another class, unfortunately lost, were given what appears to be a combined ration of 6 *khar*, but equally this could mean that the first two groups may have been present but received nothing on that occasion. If this is the case, could it possibly be that the workmen may have been present to receive their rations but for some reason the doorkeepers and doctor were not? The answer is unknown, but it raises the issue once again about how the rations were actually handed out.

There are many instances of named individuals being part of the ration list, and they were included in any position except that which occurred before the scribe. Detailing exactly who these individuals were is beyond the scope of the present study, but checking each name recorded in the ration texts against Davies' *Who's Who* reveals very little information. Where the records can

name. The exception is O. Cairo 25608 rt., where the youth is placed before the guardsmen in the order.

43 The youths were young unmarried men who were inexperienced workers, while the striplings may have been boys earning a little for their families by doing small tasks.

44 See Hofmann, in Dorn & Hofmann (eds.) (2006) for a discussion of the rations of the women.

45 Such additional duties were rewarded with additional rations. Janssen (1997: 26-29) discusses the roles and salaries for these "specialist" members of the crew. The ¾ *khar* received by the sculptor (*ṯ3y-mḏ3t*) on O. DeM 621, 7, may be another such example,.

46 Doorkeepers are discussed in detail by Černý (1973: 161-174). Their precise function is unknown but the presence of the doorkeepers with the scribe in the Turin Taxation Papyrus indicates that they provided physical support in the event of trouble arising when revenues were collected.

47 This assumes that Amenmose was the known scorpion charmer of the same name mentioned twice in O. DeM 381 and on O. Berlin 14302 vs., O. Berlin 14264 and P. Turin 2081+2095 rt. II:14.

be seen to match, the names are those of standard workmen with a couple of exceptions[48]; even though we may expect the individuals to have been workmen of importance such as the foreman or scribe this is not the case. On occasions, named individuals earlier in the list received a slightly higher ration, but the evidence is not conclusive. Why names were included in some cases and not in others may well have been down to the individual scribe writing the document and not down to the importance of the workmen, and as a result we can not get anything truly representative of any such named individuals.

Also occasionally included in grain delivery schedules, although far more prevalent in lists which primarily detail deliveries of temple supplies such as *psn* loaves and *bit* cakes, are small amounts given to kings and specific deities. The best example of an ostracon detailing such offerings is O. Berlin 14264, which details lists of *diw* on each side. Specifically stated as receiving rations are "the God" (vs. 5 and rt. 4), the "Lord of the Two Lands" (vs. 8 and rt. 8) and "the Boat" (rt. 8). Lines 6 to 9 of the recto are reproduced as follows:

6 *nty n bnr pꜣ swnw ẖꜣr ⅞*	Those from the outside: the doctor ⅞ *khar,*
7 *pꜣ iry-ꜥꜣ ẖꜣr 1*	the doorkeeper 1 *khar,*
8 *nb tꜣwy ẖꜣr ½ pꜣ wiꜣ ẖꜣr ¼*	the Lord of the Two Lands ½ *khar,* the boat ¼ *khar.*
9 *dmḏ ẖꜣr 49½*	Total 49½ *khar.*

The records indicate that the doctor and the doorkeepers were support staff "from outside" the village, even if the doctor was nothing more than a standard workman with additional duties. The Lord of the Two Lands refers to Pharaoh, and the Boat was the portable barque, which may have been present for a festival, perhaps creating a link with the deified Amenhotep I. The festival coincided with the deliveries on O. Berlin 14264. It is unfortunate that the document is undated.

§5.6 Late Ramesside Papyri

Despite the length of many of the papyri from the later years of the 20th Dynasty, there are only a small handful of documents with references to ration deliveries (see Table 3 in Chapter 4). Out of twelve papyri, four are from the Journal[49]; unlike their predecessors on ostraca, by this time they included inactivity by the crew, probably in many cases as a result of the unreliability of the ration supply, and there was no indication of any individual on watch duty. Given the length of the documents, the papyri can be looked at in terms of their overall general content and format with specific reference to the sections on rations. P. Turin 2013+2050+2061 is a series of ration deliveries (*diw* and *dni*), where the rations are specifically stated as emmer only, being introduced thus:

rt. 2:2 *bdt ẖꜣr 35 wp st diw n ꜣbd 2 ꜣḫt*	Emmer. 35 *khar*. Details of it: *diw* for II *ꜣḫt*

48 Merysekhmet in O. DeM 621 is a draughtsman (Davies 1996: 162) and Amenmose in O. DeM 381 a scorpion charmer, whose extra ration was down to his individual skills. Named individuals such as Roma (O. Ashmol. 111 and O. DeM 611), Khaemnun (O. DeM 611) and Nebnefer son of Amennakht (O. Ashmol. 111) are standard workmen, but the vast majority are unknown.

49 P. Turin 1884+2067+2071+2105; P. Turin 1898+1926+1937+2094; P. Turin 1960+2071; and P. Turin 2013+2050+2061.

Rt. x+5 and rt. 1:4 record *dni* in the same manner, the former "by the scribes of the Granary of Pharaoh" (*in nꜣ sš n tꜣ šnwt n pr-ꜥꜣ*). The use of *in* (we would expect *m-drt*) is a very strong case for the scribes actually getting physical hands-on experience in the delivery procedure, but nowhere in the other examples within this document is there anything similar. The picture of learned individuals scooping up grain and physically moving sacks around seems a bit eccentric, but it can not be totally discounted. In each case *bdt* is written in red ink, indicating a distinct heading preceding a detailed and lengthy distribution list which, when added up, does not always total what is specified in the heading. The standard method recorded on ostraca in ration distribution is evident in a longer form stressing the connection with the temple, in rt. 2:6-8 of the same document. No total is recorded, but a distribution list follows. Rt. 2:13 records rations as being distributed from a fishing boat. The variety of recording in this one text shows that there seems to have been no fixed method by which rations were noted. Despite the increased potential for more detail which was sometimes taken, there are still ambiguities in the totals and how the rations lists match up with the stated totals, and also no further insights into the process of ration distribution as it really happened.

The recto of P. Turin 1960+2071 (there are some more fragments, as yet unpublished) consists of ration deliveries but there is no fluidity in the writing. Any heading, undoubtedly relating to the Right side, is lost but an amount given to the crew (rt. 1:4) is followed by a report of "what was given to them" where the amounts recorded are unrelated to those noted previously. The same pattern is repeated for the Left side in lines 1:8-10, which would indicate this is a different way of issuing rations to men who got either ⅛ *khar* or 1/20 *khar*[50]. There is no indication whether the payments were *diw* or *dni*, but the amounts would suggest the latter even though *dni* payable "in bulk" to unidentified groups of men is very rarely recorded.

Papyrus Turin 1884+2067+2071+2105 concentrates largely on the delivery of metals and lamp wicks (*ẖbs*) with the two references to rations, dated to I *ꜣḫt* 21 and I *ꜣḫt* 26, stating that they "were placed in the Granary of Maꜥat". The second of these (rt. 2:9-12) is more enlightening as it provides lengthy distribution lists for both sides of the workforce. Where they are not lost, lines tend to start with new sentences or dates, as would be expected with Journals, but there is certainly no specific accounting terminology used within rations contexts.

Papyrus Turin 1898+1926+1937+2094 is a lengthy document indicating inactivity and consisting of several fish and wood delivery records, as well as more detailed events in the second half of the text, including mention of rations being delivered after some coercion (rt. 3:25-4:3). The direct references to rations (rt. 2:13 and 2:27) are mere statements in the same manner as those on the earlier ostraca, giving a date and stating that rations were distributed.

The other late Ramesside papyri are not from the Journal. The relevant parts of P. Turin 1906+1939+2047 are somewhat damaged but the ration lists are in the same format as those in the Journal, having a large number of men grouped together, frequent inclusion of doorkeepers[51]

50 Forty men on each side, including the chief draughtsman of the Left, were paid ⅛ *khar*, while another thirty men received 1/20 *khar*. Assuming one month's rations, this would indicate the crew consisted of seventy men on each side, plus the foremen during Years 14 and 15 of Ramesses IX.

51 It has been suggested by Janssen (1997:31) that the office of the doorkeeper may have been upgraded by the time of P. Turin 2018 (Ramesses XI, Year 8-10). Not only was he included in the ration lists more

and captains, but also the payment as "the god's offering" as in rt. 3:10 and 3:19. This either indicates reverence to Amenhotep I, the founder of Deir el-Medina, or more likely to the patron of the Peak, Meretseger. Rations were given to the sanctuaries as part of the workmen's ration list perhaps for use by the priests, but since they were very rarely recorded on ostraca, the reason for this change in this aspect of recording is not clear. The ration lists are in the same format on P. Turin 1932+1939, including the god's offering in rt. 2:3, the doorkeeper and captains. The verso of the same document is totally different. There is no heading apart from "the Right side" and no indication of rations; there follows a list of names and amounts between 1 and 1½ *khar*. We can only speculate whether this is a *dni* payment or even water, since water was also measured in *khar*[52]. The lists on P. Turin 2015 and P. Turin 2018, especially the latter, which consists of non-ration grain accounts, are short but unfortunately damaged. The references to rations on P. Turin 2097+2105 are short statements of notification of delivery in a manner similar to that on earlier ostraca. P. Turin 2002[53] is a lengthy document detailing work on the tomb, but vs. I:12-24 and II:1-6 record separate ration deliveries of emmer and barley without mention of any particular side, even though the recording is similar to other examples from the same period and includes an offering to the god within the ration lists.

One aspect of accounting, which the later papyri sometimes exhibit, is the inclusion of the *smdt* as receiving *diw*. The only examples of ostraca recording such grain payments are O. DeM 149, 8-9, which shows a group of water-carriers receiving 20 *khar*, the individual Eferikh on O. Berlin 14264, rt. 6, and O. DeM 10161, rt. 1, where the water-carriers head the list, receiving 2¾ *khar*. However, it is likely that O. DeM 149 is unusual since the grain "which was found" (*gmyt*) is unlabelled and may have been literally lying around as stock. Therefore, this can not be taken as conclusive evidence for earlier *smdt* ration administration.

The references on papyri, while still infrequent, can give us pointers to the possible administration of rations and the *smdt*. P. Turin 2018 has, after an introduction of some six lines, a recurring format taking the form of *tȝ rit wnmy/smḥw m-drt sš* … (the Right/Left side, through the scribe …), followed by a list of named individuals usually receiving 3 or 5 *khar* of emmer. These lists follow on from one another, and are often separated by a group of named individuals who receive amounts between ¾ and 1½ *khar* and these men are clearly the *smdt* for the Right and Left sides as they are sometimes, but not always, introduced as such[54].

P. Turin 2018 vs. C, x+4a	*dmḏ smdt wnmy ḫȝr 13*	Total: *smdt* of Right, 13 *khar*
P. Turin 2018 vs. C, x+4b	*dmḏ smdt smḥy ḫȝr* […]	Total: *smdt* of Left […]

The composition of both sides of the workforce is recorded on several occasions, taking the form of their profession, name (rt. A, 1a.3, shows affiliations for the first two names) and their ration

regularly, but he was paid a higher ration than previously received.

52 Measurements of water and grain are discussed by Mandeville (forthcoming).

53 This document was originally from Year 1 of Ramesses V, according to Valbelle (1985: 36 note 2) and subsequently reused in Year 7 and 8 of Ramesses IX.

54 Rt. A, 1a.3, records in full *nȝ smdt n bnr*, while other examples of *nȝ smdt* are rt. B, 2.2, rt. B, 2.15, and vs. A, 1.1.

payment. The lists are usually the same[55], with there being some variation both in the presence of individuals on the Right side and the order in which they were recorded. There is no change in the composition and order of the Left side. Totals are recorded, towards the end of the document, one for each side, clearly stated using *dmḏ*, but since the preceding lines are lost, neither can be tied up with what preceded them nor do any other complete *smdt* ration list or lists tally to 13 *khar*.

P. Turin 2062 is unfortunately damaged to a large extent, but the verso contains a ration distribution list, which although highly fragmentary, appears to be in the format expected. Following this, vs. 11 records the rations being given to the *smdt* in the same manner as the workmen, and reads as follows:

rdyt r diw n nꜣ smdt	What was given on account of rations to the *smdt*
m-drt pꜣ sš n pꜣ ḫr ẖꜣr [...]	through the scribe of the Tomb, [...] *khar*.

P. Turin 2062 possibly dates to Ramesses V, which would make it unusual for two reasons. Firstly, it is not an ostracon but a papyrus, one of the few surviving from this early on, and secondly it records the delivery of rations for both workmen and *smdt* in the same manner as ostraca record rations for the crew. This highlights the issue about survival; it would be a real chance find if this was one of a kind, which would have been highly unlikely. However, even if the recto is earlier, the verso almost certainly dates to Ramesses IX, and for this reason, the papyrus appears to be nothing out of the ordinary. It does highlight potential problems when trying to date such documents.

The inclusion of the *smdt* in the village accounting can be considered as significant and resulted in a change in recording procedure, in turn affected by different social conditions which were prevalent towards the end of the 20th Dynasty. P. Turin 2002 confirms that the *smdt* were paid by the state, but hitherto they had not been included in the ration lists of the workmen proper. If it was standard that the rations of the *smdt* were recorded, it is a strong possibility that the administration of the workforce and the *smdt*, which had previously been carried out separately, were by now combined into one single administration which may have taken place at the time of the move from Deir el-Medina to Medinet Habu[56]. As a result, this may even suggest that the role of the *smdt* may have changed slightly at this time, but this is speculation. The lack of earlier evidence for the rations of the *smdt* indicates that their associated records have never been found, or more likely, were never actually kept.

§5.7 Changes during the Ramesside Period

Even though the lack of material dictates that only limited analysis and comparisons with the other core periods can be made, it is evident that there are differences in recording technique and accounting procedure. There is enough evidence to highlight some of the changes in the way accounting was carried out, despite there being considerably less material from the time of Ramesses

55 The *smdt* are as follows. Right: scribe (*sš*) Wennefer, builder (*ḳd*) Bakenmut, woodcutter (*šʿd-ḫt*) Setbuy, gypsum-maker (*ḳḏ*) Nesamun, washerman (*rḫty*) Amenmose, washerman (*rḫty*) Ptahkha and a coppersmith (*ḥmty*) whose name is lost. Left: scribe (*sš*) Efenamun, builder (*ḳd*) Ahanakht, gardener (*kꜣry*) Ahanefer, woodcutter (*šʿd-ḫt*) Qenamun, gypsum-maker (*ḳḏ*) Pahary, and washerman (*rḫty*) Ahanefer.

56 Häggman (2002: 101).

II which can be used with the confidence of the 20th Dynasty. Other suppositions such as the possible differential effect of speech, expressions and gestures over time[57] in a society with a relatively high oral element can not be measured except perhaps with reference to the frequencies of use of the narrative style. There is not the bulk of material available from the earlier period to provide an in depth hierarchy of the workmen, in either the textual sources or especially the archaeology of Deir el-Medina itself. Comparisons between the earlier and later periods can be made by examining the formats of documents; whether they were in list forms, the presence or otherwise of different ranks of workmen, the relationship between the written amounts and with the names or classes of workmen, and the manner in which numbers were written and totals were calculated.

Table 19: Workmen categories: percentage of documents by period

	C	F	S	G	Y	W	D	O	DR	SC
19th Dynasty	0	58.8	52.9	8.8	8.8	29.4	8.8	8.8	2.9	0
Ramesses III–V	18.5	55.6	51.9	9.3	11.1	46.3	20.4	7.4	7.4	9.3
Ramesses IX–XI	50.0	37.5	37.5	0	25.0	12.5	75.0	0	12.5	0
Undated	3.2	48.4	38.7	0	19.4	45.2	22.6	12.9	0	3.2
Average %	**11.8**	**53.5**	**48.0**	**6.3**	**13.4**	**39.4**	**21.3**	**8.7**	**4.7**	**4.7**

Table 19 expands on the information shown in Table 18, breaking it down and showing the representation of each class of workman as percentages for each period. This in turn is shown in Figure 6 as a bar chart, facilitating comparisons between each period and with the average. The general trend for each class is only considerably different during the later period, and occasionally distorts the range of averages, but even so, the surviving material consists of only eight examples so one should not read too much into this. The inclusion of foremen and scribes are constant throughout the Ramesside period, but some of the lower ranked categories are less prevalent in the records during the 19th Dynasty.

There are no examples surviving of captains (the term being used in a collective manner to indicate those in charge, namely the two foremen and a scribe) as such in the ration records of the 19th Dynasty; instead they were treated individually as foremen or scribes, implying a greater degree of importance in the later periods. The greater number of names in the earlier records may be an explanation for this, but it is not known exactly who the majority of these workmen were. It can be suspected that there was a propensity to record recipients as a list of names and their corresponding amounts in the 19th Dynasty, and this may explain why there were far fewer 19th

57 Ong (1982) has studied the oral and written aspects within society, discussing all aspects of what can be termed "oral" including non-verbal acceptance of expressions and gestures and the presence of witnesses.

Dynasty individuals who were recorded with their titles of guardian, youth and doorman.

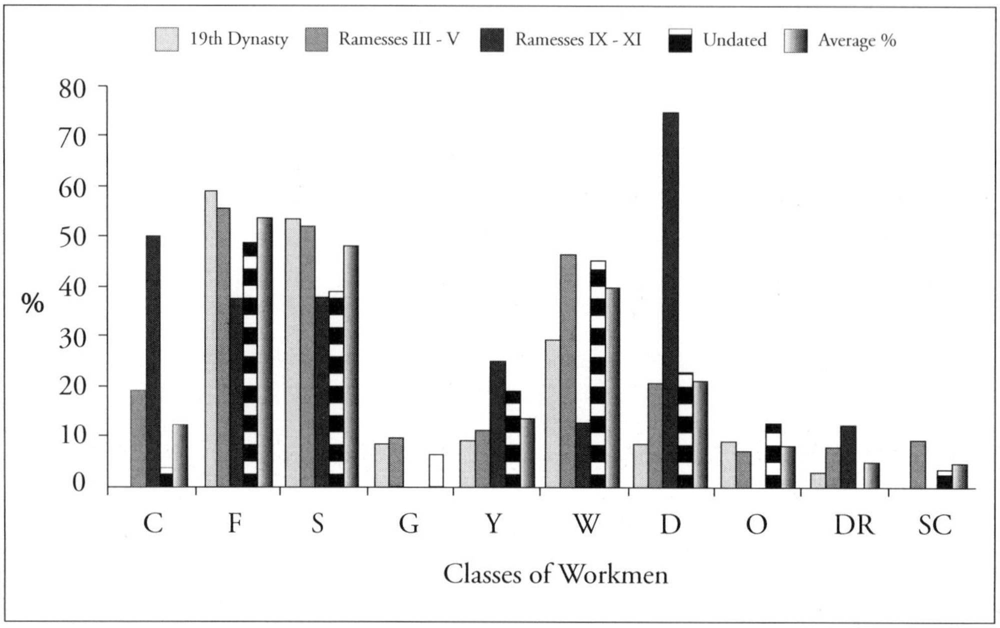

Figure 6. Categories of workmen: percentages by period

Despite us not knowing exactly what took place, it can be safely assumed that the physical process of handing out rations would not have changed noticeably, if at all, between the times of Ramesses II and Ramesses III. Similarly, a Journal must have been kept throughout the occupation of Deir el-Medina, but it is unfortunate that there are very few examples of Journal texts surviving from before Year 25 of the reign of Ramesses III. During the 19th Dynasty, the style of ration distribution lists was that of the list, where on one line the named (occasionally titled) individual was recorded with his amount[58]; later on there was an increased preference for a more continuous text with amounts and totals being written in any position within any given line. That is not to say that name lists did not exist during the mid 20th Dynasty, indeed many of the ostraca found by the Basel team around KV 18 are lists of names.

Closer examination of the material which contains at least one named individual as a recipient of rations reveals that there is a definite difference in recording techniques between the 19th Dynasty and the time of Ramesses III to Ramesses V. Table 20 shows the number and percentage of documents with named individuals as recipients of rations for three time periods: the 19th Dynasty which includes material from between the reign of Ramesses II and that of Tausret; the middle of the 20th Dynasty; and the later period which takes into account the papyri. Twenty-one

58 Examples of the list form include O. Cairo 25517; O. DeM 189; O. DeM 370; O. DeM 611; O. DeM 661; O. DeM 698 (two names on the lines, clearly defined and spaced); O. DeM 744; O. DeM 843; O. DeM 846; O. DeM 10031 (two names on lines, not spaced); O. Michaelides 34; and O. Michaelides 65. Examples from later periods or undated include O. Ashmol. 107 and O. Ashmol. 257.

out of thirty-four (61.7%) examples in the earliest period record names, the figure falling as a percentage, to between 14% and 20% for the later periods. It is easy to indicate a change in scribal practice as the reason; this is surely the case, but unfortunately the evidence does not point to anything concrete as to why records were written the way they were.

Table 20. Number of documents containing named individuals receiving rations[59]

	19th Dynasty	Ramesses III–V	Ramesses IX–XI	Undated	Total
No. of examples	34	54	8	30	126
No. with names	21	11	1	6	32
Percentage	61.7	20.4	12.5	19.4	30.2

One important change was the inclusion of the *smdt* in the accounting record. The evidence we have, although scant, suggests that their rations were treated in the same manner as the workmen's. They were rarely included on any of the ostraca, with O. Berlin 14264 being a notable exception, and limited space on this medium is a highly dubious reason for their absence. Either the records for their rations were made and kept in a separate administrative centre, or they were not kept at all. However, their presence on papyri towards the end of the 20th Dynasty indicates a change not only in accounting, but also in the administration itself.

Overall, the accounting for rations in the Journal documents does not differ a great deal over the Ramesside period. Assuming the evidence we have is representative of the complete population, the notifications of delivery are the same, the standard ration payment was the same, and the way emmer and barley were recorded did not change. Despite the low number of surviving papyri, it is clear there are similarities in the number of instances where rations were not recorded. Where they are recorded the rations were usually, but not always, delivered in the last few days of the year but it should not be viewed that the 28th of the month was the payment date. Unlike ostraca, the late 20th Dynasty papyri record rations given as "offerings to the god" as being included in the distribution lists.

§5.8 Conclusion

The work previously done on rations given to workmen has provided a solid basis for further and considerably more in-depth analysis on the amounts and recipients, so the results presented above add to the knowledge base by comparing pools of texts from specific bands of time and attempting to explain the differences, what recording procedures changed and, if possible, to get behind the reasons for such changes. It is a necessity in dealing with documentary evidence where there are gaps, especially in the time frame, that assumptions are made; without these there would be nothing to work with. Many of these, such as calculating a full delivery list based on the standard ration and the known size of one side of the workforce, can be very accurate approximations, but even so, without the data pool it would still be very difficult to come to safe conclusions. The lack

59 This corpus of documents is listed in Appendix 2.

of surviving evidence on papyrus is an example of this, and would certainly offer an opportunity to revise and even challenge these results if further documents were to be found in the future.

The analysis presented above shows beyond doubt that we do not know what a "complete delivery" was, so any examination of total amounts and subsequent calculations and analysis have to be treated with some circumspection. Suppositions have to be made to facilitate subsequent analysis, such as assuming what a full list was, based on the number of workmen in the workforce and their standard ration, and this reveals that the vast majority of ration distributions involved amounts considerably less that the expected monthly total. When the recipients of rations and the amounts recorded are examined in detail, it can be seen that there are variations during the Ramesside period even though the treatment as shown in the surviving Journal entries remains much the same. Allowing for the limited amount of surviving material and our lack of knowledge on the distribution procedure, some similarities can be highlighted, such as emmer being recorded in red and barley in black. The number of categories of workmen receiving rations on a single document remained roughly the same, even if the designations varied, averaging three throughout the Ramesside period. The standard ration for workmen did not change throughout the period, but due to both the rations being delivered in instalments and the incremental nature of the recording, they appear to show more variation from their standard amounts than would be expected.

Certain individuals were included on ration lists during one period, and not during others. For example, the captains were treated as foremen and scribes in the records during the 19th Dynasty, suggesting that the title was either used for convenience later on or it became more important over time. Individuals such as doorkeepers, guards and youths were also included more often during the 20th Dynasty, a complete contrast to named individuals. It may be that the two groups were one and the same and names were given to those who were not workmen as such, but who held positions affiliated with the workforce. The inclusion of doctors and scorpion charmers, workmen who had additional duties, in the ration lists may distort the totals as they were included in the generic lists of "men", and so were counted twice, but their continued inclusion throughout the 20th Dynasty suggests that this did not matter. Towards the end of the Ramesside period, the support staff (*smdt*) were sometimes included in the records, which suggests either that their rations records were kept elsewhere and do not survive, or that at some point during the 20th Dynasty they were included in the records of the village proper. Similarly, a small offering to one of the gods was included with more regularity towards the end of the Ramesside period, perhaps implying that by this time there was a tendency for more details to be written.

There is a significant difference between the amount of rations recorded as a total delivery, either stated or calculated by adding up the rations of each individual. This is much higher during the mid 20th Dynasty, and the reasons may have something to do with the strikes and that payments became more frequent and delivered when available. The smaller amounts during the reign of Ramesses II can, at least in part, be attributed to the length of the king's reign and smaller payments were made for tasks that were performed elsewhere and which required a fewer number of workmen.

CHAPTER 6

RECORDING PROCEDURES IN THE RATION ACCOUNTING

The content of the ration lists was examined in the previous chapter by exploring who received what and the frequencies of recording. We now move away from statistical analysis towards the finer points within the writing, the appearance of the writing and how it was laid out physically in relation to the ostracon itself. One particular matter that has occasionally arisen throughout the present study is the issue of the possible use of documents which were drawn up at least in part before the recording of a given ration distribution was completed in full. Being able to show conclusively whether or not what is known in business today as a pro-forma was used as part of the scribal repertoire in Deir el-Medina is no easy matter, and one which can not be attempted without precise examination of the original ostraca or papyri themselves. Particular attention has to be paid to the hieratic writing and the frequency of pen dips, and to a lesser extent the placement of the writing on the ostracon.

Investigation into the physical procedure of writing requires accessibility to the original documents, so the limitations are plainly evident in so far that the only available documents are a dozen rations ostraca, which were examined in well lit conditions in the basement of the Ashmolean Museum in Oxford[1]. Since this small group of ostraca is the most conveniently and easily accessible set of documents, it has to be supplemented with the photographs provided by Grandet[2] in his *Catalogue des ostraca hiératiques non littéraires de Deir el-Médinéh*—Volumes 8–11—and in Demarée's *Ramesside Ostraca*, as well as digital images found on the Deir el-Medine web site. At the same time one must bear in mind that no matter how good the photographs are, and since they are in black and white they do not show the red writing sometimes used in rations delivery texts, there is no substitute for examining the original document.

1 The author wishes to thank Helen Whitehouse, Senior Assistant Keeper of the Ashmolean Museum, for arranging and supervising access to these texts and permission to photograph them.

2 The photographs are in high resolution so may be able to add value to the discussion. Other volumes such as Sauneron (1959) only supply hand copies of the hieratic which, of course, do not show any differentials in the amount of ink deposited in individual signs and strokes.

Examination of the writing and the space used on the ostraca may also allow insights into how the scribes prepared their documents. It is not a simple matter of the scribe getting his brush and ink and simply writing the information down, but factors to consider here include the experience of the scribe in the preparation of recording, how well the scribe knew exactly what he needed to produce, the neatness of the writing in eliminating some of the possible recording techniques which did not take place, and the original selection of the ostracon itself. Some accounting procedures are more prevalent than others throughout the textual record, but also of importance is what the scribes did not do, which could either reveal inadequacies in the ancient system or highlight the lack of need for technical aspects taken for granted in modern business accounting. Many of the differences are not due to a shortage of quality in the ancient system, but because of society itself, an absence of formal state regulation and the differential need for specific information to be recorded.

§6.1 Examination of the writing

Perhaps the best way to tackle the question of whether the scribes prepared the bulk of their records in advance and filled in the ration amounts later or not, is to examine the writing on a selection of examples in turn and provide a conclusion one way or the other. Regarding the accuracy of possible results, there is a marked difference between scrutinising a photograph and examining the ostracon itself, so the two groups will be split into clearly distinct sections. Not allowing for the lack of access to the original sources resulting in a very small sample, the main problem is that the writing on the ostraca is not always legible due to fading over time and damage by rubbing and flaking. Since many of the ostraca in this category are small and fragmentary in their nature, only a selection of the photographs of the more substantial texts will be examined. The condition of the ostraca varies, with the clarity of the writing, degree of rubbing and damage to the surface and sides being factors in the effectiveness of the investigation.

§6.1.1 Original source documents examined

O. Ashmol. 21

Written in black on a large red potsherd, the writing fills most of the surface which would be one of the causes for the first signs of each line being damaged, and there are sections, particularly in lines 4 to 7, which are badly abraded. The measure of ¼ *khar* in line 9 along with the associated *ḥrp-srḳt* and *wꜥ nb* in line 3 are both written after a re-inking of the brush, and perhaps also the 7½ *khar* in line 2, though the latter is not clear. Other amounts in lines 3, 7 and 8 are written continuously from what came previously, all of which suggests that this document was written continuously in one sitting and not prepared beforehand.

O. Ashmol. 48

Written in black on both sides of a hand-sized piece of limestone, which is almost completely filled with writing. Despite the clarity of the hieratic, it is difficult to see if there are any pen dips on the distribution list written on the verso. The text is split into two parts: firstly a delivery of beer and dates, and secondly the ration distribution, which accounts for the bulk of the text. It appears that each new line starts with a new dip. This is clearly the case on the recto, which is unconnected, and this in itself may suggest reuse. The appearance of the writing indicates the likelihood that each side was written at individual sittings with no suggestion of later inclusion of any amounts.

O. Ashmol. 72

This is a shorter text also written in black on limestone, but since the beginnings of each line are missing it is impossible to analyse completely the brush dips. The surviving text appears to show that approximately five signs being written before each dip was the norm in this example, indicating a possible pattern as to when the brush was dipped and suggesting that the document was written continuously. The total in line 4 is faint but appears to be in the same handwriting and was not started by a new brush dip, so its use as a pro-forma is highly unlikely. There is a considerable amount of unused space on the ostracon, which may indicate that this document may have been written at short notice with a less than adequate ostracon.

O. Ashmol. 107

The relationship of the writing to the recto of the ostracon is such that the ration list fits neatly onto the stone face, so it is likely that this small, rectangular piece of limestone was specifically selected from a supply of unused and previously stored ostraca. Badly eroded in places, the writing is in black and consists of a complete list of names and associated amounts. Even with a distinct heading, there is no clear indication of any dips, so we must assume that the ostracon was written all at once, and in contrast to many of the absence lists, there are no check marks, which would indicate that the list was not drawn up for any other future use. However, the verso consists of another unrelated literary text so this is another example of the reuse of an ostracon.

O. Ashmol. 108

The writing is on both sides of this potsherd; that on the verso is nowhere near as clear as the recto because of the rougher surface of the inside of the vessel. There is very little unused space on either the recto or the top half of the verso (the bottom half is unused), so perhaps the ostracon was taken from storage prior to use. Where the scribe re-inked his brush on the recto is clearly differentiated in many places, for example *m wnn* (line 2), twice in line 3 (the start and the amount of 100), *wp sn* (line 4), the start of line 5 and perhaps again half way through on the *m* and probably the amount in line 6. Two amounts being written after a new brush dip may suggest the possibility of a pre-written document but there are several examples of amounts where there was no brush dip so this seems unlikely.

O. Ashmol. 111

The writing on the verso of this slab of limestone covers most of the stone face, is very clearly formed, and is written in both red and black. The first line acts as a heading: date + *wḥm* + *diw wp sn*, and interestingly only the word *wḥm* "repetition" is written in red, which usually denotes emmer as opposed to barley. What follows is a list of names and ½ *khar* amounts and, as with O. Ashmol. 107, there are no check marks in the text. The next word written in red is *dni*, which starts line 4 and the ½ *khar* per man and the total. The amounts which follow are also written in red, as is the total in line 7. This is not unusual, but it can show the order in which the content was written, since each black section in between the red values starts with a new brush dip. If the scribe had prepared this document in advance, then we would expect to see brush dips at more irregular intervals throughout and not only at the start of the black sections. Therefore, it is highly probable that the document was written continuously at one sitting with two brushes, one for each colour.

O. Ashmol. 184

A piece of pottery, written primarily in black with some amounts in red, each line of which appears to start with a new brush dip, as do the signs after the red amounts. Close examination of the writing reveals that at least occasionally the scribe wrote a line and left a gap for an amount but whether or not this was done in advance we can only speculate. On at least two occasions—the first amount in line 4 and more clearly the sub-total in line 6—the amount appears to have been written in black and overwritten in red. At the end of line 2 *wḏꜣt=f ẖꜣr ¼* is scribbled off the line, not a continuation of the previous details but more in the manner of a memorandum or reminder that the full ration had not been paid. This is the same distribution list as that on O. DeM 376. Unfortunately, since it has not been possible to examine the latter text, a comparative analysis of the handwriting of these texts, which may have revealed which document was compiled first, could not be undertaken. There is a margin of blank space on the left side of the ostracon, which may indicate that either the scribe was not experienced enough at his job to make his writing large enough to completely fill the space, or that the ostracon itself was hastily selected prior to recording.

O. Ashmol. 200

The writing on this limestone ostracon is such that it is difficult to ascertain where the brush dips were, apart from a couple of instances on the recto; *ẖꜣr* in line 2 and *ḫꜣꜥ* in line 3 but since these were not amounts nothing can be proved.

O. Ashmol. 257

A short but complete ration distribution list, written in black on a piece of pottery. There are no evident differentials relating to brush dips. A total of emmer is written to the left of line 4 probably due to a lack of space at the bottom of the ostracon, which is the result of the limestone breaking. This line possibly appears to be in a different hand; if so, this could be evidence that there was in this case a further check on the document, but the evidence presented in the present study on a wider scale has shown that any auditing and checking by higher authorities did not take place. Since there is a large percentage of the writing space unused, and also, the total was originally written in red and later written over in black, so perhaps it was more likely that the document was used as a draft on a spare ostracon.

O. Ashmol. 262

It is impossible to make much of the writing because the surface of the limestone is littered with pockmarks or darker dirt, dust or micro-organisms in the grain of the stone. The writing was originally clear and relatively large, filling the stone's surface comfortably, but what can now be seen reveals little in terms of minute detail; even so it is still clear that the writing has no discernable differentials in brush dips.

O. Ashmol. 277

Written on a small piece of limestone, this very short memorandum consists of a balance of grain and dates to be delivered. There are no differentials in writing, although line 1 appears to be squeezed into the main text content, probably as a heading inserted after the rest was completed.

O. Ashmol. 1139

The space at the top and bottom of this document is empty and the position of the writing seems to indicate a poor choice of ostracon, but this may be due to a low supply and short notice given to the scribe prior to making his composition. Perhaps this list may be an example of the supply of grain not being predictable; speculation of course since we are hindered by our lack of knowledge of how frequently the donkey trains arrived. A short but complete ration list written primarily in black with some amounts in red, the main point of interest is the number of instances where the black writing overlaps the red. This is evident twice in line 2, twice in line 3 and once in line 4. The sign for *khar* may have been added after the grain amounts, even though there is no reason why this was done. In line 2, the amount of rations given to the scribe is left blank; whether this was omitted in error, omitted deliberately as the individual did not get any grain, or omitted due to the document being written in advance is unclear.

§6.1.2 Examination of high resolution black and white photographs

O. BM EA 50726 rt.[3]

The text on this piece of limestone, which consists of a lengthy ration list, is faded, and much of the surface is badly abraded whilst some of the edges are broken. Some signs, which are heavy, remain but these are insufficient to show any differentials in the writing or any locations of brush dips.

O. BM EA 50739[4]

This limestone ostracon dates to the 19th Dynasty, and is written on both sides. A small amount of writing is lost at the ends of the lines, but despite this the script fits onto the surface except for the top part. The top was not broken off, so the scribe made no attempt to shape the ostracon to fit the writing. The recto reveals no differentials within the writing, but there are some amounts in red on the verso. Traces of writing can be seen between all the lines on the verso so this is a good example where one side of an ostracon is reused.

3 Demarée (2002b: Plate 120).
4 Demarée (2002b: Plates 141-142).

O. DeM 712[5]

This potsherd records small deliveries of emmer covering a number of days, which are not always sequential. The dips appear to be at the start of lines, but the fading of the writing renders this unclear. The writing, which fills the ostracon, is fairly level, but as one goes down the lines the extravagance of the signs denoting the day becomes noticeably less pronounced. All this suggests that this ostracon was written up at the same time and not on a daily basis.

O. DeM 734[6]

A fragment of a distribution list written on pottery, the photograph reveals no discernable dips except for the *n* in line 1, but the amounts do not appear to be written after a fresh dip.

O. DeM 737[7]

Written on pottery, the beginnings of the lines are all intact, but even so, from the photograph the differentials in dips appear to be more as a result of fading rather than due to the nature of the content, since there seems to be no pattern to their use. In line 2 the signs for *wnmy* and *ẖ3r* appear to be made with fresh dips, and also *ḥmt* in line 5 and *dni* in line 10, with the latter being a heading for a new section of text. Two faint signs in between lines 5 and 6, and 8 and 9 are, according to Grandet, ticking marks, though there seems to be no obvious reason for their presence here and not elsewhere in the text. The lines are neatly spaced on the ostracon, but the ends of the lines are lost, making it impossible to tell how much space remained unused.

O. DeM 738[8]

A small fragment of pot, recording the opening two lines of a delivery list, it is impossible to determine where the brush was dipped. The writing appears slightly rubbed in places, making any possible differentials in the writing difficult to spot.

O. DeM 739[9]

This fragmentary ostracon consists of two fragmented pieces of a potsherd; there is no indication of any locations of brush dips or any differentials in the writing. The content is more narrative in style than a standard delivery list, so undoubtedly this was written in one sitting and no amounts were inserted at a later date.

O. DeM 838[10]

The writing on the recto is neat, but does not cover the surface of the limestone, which is damaged in places. This ostracon is interesting for two main reasons. Firstly, it is one example where the

5 Grandet (2000: 111). The ostracon has been broken into three pieces but this does not detract from the photograph, which does not reveal any differences between the pieces in the writing's survival.

6 Grandet (2000: 136).

7 Grandet (2000: 139). For the note on ticking marks, see p. 33.

8 Grandet (2000: 140).

9 Grandet (2000: 141).

10 Grandet (2003: 205).

signs have been written over again because the ink of the original signs *ꜣbd 4* in line 1 was too light[11]. From the photograph, it appears that all the dates were written in lighter ink, but with no logical reason why this should have been done it must be highlighted as an example where using a photograph is inadequate and verification would need to be done by examining the original object. Secondly, the photograph shows clearly that there was a large black dot at the start of each line. The word *ḫbꜣ* in line 1 as a heading after the date records a subtraction or reduction[12] in rations of between 1¼ and 1½ *khar* for each of four days, so rather than being proof of auditing these marks served as a reminder to the scribe that the associated reduction in rations was made physically. It is unfortunate that there is no indication as to who received the reduction.

O. DeM 841[13]
Only two of the three potsherds that formed this ostracon have survived, hence the text is incomplete. Written in the centre of the ostracon, the writing is clear and well-inked and despite many instances of the use of small *ro*-fractions recording rations for the epagomenal days, there is no indication from the photograph of any brush dip locations, even if the amounts calculated were precise.

O. DeM 842[14]
A fragment of pottery, the writing is fully inked and clear. The titles of foreman and scribe are recorded, but any amounts may have been recorded at the bottom, which is missing.

O. DeM 843[15]
This limestone ostracon contains a list of individuals and amounts between 1 and 1½ khar of grain to be given to them in order to complete a ration delivery. The use of *pꜣy=i diw*,"my rations", indicates that the writer was the person responsible for the distribution. The columns are again neatly aligned and for the most part clearly inked with some exceptions which appear to be faded, implying that even in this relatively early period of the village's existence the ostracon was written in one sitting and not prepared in advance. Half of the surface is blank except for two names and amounts which follow on from the main list. This perhaps implies that, on this occasion, the scribe was not sure of the size of ostracon required so he chose one which was larger than needed.

O. DeM 844[16]
Written on both sides of a potsherd in two joining pieces, this ostracon is an unusual document

11 Grandet (2003: 17).
12 Lesko (2002. 354).
13 Grandet (2003: 210).
14 Grandet (2003: 211).
15 Grandet (2003: 212). The list of recipients is extensive, covering twelve individuals from both sides of the workforce during the first half of the reign of Ramesses II. Despite the names being very similar to those on the absence list O. BM EA 5634, there are no check marks here.
16 Grandet (2003: 215, 218).

consisting of lines of dates and the number 1 at the end of each line, which may represent 1⁄16 *khar* based on the total in line 5. Since the first lines are damaged, it is not certain whether it relates to rations owing or delivered. The amounts are neatly situated in a column but the long lines and large dots between these and the days follow directly from the day numbers resulting in a space of variable length before the amount. This may be evidence for advance preparation but from the photograph it is not clear whether the amounts were written at the same time as each line or at the end as the brush dips.

O. DeM 845[17]

The writing on this piece of limestone is clear with fresh dips with *dni* at the start of text (line above is lost) and *s* at the start of line 2. The photograph suggests that the *khar* sign which follows may also be after a new brush dip and also line 3 appears to be lighter, but only by examining the original can this be clarified.

O. DeM 846[18]

A small fragment of pottery where the dates in lines 1 and 3 may have been written in lighter ink, but this is not certain. The writing is generally clear but there is no real indication from the photograph of any new brush dips with the probable exception of the *diw* sign at the start of line 2.

O. DeM 848[19]

This ostracon is a small fragment of pottery which is missing the start of each line due to breakage. The writing is blotchy and haphazardly arranged with the amounts, which do not tally up, written to the right of two lines indicating the location *p3 ḫtm n p3 ḫr*. A total is written perpendicular to the rest of the text. Despite this, it is impossible from the photograph to ascertain the locations of any brush dips.

O. DeM 849[20]

The first list on the recto of this piece of limestone is relatively complete except for the bottom, consisting of a date, a list of titles (the foreman has been crossed out with no amount recorded) and their associated ration payments; the second list is lost due to breakage. Examination of the photograph suggests that this ostracon may be the most likely to indicate possible dips on the *khar* signs throughout, but even so it is still not convincing. Without examining the original it is impossible to determine whether this is due to brush dipping or the fading of one side of the recto. Only some amounts survive in part on the verso.

O. DeM 852[21]

This large piece of limestone is written on both sides which consist of a heading plus two columns

17 Grandet (2003: 221).
18 Grandet (2003: 222).
19 Grandet (2003: 224).
20 Grandet (2003: 225).
21 Grandet (2003: 228-230).

of names and amounts which suitably fit the unusual shape of the stone. The writing is generally fuller on the recto, but there are no differentials in the amount of ink used. The indentations of both columns are straight even if the lines do not carry over, which strongly suggests that this was not a pro forma. The writing on the verso is less neat and appears to be lighter in places, although whether this is due to fading or the surface of the limestone is not clear from the photograph.

O. DeM 853[22]
Both sides of this small piece of limestone consist of clear writing with full ink throughout indicating that without doubt it was written in one sitting. Some signs on the verso are unconnected, implying reuse of the ostracon.

O. DeM 10031[23]
Written in such a way that the surface of this small piece of pottery is neatly filled, the text is relatively complete except for the beginning of each line, and the writing is predominantly black with amounts in red, indicating emmer. It appears from the black and white photograph, which does not show the red writing well, that the scribe wrote the first black section, then the red amount and carried on alternating until the document was finished. The brush dips seem clear, at the start of every black section.

O. DeM 10032[24]
The writing appears crammed into a small space, indicating the probable low supplies of ostraca from which to choose. The top part of the delivery list is complete on this fragment of pot, the writing becomes less clear towards the bottom, but the photograph does not indicate whether this is due to the scribe not filling his brush with ink or more likely as a result of fading.

O. DeM 10033[25]
The writing on this fragment of pot is faded and possibly rubbed in places, so apart from the writing of the titles of the foreman and scribe in lines 3 and 4 it is impossible to pinpoint the locations of any brush dips. Based on the size of space between the lines, the relative height of the writing, and the script intruding into the left side column, it appears from the photograph that some lines have been inserted afterwards. This may well account for the error in the figures (see §7.1).

O. DeM 10034[26]
The photograph suggests that there are fresh brush dips in all three lines; *in* in line 1, *dmḏ* in line 2 and *wḏ3t* in line 3, but these are not conclusive. Again only by examination of the ostracon itself will we know whether these are fresh dips or differentials due to fading of the writing.

22 Grandet (2003: 232-333).
23 Grandet (2006: 223).
24 Grandet (2006: 223).
25 Grandet (2006: 224).
26 Grandet (2006: 225).

O. DeM 10036[27]

It is unclear why the scribe chose to write with such a large margin. Unfortunately most of the ration amounts have been broken off the surviving part of the pot, and what remains reveals little as to how the recording was carried out. The writing becomes larger towards the bottom of the ostracon. Apart from the start of each line, the photograph indicates possible brush dips on the sign for *it* in line 2 and *smḥy* in line 4; both of which can be headings or sub-headings. There is fading of the writing in lines 3 and 6, and the total in line 7 is very light.

O. DeM 10039[28]

This limestone ostracon is a small part of what appears to have been a substantial text in a more narrative style as opposed to a list written on the recto; much of the verso is lost. There is what appears to be damage from rubbing over much of the surface, thus obscuring the evidence for brush dips. The few amounts that remain carry on from what came before and therefore the text is not part of any pre-prepared documentation.

O. DeM 10040[29]

Written in the centre of this limestone shard, the text on this badly abraded ostracon is in black and red, but as is always the case, the red writing does not show up on the black and white photographs. There appear to be brush dips at start of the black after the red amounts, but this is obscured by the surface damage; even so this writing was probably written at one sitting.

O. DeM 10161[30]

A small piece of a pot written on both sides; the top of the verso and bottom of the recto are missing. The surfaces are rubbed in places; from the photographs it is impossible to gain any information relating to brush dips.

O. DeM 10162[31]

Three joining fragments of pot, the first part of the delivery list and the start of the surviving lines are all lost. The writing is clear, the *dmḏ* sign and those following are darker, so the delivery list seems to have been drawn up first, with the total included to the left as an afterthought, rather than underneath.

O. DeM 10163[32]

The writing on the surface of this flat piece of limestone is somewhat cramped; it appears that the ostracon is more or less complete except for a missing piece at the end of the rows, but the beginnings are intact. This may indicate a poor choice of item upon which to write, or an expe-

27 Grandet (2006: 227).
28 Grandet (2006: 229).
29 Grandet (2006: 230).
30 Grandet (2011: 270).
31 Grandet (2011: 271).
32 Grandet (2011: 273).

rienced scribe being able to record what he wanted on what was available at the time. From the photograph, there is no indication of any differentials in the writing.

O. DeM 10164[33]

This list details individual recipients and their rations written in two columns, but unfortunately the surface of the limestone is broken away towards the left side, so many of the names are lost in the second column. The writing itself is not arranged neatly, but the amounts are noticeably lighter on the black and white photograph, suggesting red writing rather than black. There is no indication of whether or not the document was written at one sitting, nor of any brush dips.

O. DeM 10165[34]

The surface of this limestone ostracon is badly flaked, resulting in an irregular surface, and in addition to this, the ends of the lines are lost. Although the writing is legible, it is impossible to examine it for any differentials due to its poor condition.

§6.1.3 Examination of digital images[35]

O. Berlin 10661

The writing is on the outside of a piece of grainy pot, with large gaps between lines 4 and 5. Examination of the content indicates that the ostracon is incomplete, with the beginning and the end of each lines being missing. Written in black, the writing is faint, and as a result it is impossible to pinpoint any instances where the brush has been dipped.

O. Berlin 11249

The pot of which this ostracon was part is finely made, but only the top part of the delivery list survives. The writing is clear and uniform throughout and fits within the surface of the ostracon, although the lines are not straight and the gaps between them are not the same in height. There appear to be no differentials within the writing; even the numbers do not appear to have been entered after the brush was dipped. There are instances where other signs remain darker, such as at the start of line 3 and the end of line 4.

O. Berlin 12294 vs.

A large part of a lengthy delivery list dating to the reign of Ramesses II, the writing on this piece of limestone appears to fan out slightly from right to left in order to fill the surface. The writing is faint in places due to abrasion and age, but it is neatly written with signs clearly defined. Signs at both ends of the lines are lost, rendering any inferences as to where the brush was dipped very uncertain.

33 Grandet (2011: 274).

34 Grandet (2011: 278).

35 These seven documents are all available at Deir el-Medine Online: www.lmu.de/dem-online.

O. Berlin 14210

This fragment of pot contains the bottom part of a delivery list of unknown length, less the beginning of several of the lines. What remains is clearly and neatly written, with no evidence of brush dips before the numbers (including the error in line 5), suggesting that the document was written at one sitting. There is space at the ends of the lines, so the space was not completely utilised. The numerical mistake in line 5 is no different in appearance from the rest of the writing, implying that the scribe was not aware of his error.

O. Berlin 14219

Consisting of a short ration delivery list, the writing is not neatly executed, although this may have been due to the rough texture of the surface. The signs at the beginning of the lines appear darker, which may indicate the frequent dipping of the brush, perhaps by a less experienced scribe. The total of line 7 was not entered at the bottom of the ostracon, or even at the end of lines 2 and 3, where there would have been space, but obliquely crammed in at the end of line 5. This does not seem to be the action of an experienced scribe.

O. Berlin 14264

This ostracon contains a ration delivery list on each side, and is a relatively round piece of limestone with some rubbing and chipping of the surface, especially on the verso. In addition, there is differential survival of the writing where the stone has absorbed the ink. The writing on the recto is neat, with space unused on the left side of the ostracon, perhaps indicating that using the vertical space efficiently may have been more important than horizontal space. Lines 4 and 5 could easily have been entered as a single line. The verso is in worse condition, but most of the surface has been used. There is no indication anywhere of where the brush was dipped, as where the signs appear darker seems to depend on the preservation of the surface itself; for example, on the digital image the bottom left part appears shinier and the writing darker.

O. Berlin 14302

The lengthy delivery list on the recto of this ostracon is neatly written throughout the space of the surface, but the limestone is somewhat degraded with small pitting marks. The writing is badly abraded in places, so it is impossible to show where the brush was dipped. The verso is badly chipped with much of the text being lost.

O. Berlin 14842

The limestone has been weathered, but the writing on the recto is still perfectly legible, even if faint in places. The date is dark, perhaps due to survival; the rest of the writing is generally uniform except that the amounts were all written in red ink. Close examination of the digital image suggests that dips were made after the ration amounts; this and the amount of space used by the red writing, where signs appear continuous, both suggest that the document was written at one sitting and the amounts were not entered afterwards. The verso continues in the same style, but is badly damaged.

§6.2 How did the scribes prepare their documents?

The first thing that had to be done was to select a suitable item on which to write. Generally speaking, most of the material that was found in the Grand Puits was pottery, while that unearthed in the Valleys of the Kings and Queens consisted of pieces of limestone. This was natural since stone was readily available in the vicinity of the tombs and pottery was found close to the village. It is not clear how the appropriate item was chosen, but there was a supply of suitable limestone slabs which were both the right size and had a good surface on which to write. But whether the scribes or other workmen occasionally hunted for them or picked them up as and when they were needed is not clear. The former would be the most logical, but there is no evidence of a storage area, which may have contained many unused pieces of limestone. This storage area may have been either individual huts or the Enclosure itself[36]. Pottery was more straightforward as the availability of broken pottery was such that a suitable ostracon could be created on the spot. The close examination of a selection of ostraca reveals the differential positions of the writing on the stone or pot faces can perhaps be explained by the amount of blanks available; when supplies were running low either a smaller piece was chosen or a quick search took place for something to write on.

The evidence examined above indicates that the scribes did not use pro-forma documents in as much as the physical object was not written up beforehand. However, it is more likely that they had pre-planned texts in mind, and the experience gained of writing texts over the course of time would allow the scribes to choose an appropriate unused ostracon upon which to write his record. From the small sample detailed above, it appears that there was more unused space on the faces of stone than pottery. There seems no obvious reason for this, as stone could be chipped away more easily after the writing was completed, but there again, it may have been deemed pointless. More likely is the experience of the scribe; with practice he would be able to fill the side up with minimal effort. The ostraca which have been examined physically or by photograph have one general thing in common[37], which is that the writing seems to fit into the ostracon almost every time. The limestone could be chipped away at the edges to make a suitable size, but for pottery the breaks are clean and lack the smaller and more serrated edges. Therefore it does seem that in the pottery examples at least, the scribes chose their ostracon having a good idea of what they were going to write and a good estimation of the size of script and the amount of writing needed for an individual record.

The writing itself allows us to speculate as to the timing of the writing in relation to the physical handing out of the grain. There are very few examples where the ration amount was missing within a ration list, so writing prior to distributing the rations was not done. If the grain was given out first, and the scribe subsequently recorded the distribution, then the scribe was relying both on a good memory of who received what amount, and this may account for some of the mistakes in the records. If the scribe recorded the distribution at the same time, then he would

36 This could be treated as one piece of evidence against the use of the *ḫtm* as a storage area. If the recording was carried out there, it seems probable that there would be unused stone ostraca present. On the other hand, the unknown location of the *ḫtm* may be due to the absence of such finds, and if found, they may prove the location of the structure.

37 Also true in Černý & Gardiner, *Hieratic Ostraca*, and López, *Ostraca Ieratici*, assuming the transcriptions mirror the hieratic in position.

have had to write very quickly, undoubtedly resulting in a messier script and a higher probability of mistakes. Despite only a small number of ostraca being available for examination, the neatness of the writing is such that the latter suggestion is unlikely, since the majority of these ostraca show a neat hand. We do not know, of course, how long a delivery took to complete, so on the basis of the evidence presented, the scribe probably recorded the amount as the grain was distributed, perhaps as it was called out by the person issuing the grain, slowly enough to allow him to record every detail as fully as required, allowing him to redip the brush and calculate totals at the point of distribution.

§6.3 Closing the books and ending the period

Closing off one period and starting another is a procedure fundamental to accounting today, but only a small number of ostraca and papyri are available to allow examination of any equivalent practices in Deir el-Medina. This is not surprising since the majority of the texts are by their very nature lists recording a single ration distribution, but even so there are a handful of examples that record ration activity on more than one date. Donker van Heel[38] has discussed a small number of examples relating to lamp wicks and the inactivity of the workforce, but the notion of closing the books in a rations context is not the same, and may not even be appropriate within the material under examination. The scribes wrote the records, but it is impossible to establish how long they were kept since there is a lack of direct evidence for a specific storage area and the possibility of the records being written for and checked by higher administration being remote. This has implications as to whether techniques of ending one period and starting the next were intentionally carried out, and if the scribes of the village did not set out to do this regularly, what can be gleaned from those instances where a ration delivery was recorded for more than one day or month.

For the most part, ration lists were drawn up after a day or month, and completed by a total at the end. A good example is O. Ashmol. 274, which records deliveries on various days; despite the ends of the lines and therefore the amounts being lost, the dates recorded are IV *prt* 10, I *šmw* 14, I *šmw* 20 and II *šmw* 13[39]. The entries are straightforward, each consisting of a date and notification of a distribution of *diw* by a water-carrier or other individual, and the records for each day being entered onto a separate line with no formatting or other indication of any distinct separation. The same seems to be evident when the lists are longer and consist of detailed lists of recipients. The three ration deliveries on O. Cairo JE 72455 rt. start on lines 1, 3 and 5 with dates each a month apart from the previous list, and only the first indicating a day of delivery. This may suggest that the document was written in its entirety at one single point in time, though only examination of the ostracon can confirm this with more certainty. Even allowing for the damaged sections of writing, each list consists of two lines so no closing off of a month took place. Rather, any closing off, if it can be termed thus, is generated by the completion of a delivery rather than a span of time. A similar situation is recorded on O. DeM 621, which records five deliveries to the Right and three for the Left. No days are stated but the months precede a standard list for each record, and each list is recorded on a separate line. Once again, only by examining the handwriting

38 Donker van Heel (2003: 67).

39 These dates are after that of IV *prt* 13 in line 3, which arouses suspicion of an error in the dates of either this or IV *prt* 10 in line 5.

could we attempt to say whether each line was added some time after the previous line[40].

Ostracon DeM 712 records a series of at least seven small emmer amounts, one day's delivery per line; examination of the photograph supplied by Grandet[41] indicates that the writing was clear and well aligned and was written by the same scribe. In common with today, where hand-written lists added to over a number of days or months almost always reveal slight variations in writing appearance even if the same person was responsible throughout, there is no reason to believe that things were different in ancient times. O. DeM 712 would, on this basis, have been written at one instance and not added to over the course of the two months in question. Where rations were included amongst other consumables such as O. IFAO 300, there was no difference in the format of the ostracon. Here, deliveries were recorded for three successive days: wood on Day 7, loaves and beer on Day 8 and *diw* on Day 9 of III *prt*, so different consumables were treated in exactly the same way. Having said that, this ostracon was part of the Journal for Year 27 of Ramesses III, so this would not be anything unusual. Each record for a given day was recorded on an individual line or lines, with the next day's record written on a new line.

Sometimes there were separations which were not recorded in this manner. In these cases, the most common means was to record each distribution on a different side of the ostracon, as was the case with both O. Cairo 25685 (dated IV *prt* 28 and I *šmw* 7) and O. DeM 381 (dated II *prt* 12 and II *prt* 22). Where space allowed, there was the possibility of recording two deliveries on the same side in separate columns. O. DeM 852 rt. shows this distinctly, where the heading on line 1 together with the associated names and small amounts are written in standard column form. To the left side of line 2 is another heading for another list of names recorded in the second column, which is written to the left of the first column. This also strongly suggests that the entire side, and perhaps the verso, which records another separate delivery, was written at the same time and not when the deliveries were dated[42]. The same can be said of O. Turin 57072 rt. The first three lines may be unrelated; the remaining lines of this column and the second indicate an amount delivered on a given month and an associated balance. The only constraint here is the amount of space available, and in addition there is no clear indication of anything unusual. Three complete lists, two dated I *3ḫt* 30 and one dated II *3ḫt* 30 are recorded on O. Munich ÄS 397; they exhibit some distinct accounting terminology but are all written so they start a new line. The first two are undoubtedly connected, but the second is unrelated. In all these instances, it must be borne in mind that we do not know whether the scribe wrote his records at one time or not; we can suggest that he did, but without examination of the ostraca themselves, this is not stated with complete certainty.

All the documents examined so far have been ostraca, but the evidence from papyri is no different; the space allows for both more detail within each list and longer ration lists in terms of

40 Unfortunately many of the month numbers are missing, even if the season is clearly stated as *šmw* each time. For the Right, both line 1 and line 5 record I *šmw*, but the other three months are not clear. For the Left, lines 6 and 8 record the same month, if Sauneron's transcription is correct, sandwiched by a delivery for II *šmw* in line 7. Taken as it is, the document was written at one sitting.

41 Grandet (2000: 111).

42 The first date is *šmw* Day 5; the record of the month is lost but is likely to be IV since the second column is dated to IV *šmw* Day 11. The verso dates to I *3ḫt* 5.

composition and the number of days, but the form is still the same within the ration sections. The papyri suffer from the problem of damage to the majority of the pages, resulting in partial lists and the added complication of many of the dates being lost even if the sense is obvious. A relatively complete example is the verso of P. Turin 2097+2105, which is of significant length; even allowing for part of lines 1-5 being lost, there are still four successive lists, each recorded on a new line and covering two lines. The *diw* were for each month of *šmw* and the interval between each was very close to one month. A similar layout is recorded on P. Turin 2081+2095 rt. where only partial dates remain due to the right side of the papyrus being damaged. Col. I has five[43], perhaps more, *diw* and *dni* lists which start on a new line and follow one after the other. Some of the dates can be read as IV *šmw*, which adds further strength to the suggestion that ration lists were closed not by a date or time period, but by the distribution itself. Column II, where the damage is on the left side and the dates are written in full, including the regnal year, follows the same pattern.

Other papyri are no different. P. Turin 2013+2050+2061 is related predominantly to rations, where the lists are dated and one list follows another. Even if many of the dates are lost due to the often fragmentary condition of the text, each delivery starts on a fresh line, sometimes after a complete date including the regnal year. Of the legible dates, which tend to state not the date the document was written on, but the date the delivery related to, deliveries cover III *šmw* through to III *3ḫt*, and the treatment of the lists is the same every time. There is no difference on the treatment of ration lists on P. Turin 1906+1939+2047 and P. Turin 1932+1939.

The Egyptians knew how to close accounts at the end of each period and how to carry forward balances into the next[44], but with rations this was not what happened. These examples, on both ostraca and papyrus, have shown conclusively that the books were not closed in the manner we would expect today. One could argue with some justification that there was no such concept as closing off accounts in a rations context. No individual accounts are present which indicate a balance being present at the end of one period and carried over into the next. Whereas the Journal was written ideally as monthly documents where the calendar month was the key "shutting down" period, this is not true for ration distribution lists. Space was a factor which influenced what could be written, but the close down was based on the completion of an individual delivery and the date was irrelevant. Similarly, apart from the Journal[45], starting a new period was a concept that was not used in ration accounting in Deir el-Medina for the same reasons. There was a lack of need for period-based records on a daily basis in a society where there was a tendency to write fewer details and such records would be deemed superfluous in the absence of external auditing and administrative checking.

43 Those starting on lines 5, 7, 10, 12 and 15 are clear, even if the date is sometimes lost. The possible lists are those which start on lines 2 and 14.

44 Asserted by Ezzamel (1994: 237) based on documents from elsewhere such as the Abusir Papyri.

45 Although the Journal was not a ration document, it has to be considered due to the frequency of references to ration deliveries as well as providing much dating evidence.

§6.4 Emmer and barley: recorded separately or together?

The standard methodology in ration accounting was that emmer was recorded in red ink and barley in black, but the material does not always exhibit this procedure[46]. Without examining the documents themselves, we are often relying on the accuracy of the transcriptions in Černý's *Notebook* and Kitchen's *Ramesside Inscriptions* as a means of separating grain types. It is impossible to verify how often this scribal procedure was not carried out, but by looking at the amounts we can examine whether for the most part the two staple cereals were split up in the records or treated as one figure. In addition, it may be possible to investigate whether there was any change in technique over the course of the Ramesside period, although the limited sample size is unlikely to narrow things down further than stating that the change happened some time during the 20th Dynasty[47], if this is indeed true. An additional problem is that since many of the ration texts record small amounts of *diw* and *dni*, such as ¼ or ½ *khar*, it is almost always impossible in these cases to tell which type of grain is being distributed.

Apart from the colour differentials, there are two ways of knowing with certainty whether a distribution was of emmer or barley. The first is obvious; where it is explicitly stated as such, with eleven documents listing a distribution either stated as being emmer (*bty* or *bdt*) in a heading or a labelled total[48]. In addition, O. DeM 621 and P. Turin 1932+1939 have individual lists stated to be emmer and barley, the only examples available with both grain types distinctly headed[49]. Examination of these texts accentuates the problems in identifying cereal type, even though this is known, the amounts are often not those that would be expected. The inherent nature of the ration distribution procedures in basic and additional payments is itself problematic, as there is often no way of indicating which is which, without explicit specification. On the question of time, there are Group II, Group III and Group IV examples so together with the limited evidence available, this only shows that headings and labelled totals were used throughout the Ramesside period, or at least until the use of ostraca started to diminish, since the number of surviving papyri is too small to prove this was standard procedure towards the end of the 20th Dynasty.

The second discerning feature is exhibited in several examples which record the foreman's ration as 5½ *khar*,[50] so it is obvious that payments in these cases are emmer. Other examples are not so clear-cut. O. Cairo 25592 records a *dni* payment to the foreman and scribe as 4 and 2 *khar* respectively, which would indicate the probable, but not definite, payment of emmer since these

46 Two examples are P. Turin 1906+1939+2047, rt. 3:12, where the distribution of emmer, stated as such, is not underlined by Kitchen (*Ramesside Inscriptions* VI:626) and P. Turin 2081+2095, rt. II:13 where the delivery is written in black (unless Černý's transcription is incorrect. This is unlikely since he has copied the other emmer payments in red) except for the month and day numbers.

47 Černý (1954: 919) states that the red notation for recording emmer disappears during the 20th Dynasty, but when exactly and whether this was a gradual or sudden change is not specified.

48 O. DeM 179 (Group II); O. DeM 182 (undated); O. DeM 276 (Group III); O. DeM 712 (undated); O. Strasbourg H110 (Group II); O. UC 39626 vs. (Group III); and P. Turin 2013+2050+2061 (Group IV).

49 O. DeM 621 is composed of two ration lists; the recto records a distribution to the Right, the verso to the Left. Each is further separated into two lists, one for each grain type.

50 O. Ashmol. 1139 (undated); O. Cairo JE 72455 (undated); O. Cairo JE 72457 (undated); O. DeM 177 (Group II); and O. DeM 179 (Group II).

amounts are above the standard barley ration. The same amounts form part of the *diw* payment recorded on O. Cairo 25698, showing that amounts could be the same, no matter when the distribution was made. A small number of examples record the foreman's ration as 7½ *khar*[51], which is merely the emmer and barley rations added together and not what would be considered to be a significant ration rise, since the standard ration payment remained constant throughout the Ramesside period[52]. The only positive statement which can be made is that combining the emmer and barley rations into one entry in the records was done infrequently, and that it did happen at least until the mid 20th Dynasty.

Barley is also recorded in the same manner, usually denoted as *it m it* as on O. DeM 181, 3, O. DeM 611, 2 and P. Turin 1906+1939, vs. 1:2, 2:12 and 2:19. As used on O. Cairo JE 72457, rt. 5, O. Cairo 25809 and O. DeM 177, 6, where the foreman receives 2 *khar* and the scribe 1 or 1½ *khar*, the word *it* may be an abbreviation for barley rather than being a generic word for grain as on P. Turin PN109, 4, which "reports the grain" and this comprises totally of emmer. The meaning is not always clear as this term is used to indicate the grain given to temples as offerings and deliveries of rations from outside to the village *ḫtm*. Together with the lower standard amount, this can lead to uncertainty in determining whether the payment was actually barley or emmer. A good example of this is O. DeM 577 rt., which records a distribution of small amounts of *it*. This is doubly confusing, as the verso of the same document records a similar list without a heading or labelled total, followed by a further list, this time stated explicitly as barley, so what the other lists composed of is ambiguous. Once again this highlights the erratic nature of the amounts paid to the workmen and brings into consideration the repeated question of how exactly the rations were given out - on an ad hoc basis or distributed by the officials at the *ḫtm*. This question may be answered in part by investigation of any archaeological evidence for silos and their possible capacities within the village, and is one to which we will return in due course.

Another half a dozen ostraca[53] indicate emmer and barley by splitting them up in the same list in the form (A, B), where A and B are the amounts of emmer and barley respectively, as exhibited in the following extract from the recto of O. Cairo 25608:

> 3 The foreman 2, 5½ *khar*.
> 4 The scribe 2, 5½ *khar*
> 5 17 men, each 1½, 4 *khar*, making 25½, 68 *khar*
> 6 2 youths, each ½, 1½ *khar*, making 1, 3 *khar*

Even here there is no consistency in the methodology as some of these documents record emmer first, and others barley. On O. Cairo 25689, 2, the scribe is the only person who receives a split ration, so a delivery consisting of equal proportions of emmer and barley was not adhered to and

51 O. Ashmol. 21 (undated); O. DeM 180 (Group III); O. DeM 386 (Group II) where the scribe gets paid one side's rations of 3¾ *khar*, and P. Turin 1880 (Group III).

52 Concluded by Černý (1954:920) based on a large sample of individual ration payments over the 19th and 20th Dynasties.

53 O. Ashmol. 184 (Group II); O. Cairo 25608 (Group III); O. Cairo 25689 (undated); O. Cairo JE 72455 (undated); O. DeM 376 (Group II); and O. Turin 57429 (Group II).

workmen did receive variable ration amounts. Without a larger pool of examples, there is no way of checking whether such a payment had a counterpart which, when added to the original, consisted of a month's full ration.

It may be expected that the later papyri, given their increased size and possible level of detail recorded, would show a much clearer methodology in the way the grain types were treated. In some cases the damage hinders the reading of the text, but the majority of the distribution records of emmer on the surviving documents are underlined in the transcriptions (red ink on the original), which would contradict Černý's statement that the red notation disappeared during the 20th Dynasty[54]. Without this colour differentiation, we would have great difficulty since the amounts recorded in many lists are either not the standard ration or are small and in essence unrevealing. What is clear is that there was no fixed format to which the scribes had to adhere, and that it did not matter which variation was used.

§6.5 Other procedures not implemented

Apart from the concept of double-entry bookkeeping[55] and the closing of the books at period end, which have been discussed above, the emphasis so far has been on those procedures which were utilised by the scribes in their ration accounting. However, also of interest are those techniques which are prevalent in modern accounting that were not used in Ramesside Egypt, or at least those for which there is no evidence in the textual record of Deir el-Medina. Naturally, not every practice will be examined, instead only a selection of the more widely used accounting conventions will be looked at, and these have to be restricted to those relevant to rations in an ancient context.

Out of the five basic accounting concepts widely used in modern accounting in the United Kingdom[56], only the concept of consistency can be readily applied to ancient Egyptian ration accounting. The evidence presented indicates that for the most part distribution records have been written in a uniform manner, although the scribes have exhibited a small degree of freedom in the terminology and vocabulary used, such as whether workmen are named or not and the frequency with which totals are included within the document. As scribes became more experienced, they were able to know in what manner to write within the constraints of space and information requirements so each scribe in turn had his own methodology which varied slightly with that of others. Consistency is generally there, but the absence of businesses renders the other four concepts immaterial in this ancient setting.

One notion important today is that of stock valuation, where all stock is given a value according to one of a number of methods, and this affects the order in which items or bulk commodities are moved out of storage. When the grain arrived at the granary in Thebes or that in the village Enclosure, there is no evidence for the scribes making periodic checks on the amount of grain

54 See note 47 above.

55 See §1.3 above.

56 See Wood & Sangster (1967: 98-100). The Companies Act of 1985 in the UK enforces five fundamental accounting concepts: going concern (where a business continues for the foreseeable future), consistency (everything is done the same way for all items), prudence (gains and losses are not over or understated), accruals (revenues less expenses equals net profit) and separate determination (for each asset or liability).

held there at any one time. There was never any checking of existing grain supplies prior to the addition of fresh produce arriving from the fields; the arrival of the grain was noted and that was enough. Of course grain had a value[57], and this varied according to whether it was early or late within the Ramesside period, but interestingly, the prices of emmer and barley were generally the same[58]. There is nothing in the textual record stating that a certain amount of grain was held in a specific granary, and this proves beyond doubt that even though grain did have a value, this value was not applied to state supplies and stock.

There is a huge difference between Ramesside Egypt and the developed world today in defining what a wage was, and this in turn accounts for how taxation was dealt with. Today, taxation and other expenses are deducted at source from the monetary wage; in other words the worker never actually receives this part of his wage. In Deir el-Medina, a ration wage was an amount of grain which was given to a workman for a specified period and nothing was deducted prior to this. Taxation was a deduction levied not to every working person in the land, but as every tax known was a grain tax[59], it must be considered to be a payment made by the grain farmers and perhaps everyone who produced physical items in arrangement with the state officials, and taxation came under the control of the vizier. The period the tax related to, the amounts and the location which the revenues should be delivered to[60] were often stated, but never in the ration record since there was simply no taxation on rations.

The grain brought to the village from the granaries of Thebes was sometimes recorded in the Journal, but only as a notification such as the entry on O. DeM 34, rt. 11, which merely notes "the distribution/giving of *diw* for the crew through the water-carrier". It is likely that the arrival of rations was not deemed important enough from the point of view of the administration to record at this stage, so as a result there were never any goods in notes to match up with the receipts of grain, and no corresponding day books to record goods received in. Other commodities such as wood and fish were delivered on a quota basis, where each fisherman or woodcutter had to deliver a specified amount of his commodities, and the material records these in abundance[61]. There is no such equivalent for grain, although ration grain is classified more as a commodity than a wage due to our modern treatment of wages in accounting, no quotas existed for ration deliveries. The importance lay in the workmen getting their rations, and not who was accountable for them, whereas for fish and wood there were personnel who were solely responsible so it was in their interests as well that quotas were used and recorded.

57 Measured in *deben*, a comparison of the value of a commodity with a given weight in copper (Janssen 1975a: 101). Occasionally the *sniw*, a comparison with an object of silver, was used. The relative value of the two measures was not constant throughout the Ramesside period, but the approximation of 1 *sniw* to 5 *deben* can be accepted (*ibid.*, 108).

58 Janssen (1975a: 129).

59 Janssen (1975a: 548). There is no Egyptian equivalent for the modern concept of "taxation" but instead several words designate different aspects of the revenue collecting procedures (Janssen 1975b: 173).

60 Stated by Ezzamel (2002: 37) based on texts such as P. Lansing, P. Harris and P. Wilbour, but the accountability being traced to every individual is not always present. This may be due to records not surviving or perhaps the accountability process was not fully developed in terms of recording.

61 Discussed by Janssen in his chapters, "The Woodcutters" in Janssen, Frood & Goecke-Bauer (2003: 1-28) and "Fish and Fishermen" in Janssen (1997: 37-54) respectively.

In modern accounting, wages are treated as a company expense and have their own section in the Trading and Profit and Loss Account of a company. With no such concept existing in the Egyptian state, ration wages were formally not classed as a state expense as such, but this statement is based on the absence of evidence for accounts belonging to the temples and administrative centres in Thebes and has to be treated with circumspection. Balances (*wḏ3t*) were used as part of the recording within the distribution system in the village, but it is not known whether the same applied to rations as they left Thebes. We would probably suspect not, but without any evidence either way it is pure speculation. Monthly accounts are critical in the running of any modern business, and certainly there is no example in the ration material that has a balance carrying forward from one period into the next, although with wages that is no surprise. Within the temple accounts, since ration wages were in effect a product, this would have been easily possible but not necessary for the efficient running of central administration.

Apart from internal checking, it is a legal requirement today that financial statements and accounts of a business are audited independently to ensure that the state of the company is reflected fairly and that nothing untoward has taken place. No such requirements were placed by the Egyptian state on viziers, overseers or other figures of authority so the suggestion of any form of checking in the textual record is based on internal need which fostered the daily running of society. Absence lists dating from the late 19th Dynasty frequently include check marks, but there is little in the ration material which shows check marks were used on at least a semi-regular basis, even though their use at the point of physically measuring and handing out rations would have served as a control over the recording of the ration distribution procedure. The frequency of mistakes in the records, which will be discussed in due course, reveal an alarming lack of proof reading. Despite the fact that grain rations were state property, there is no evidence whatsoever that there was any auditing carried out on the accounts and distribution lists.

§6.6 Conclusion

The subject of documents being prepared prior to the event of ration payment and physical examination of the writing are subjects which have not been approached before. Therefore, the present study will both contribute to the knowledge base and open up many avenues for future research. Similar approaches can be made on texts which detail other commodities as well as those from other genres such as wood, fish and temple supply deliveries and also private letters. It is not without its dangers, however, primarily due to the small number of documents available for examination and the many gaps in our knowledge of where and when the scribes did their recording in relation to the wage rations being paid. If access becomes readily available to the papyri in Turin or the O. DeM series of ostraca, for example, then firmer conclusions will be possible, even though the ambiguities in the physical procedure of distribution would still remain.

Any conclusions made concerning any prior preparation on the part of the scribe are based on a small number of ostraca viewed, together with a number of black and white photographs, which have several drawbacks, despite their high quality. Firstly, the photographs do not discern between damage due to fading of the ink over time and that due to surface rubbing, both are frequent occurrences and equally likely. Secondly, photographs do not show up the differences between red ink and naturally fading writing, so we are reliant to an extent on transcriptions of the hieratic which show the red amounts, and because of this red ink can easily be mistaken for fading or a lack of ink on the brush. Similarly, there is no indication whether the scribe wrote over the sign again for clarity in the event of ink running out as we would today. Thirdly, the materials used for ostraca were limestone and pottery, and photographs do not indicate which type absorbs the ink better, whether the pottery was glazed or the limestone was particularly difficult to write on. It would seem logical that limestone would be more porous, but on the other hand pottery appears to rub more easily than limestone. Finally, with the original, there is the chance of very close scrutiny where minute details can be looked for which may not show up in a magnified black and white photograph.

Despite these drawbacks, we can say with a high degree of confidence that the evidence presented here indicates that the scribes of Deir el-Medina did not prepare any of their records in advance. Within a distribution list, there are very few instances of names or titles being recorded without an accompanying amount. Where it is possible to identify fresh brush dips, these do not show a tendency for signs representing amounts; where there is emmer recorded in red, the scribe appears to have written the document from the start, and when red ink was required he put the brush aside, used a new one to write the red amounts and carried on with the original brush, usually with a new supply of ink. Writing is of course variable in appearance, thickness and frequency of pen dips, so with the number of different scribes who performed the recording there were undoubtedly differences. For example, what may appear as a new stroke in the writing on one ostracon may not be the same on another. What seems far more likely is that the distribution was carried out slowly enough and with enough pauses to allow the scribe to record the complete ration payment without having to rely on memory or a fast and neat hand, and this fits in very well with the situation portrayed in many models of granaries from the Middle Kingdom, where the scribe sits and writes while grain is brought in or out of the granary.

As we would expect, there are several ration accounting procedures that anyone running a business today would take for granted which were not performed in Ramesside Egypt. There was no official framework recommended by the state for the compliance of recording techniques; although scribes were well trained in literacy and numeracy, they recorded what they needed to in their own manner, which was pretty much uniform throughout. Rations did not consist of money, but consumable produce allocated by the state for the workmen. This may be one reason why ration accounts required no closing off and carrying forward of any outstanding balances, so the need for strict periods was just not there; once the rations were in the possession of the workmen they ceased to be of any further interest to the state. In common with government departments today, wages got paid out of taxation, but taxation was itself treated as a commodity, which of course it was.

CHAPTER 7

RECORDING ERRORS

The final chapter which explores the content of documents in detail seems to be a natural progression from the assessment of the writing performed in the previous chapter, and one where what appear to be errors survive in the ration record. It would be natural and correct to assume that the ancient Egyptian scribes made mistakes, and without correcting agents the mistakes are there to allow us to attempt a full examination. However, the approach taken here is not to assume that everthing that does not tally is an error; instead to identify the numerical inconsistencies and explore the possibility that scribes avoided complicated fractions by "adding a bit" to the totals. This creates the additional requirement to get behind the totals indicated by the use of *dmḏ* and to further investigate the frequency that this particular word is associated with a numerical imbalance.

Being able to inspect the original document would help significantly in unearthing the reasons behind the errors, for example, whether there was any effect on the accuracy of recording if documents were prepared in advance or not, and whether there were any check marks to indicate the likelihood that records were checked after their drafting. Even though the evidence presented in §6.1 strongly suggests that neither of these procedures took place, we should not discount the possibility that a larger sample would lead to a different conclusion. Therefore, the documents examined in §6.1 which contain one or more numerical irregularities will be checked on an exploratory basis to see if there is any suggestion that pen dips effected the presence of errors, but only in the cases where the original ostracon has been examined, as photographs are not reliable.

A variety of errors are present in the administrative record, including mis-spellings of the names of workmen, transposition of signs, omission of signs and watchmen and errors in the dates[1], but only those which are directly relevant in ration accounting will be scrutinised here. These consist of possible addition and multiplication errors, omission of recipients and confusion with the grain type and in common with the present study as many examples as possible will be looked at, but even so there are instances where it is not possible to discern the presence or otherwise, of an error. It is impossible to state what proportion of the material shows one or more

1 This section expands on those discussed by Janssen (2005), who assesses the accuracy of the administrative ostraca as a whole, as well as providing a short selection of errors relating to grain rations.

accounting errors since there are many texts which are either fragmentary. Those texts that are broken, or damaged to such a degree so as to render the lines, amounts and totals as doubtful, have not been taken into account. This is especially true with papyri, as many ration amounts are lost in the folds, edges and destroyed sections of the documents. The material is split into lists consisting of texts showing each type of numerical error along with the associated explanations for the mistakes.

§7.1 Errors in the totals

The most frequent type of discrepancy appears to be in the calculation of the total (both *ir.n* and *dmḏ*) of a given group of recipients' rations and many of these would surely have been spotted if the records were drawn up with more care, or checked afterwards. The fact that there are so many of them, given the size of the corpus of the rations material, strongly suggests that there was no check whilst writing them[2] and that there was no subsequent auditing by the internal or external administrative officers. The precise expression used to show the total is examined to check for any correlation between errors and the word used. The following texts show errors of this kind, with some probably resulting from inaccuracies in the number of men paid or their ration, in addition to faulty mathematics.

- O. Ashmol. 48, 5: 26 men, each ½ *khar* making 8. Either the total (*ir.n*) should be 13 or there were 16 men instead of 26. Line 6 continues with 8 men, each ¼ *khar* making 3. It should be 2. Examination of the original writing does not shed any light on the error in relation to pen dips.
- O. Ashmol. 111, 4: 8 men, each ½ *khar* making 4¼. The total (*ir.n*) should be 4. The totals (*dmḏ*) to named individuals which follows is totalled in line 7 as 4¼ *khar* but the signs immediately preceding this are lost. At the end of the line there appears to be 1 *khar* scribbled down twice which does not seem to have any relevance to other ration totals. Examination of the ostracon itself reveals that there is smudging on line 4 and again on line 7 (the total after the *dmḏ* sign), which seems to indicate that the scribe was aware of his mathematical error and tried to correct it but only after he had written out the whole text. This, along with the error at the end of line 3, which has been erased by the scribe, indicates that scribes did correct their mistakes probably as they went along or upon completion of their recording.
- O. Cairo JE 72455, rt. 1: 21 men, each 4 *khar* making 94. This should be 84, and the mistake is carried forward into the total (*ir.n*) in line 2. The error is the same as that in O. Ashmol 48, an extra 10-sign being written.
- O. DeM 181, 2: 61 men, each 1¼ *khar* making 75½. The total (*ir.n*) should be 76¼.
- O. DeM 182, 5: 16 men, each 3 *khar* making 51. Either the total (*ir.n*) should be 48, or more likely one man has been omitted.
- O. DeM 345, 3: 39 men, each ¼ *khar* making 9. The total (*ir.n*) should be 9¾, or else the correct number of men is 36. Whichever is correct, the total (*dmḏ*) in line 4 of 118¾ is too low as the preceding amounts add up to 125½.

2 This can only be verified under examination of the original ostraca or papyri themselves by checking for erasures or alterations.

O. DeM 376, 14[3]: 17 men, each 3¾ *khar* making 69¾. This (*ir.n*) should be 63¾.

O. DeM 378, 3: 56 men, each <blank> *khar* 1⁄16 *oipe* = 12 1⁄64 *khar*. The missing payment is unlikely to be ⅔ since this fraction was never used with ration payments. The total may be an addition of amounts for a group of men for whom the scribe did not break down their ration payments. It may have been to save time and effort, but the 1⁄16 *oipe* element in the total may have sufficed as an unmeasured amount to represent the whole amount "plus a little". In other words, this may represent a mathematical approximation of a real activity by which the scribes avoided the use of complicated fractions. Line 4 is correct, but line 5 continues with 67 men x 2¾ *khar* = 24¼. This latter ration payment is doubtful since it appears at the end of the line and may be partly lost with the fraction element written below the text of the main line. The total in any case is too low.

O. DeM 10033, 6: 17 men, each 5¼ *khar*, making 87½. This total (*ir.n*) should be 89¼.

P. Turin 1884+2067+2071+2105, rt. 2:11: 47 men, each 1½ *khar*, making 71½ *khar*. The correct total (*ir.n*) is 70½.

P. Turin 1906+2047+1939, rt. 3:9: 65 men, each ¾ *khar* making 48 *khar*. This total (*ir.n*) should be 48¾ so either the fraction was not written or the payment to one man was not accounted for. This is carried forward into the total (*dmḏ*) following in line 3:10.

P. Turin 2081+2095, rt. I:13: 32 men receiving 1 13⁄16 *khar* each comes to 60, not 48. Allowing for the ⅛ as an error and the total (*ir.n*) to be 54, it is still incorrect. The question raised about small fractions representing a small extra unmeasured amount of grain resurfaces in this example.

§7.2 Addition errors

Errors in the addition arise simply by adding the amounts after a list of names and many documents contain addition errors which range from an omission of one or more individuals in the preceding list to those which bear no relevance to what came before. As with totals, the mathematics is incorrect so a simple check or proof read would enable the error to be corrected.

O. Ashmol. 257: the totals (*ir.n*) of lines 2-3 and 4-5 not included, while the final emmer total (*dmḏ bty*) is recorded to the left of the main text as 63¾ and not 61½. One possible explanation is that the difference of 2¼ *khar* is that of the scribe, who was incorrectly omitted from the list, but close examination of the original document reveals that the emmer total was written in an alignment which was off centre and almost certainly was in a different hand. The rest of the text was written in red ink and has been overwritten in black which brings to mind whether this document was an example of the use of drafts. Line 7, which is lost, may include the unrecorded total of Pentaweret, who may himself have been a scribe, in line 6.

O. Ashmol. 1139, 2: the scribe's ration is not shown. The total (*dmḏ*) at the end of 2¾ *khar* may be his, if so then the final total (*dmḏ*) in line 4 is correct.

O. Berlin 14210, 5: 40 men each receiving 4¾ *khar* should total 190 and not 188 as recorded on the ostracon. This is not due to any individuals being omitted; the only explanation is that

3 Errors relating to O. DeM 376 and O. Ashmol. 184, which record the same delivery, were examined in detail in §4.3. Having both ostraca indicates the possible errors which could occur with what appears to be a straightforward distribution of rations.

there was a loss of concentration by the scribe, since the captains in lines 2 and 3 receive a total of 18 *khar*.

O. Cairo 25517γ, 23: total 15 *khar*. This is a lengthy list of twenty-one names and their associated amounts of ¾ *khar*. The sum for these men is 15¾. At the bottom is written *dmḏ ḫ3r* 15¾ + (*ipt*) ¼ + 1⁄32, the fractional elements of which seem to have no relevance to the list. These probably relate to an incidental and unmeasured amount of either the same or a different type of grain, so technically they are not errors *per se* but an intentional part of scribal protocol.

O. Cairo 25620, 4: the total (*dmḏ*) is shown as 31½ *khar*, but the amounts add up to 33½. This may be due to the omission of one individual but 2 *khar* of barley is not a standard ration. Perhaps the amount was taken by the person in charge of the physical delivery, or perhaps it represents creative accounting.

O. Cairo 25689, 7: the total (*dmḏ*) is shown as 71¼ *khar*, but the amounts add up to 73¼, the same difference of 2 *khar* as in O. Cairo 25620, with the same possibilities of adjusting the figures or the deliverer taking his payment.

O. DeM 177, 2: this example records what appears to be 18½ men, each 4 *khar*, making 72 *khar*. This may indicate half a ration for one man, but only by ignoring it does the total (*ir.n*) add up correctly. The total (*dmḏ*) in line 3 total is incorrect, while the preceding amounts indicate ¼ *khar* was omitted at the end of this total.

O. DeM 381, rt. 9: total 92 *khar* (or 91½ as the writing is doubtful), balance 1. When added up, the sum of the preceding lines is different, at 98¾, for which Janssen has proposed that if the 7¼ *khar* in line 8 is omitted, the resulting total may be correct[4].

O. DeM 383, 7: total of all expenses (*dmḏ h3w nb*) 55 *khar*. The preceding lines total 51½ but if the foreman's ration is missing then the total is ½ *khar* out. The amount was double that of the scribe's for an individual side of the workforce; in this example recorded in line 2 as 1½ *khar*.

O. DeM 621, rt. 4: total 21 (*khar*) 1⁄16 (*oipe*), 27 (*khar*) 1 1⁄16 (*oipe*). From the preceding amounts, the total (*dmḏ*) should be 48, creating a difference of 1⅛ *oipe*. Perhaps one individual's payment was not recorded, or more likely the amount was deemed accurate enough to be acceptable or either deliberately recorded as an unmeasured difference.

O. DeM 737, 12: total 29¼ *khar*. Despite the rations for each of the 35 men noted in line 10 being lost in line 11, as Grandet points out[5], 29¼ divided by 35 is not a simple fraction. If this was ¾ *khar* per man, the total (*ir.n*) would be 26¼ and not 29¼.

P. Turin PN109, rt. 4: a report of grain delivery recording 74¼ *khar* + 1⁄10 (using the *r*-notation) + 7 *khar* and a total of 81½. The scribe seems confused by the fraction and may have meant ¼ instead of 1⁄10; this rendering is uncertain but it does seem to be the only explanation. If this is not read, then either the ½ or ¼ is incorrect.

P. Turin 2013+2050+2061: the first part of this document is significant as it records a series of errors within a short, if not completely understandable, section of text. It reads as follows:

> [rt.1:4] Emmer: 48 *khar*. Details of it (*wp st*): *dni* for IV *šmw*.
>
> [rt.1:5] [...] foreman Nakhtemmut 1¾ *khar*, scribe Hori of the Tomb 1¾ *khar*, foreman Hormose 1¾ *khar*.

4 Janssen (2005: 151 n. 27).

5 Grandet (2000: 33).

rt.1:6 [...] total (*dmḏ*) 6¾. 64 men, each ½ *khar* making 32 *khar*. Total of all expenses (*dmḏ h3w nb*). The distribution of rations for I *3ḫt*, 37¼ *khar*.
rt.1:7 [...] 39¼ *khar*. *dni* for III *šmw*, 19 men, each ¼ *khar* making 4¾ *khar*. 20 men, each [...] *khar* making [...].
rt.1:8 [...] making ¾ *khar*. Total 13(?)¾ *khar*. Total of all expenses (*dmḏ h3w nb*), in its entirety (*r-ḏr=f*) *khar*.

The total of the first ration distribution (IV *šmw*) is stated in the heading, but there is no breakdown unless the lost sections are significantly long. If these details are lost, then the total "of all expenses" in rt. 1:6 is erroneously omitted and the next distribution is that for I *3ḫt*. Otherwise, this phrase may relate to the following month but even so it is a unique combination of terminology which is not evident elsewhere in the rations material. If the rations for the three named workmen are added to the 32 *khar* then the total is 37¼ *khar*, which is what is stated as being the delivery for the following month. If the error is in the date, then the total of 6¾ *khar* would be redundant; even allowing for the lost section the scribe has undoubtedly muddled up his ration recording. At the end of rt. 1:8, the total is completely omitted.

In addition to these errors, O. Strasbourg H110 verso has several addition errors which result from the repeated use of fractions which do little but to confuse the scribe. Totals are incorrect, for example twice (both are *dmḏ*) in line 5, vocabulary is missing (*ir.n*) in line 3, and an individual is probably omitted in line 2.

§7.3 Omission of words

There are examples where the scribe has simply not written down amounts, numbers of workmen or connecting words. In extreme cases, even the omission of one word can lead to confusion in what was actually meant, as has been demonstrated by P. Turin 2013+2050+2061 (§7.2 above).

O. Ashmol. 107, 3: ½ *khar* is added after the foreman's payment of ½. This may be a simple and inexplicable duplication error, or an amount of emmer as opposed to barley, but there is no total surviving to support this.

O. Ashmol. 107, 5: records forty men each receiving 20 *khar* with no accompanying total. This could either be an omitted total of 800 *khar*, or far more likely, an omitted amount of ½ *khar* per man, with 20 *khar* being the total. The ostracon is abraded in many places so close examination of the writing provided no additional information.

O. DeM 34 + O. Heidelberg 567: is a Journal ostracon, and proves that the Journal was not free from error. On two occasions, rt. 11 and vs. 4, there is written an amount per workman which, when taken with the total, implies the presence of 21⅔ and 46⅔ men respectively. Any differences between individuals of different status were presumably not recorded but pooled together into one entry.

O. DeM 141, 3: omits any amount after *dmḏ*.

O. DeM 149, 4: omits *wꜥ nb* "each", but the sense is still clear.

O. DeM 177: records multiple deliveries without the consistency in standard recording. No totals are mentioned for the deliveries in lines 5, 7 and 8; perhaps after getting it wrong in line 3 the scribe gave up trying.

O. DeM 10034: is a text which is extremely difficult to make any sense of, and is reproduced in translation for ease of reference:

[1] *ꜣbd 3 prt sw 25 dit diw in sš*	III *prt* 25. Giving rations by the scribe
imn-nḫt sš ḥri ẖꜣr	Amenakht and the scribe Hori,
[2] *50¾ dmḏ 66¾ 61¾*	50¾ *khar*. Total 66¾, 61¾.
[3] *(sw) 27 ẖꜣr 180¾ wḏꜣt ẖꜣr 66¾*	(Day) 27. 180¾ *khar*. Remainder 66¾ *khar*.

After a standard heading, totals are stated but without any accompanying distribution list. There is no indication whether amounts are erroneous or not, but this example seems to back up suggestions that incomplete information may appear to be just that in modern eyes, but to a society where people did not commonly rely on written details, the administration would know what was meant.

§7.4 Omission of individuals

Some documents show errors which result from the likely omission of one individual from the distribution list; these can usually be worked out from the standard amounts a workman was paid.

O. Ashmol. 184, 4: 17 men, each 4½ *khar* making 68. Either the total should be 76½ or more likely the ration was 4 *khar*, which was the standard emmer payment for one workman.

O. Cairo 25608, 11: total 32½ *khar*. This should be 34, and indicates the probable omission of one man, with 1½ *khar* being the standard barley payment for one workman. The next line totals 84¾ *khar* instead of 88¾, indicating the probable omission of one man, maybe the same individual, from the record.

§7.5 The frequency of errors

Estimating the frequency of errors in the corpus of ration documents is not easy for three main reasons. Firstly, the amount of material available is not vast, so any results must be treated with caution as to their reliability. Secondly, some criteria need to be established as to what is included and what is not, in order to provide an unbiased result and to lessen uncertainty in relation to fragmentary records. Where a document covers a broad range of subjects, only the ration element is included and any error which exists outside of this constraint is not taken into account. With one exception, Journal texts have not been included on the basis that they almost always consist of one line indicating that a delivery took place[6], and including these would skew the results significantly towards a lower error frequency. Other texts are fragmentary to the extent that either a significant portion of a larger document is lost or the ostracon is a small fragment[7], or the text

6 The only Journal document consisting of an error in a rations context is O. DeM 34; this is included.

7 O. Ashmol. 72; O. DeM 188+373; O. DeM 301; O. DeM 388; O. DeM 661; O. DeM 734; O. DeM 735; O. DeM 742; O. DeM 743; O. DeM 744; O. DeM 745; O. DeM 746; O. DeM 837; O. DeM 850; O. Michaelides 34; O. Qurna 656/4; O. Qurna 659/4.

is itself merely a one or two line entry with no ration calculations[8]. By including fragments it is not clear whether there is an error present or not—and this includes papyri as well as ostraca. The only way to remove this uncertainty is to not include such pieces in the results. With the single line examples, although they may be ration texts there is no possibility of them having a relevant error which can be identified. The third reason concerns whether the error really is an error, or a mechanism by which the scribe indicated that a small extra amount was included in the delivery, in which case the errors should instead be described as numerical irregularities.

A complete list of texts for which it is possible to ascertain errors or numerical differences in a rations context is provided by Table 21, which indicates texts which are free from error and those which contain one or more errors. Errors in spelling, transposition of signs, duplication of signs and the like, which do not have any bearing on the rations paid, are not taken into account. One hundred and thirteen examples are included, of which eighty-one have no errors and thirty-two have one or more errors. In percentage terms, this equates to approximately 30% of all non-Journal ration texts having an error in the figures or an omission of one or more words. This may seem high, especially given that corrections such as those on O. Ashmol. 111 are not taken into account, but what was deemed an acceptable margin and frequency for error was undoubtedly higher in societies such as Ramesside Egypt than in the modern western world. Five out of the ten papyri which detail complete ration distribution records contain errors; apart from there being longer lists on many papyri it is not obvious why the error level is considerably higher on papyri than ostraca. It does not appear that the use of *dmḏ* or *ỉr.n* had any effect on whether any given document contained a numerical difference, since many of those listed in the first group under "no errors" in Table 21 contain both words and the majority of these record convenient and easy to follow summations.

Table 21: Documents with and without errors

No Errors		Error in totals	Addition error	Omission
O. Ashmol. 21	O. DeM 386	O. Ashmol. 48	O. Ashmol. 257	O. Ashmol. 107
O. Ashmol. 131 vs.	O. DeM 387	O. Ashmol. 111	O. Ashmol. 1139	O. Ashmol. 184
O. Ashmol. 200	O. DeM 577	O. Berlin 14210	O. Cairo 25517γ	O. Cairo 25608
O. Ashmol. 262	O. DeM 591	O. Cairo JE 72455	O. Cairo 25620	O. DeM 34
O. Ashmol. 274	O. DeM 611	O. DeM 181	O. Cairo 25689	O. DeM 141
O. Ashmol. 277	O. DeM 638	O. DeM 182	O. DeM 177	O. DeM 149
O. Berlin 11249	O. DeM 640	O. DeM 345	O. DeM 381	O. DeM 177
O. Berlin 12294	O. DeM 698	O. DeM 376	O. DeM 383	O. DeM 10034
O. Berlin 14219	O. DeM 707	O. DeM 378	O. DeM 621	
O. Berlin 14264	O. DeM 712	O. DeM 10033	O. DeM 737	

8 O. DeM 737; O. DeM 738; O. DeM 747; O. DeM 847.

No Errors		Error in totals	Addition error	Omission
O. Berlin 14302	O. DeM 739	P. Turin 1884+2067 +2071+2105	P. Turin PN109	
O. Berlin 14842	O. DeM 838		P. Turin 2013+2050 +2061	
O. BM EA 50726	O. DeM 839	P. Turin 1906+1939 +2047		
O. BM EA 50739	O. DeM 840			
O. Cairo 25280	O. DeM 841	P. Turin 2081+2095		
O. Cairo 25592	O. DeM 842			
O. Cairo 25685 rt.	O. DeM 843			
O. Cairo 25698	O. DeM 845			
O. Cairo 25809 rt.	O. DeM 846			
O. Cairo JE 72457	O. DeM 848			
O. DeM 179	O. DeM 849			
O. DeM 180	O. DeM 10032			
O. DeM 184	O. DeM 10036			
O. DeM 186	O. DeM 10039 rt.			
O. DeM 189	O. DeM 10040			
O. DeM 252	O. IFAO 300 rt.			
O. DeM 272	O. Michaelides 65			
O. DeM 276	O. Michaelides 73			
O. DeM 312	O. Munich ÄS 397			
O. DeM 329	O. Strasbourg H110			
O. DeM 370	O. Strasbourg H117			
O. DeM 371	O. Turin 57072			
O. DeM 374	O. Turin 57429			
O. DeM 375	O. UC 39626 vs.			
O. DeM 377	O. Varille 39			
O. DeM 379	P. Turin 1880			
O. DeM 380	P. Turin 1932+1939			
O. DeM 382	P. Turin 1960+2071			
O. DeM 384	P. Turin 2002			
O. DeM 385	P. Turin 2015			

§7.6 The acceptance of errors and validity of the document

Questions must be asked about the validity and relevance of mistakes and why they should actually matter in the context of an administration system which left many gaps within its procedure. As the many unusual and precise measures suggest that the scribes did not necessarily record the weighed out payments exactly, and there is no evidence that the rations were always weighed, all this suggests that the records were protocol and were part of a system which should in theory have worked from beginning to end but was in reality flawed and contained a high amount of approximations. The mistakes did not appear to matter to the internal or external administration as they would in today's accounting, highlighting the absence of controls or auditing by officials, and the severity of the errors was not high, indeed the majority of the errors can be regarded as trivial to the recording system, being a small amount of *khar*. Many of these instances may not have been errors, but roundings to approximations of an unmeasured portion of a delivery used to avoid exact fractions. However, on the other hand it could perhaps be argued that the presence of so many mistakes would lessen the value and usefulness of the records to both types of administration. This was not the case, since whether the grain was recorded short or not at all did not matter to the scribes, suggesting that the documents were not drawn up for the administration but for the workmen. The notion of a society with a high oral content is returned to, and the important matter was that goods and payments were received, and the document was roughly accurate. Errors do not indicate anything to the contrary and certainly did not invalidate the document, and the importance of documentary requirements for the end users of the records is highlighted.

The physical changes in the writing can only be looked at by examining the original documents. Even good quality photographs and images, such as those in Grandet's *Catalogue des ostraca hiératiques non littéraires de Deir el-Médinéh*—Volumes 8–11—and on Deir el-Medine Online, can not reveal changes in pen, differentials in ink deposited from different pen dips, the use of pro formas and the use of marks as an aid to checking[9], and to see whether events took place such as rations being given out to an individual on a regular basis, such as the details on O. Turin 57072. The low frequency of marks in the ration material suggests that the ostraca were not for the benefit of the administration, but used as receipts for the workmen, and served as proof that the workmen got their rations and they were happy with this. However, the complete lack of examples in the ration corpus detailing only one man as receiving his rations sheds doubt on this. Either there were one or more individuals who were in charge of such "receipts", or as seems more plausible, the ration ostraca were reminders as to the amount of grain available which had been delivered fairly and accurately to the workmen. It is also impossible to discern whether the accuracy of an individual ration text is affected by any of these factors without inspection of the original ostraca. As a result, examination of the errors taken in a wider context can only reveal generalisations in the scribal process as to why the degree of error was so high, whether it mattered to the administration, and why the errors happened. Unfortunately the distribution of the find spots of the ostraca shed no further light on this since they were not found in the locations where they were first discarded.

§7.7 Conclusion

When dealing with accounting systems from any society, its flaws and the degree of error within the system and the end product are areas which would form a crucial part of any study aimed at least in part in discussing its efficiency and effectiveness. We are fortunate to have the number of surviving records available that we have, allowing us to make an attempt to assess the frequency,

9 While this is evident in many texts from Deir el-Medina, there is little in the ration material to suggest scribes systematically checked ration lists. P. Turin 2084+2091 is one example where check marks are present before each of the names. Also the Necropolis Journal (*KRI* VI, 567-568).

severity and relevance of any errors. The present study expands on the study by Janssen[10] by adding to the list and splitting it into broad categories enabling the information to be readily available for any future research, but does not assume that every numerical irregularity contained in the records is a scribal error.

The broken condition of many texts renders it problematic in determining the frequency of errors in the ration corpus but at a very rough guess, between a quarter and a third of the documents recording ration distributions have an error of one kind or another; perhaps 30% based on the sample presented above. Errors in the spelling of names are not taken into account; those errors which are included are accounting mistakes and are primarily mathematical, either the multiplication or addition is incorrect, or there is at least one individual omitted from the list. Other errors involve omission of terminology and words, transcription of signs where individual signs have been erroneously included and the occasional example where the wrong colour of ink was used. Fraud was a real possibility, as there are texts, such as O. Leipzig 2, about problems with the correct or incorrect *oipe*-measure being used. Unfortunately, the documentation which consists of errors is not extensive enough in its availability to enable us to fully look for any relationships between errors and pen dips, so this question remains unanswered.

The question of reality is a significant issue in attempting to get behind inconsistencies in the calculations. Most documents use both notations for totals, *ir.n* and *dmḏ*, and there appears to be no noticeable difference in errors resulting from the use of one word over the other. It is the case that many examples do record an imbalance in the *dmḏ* when the previous totals were added up, but the presence of small and precise fractions on several occasions leads us to suspect that part of accounting technique was to use a small fraction such as 1⁄16 of an *oipe* to denote an unmeasured element which was a small approximation of reality, whilst at the same time avoiding complicated mathematics.

The presence of a relatively large number of errors can reveal insights into the ration delivery procedure. Based on the number of originals examined, there does seem to be a relatively low amount of visible corrections which include smudging, erasing of signs or a rewriting of signs or words either in the same colour or a different one. The majority of mistakes can be traced and corrected easily by us today, but the relative infrequency of corrections actually visible and the ease of checking which indicates that there was no checking or auditing of the material. This would add an extra layer to the bureaucracy of a process which already involved temples, silos, the *ḫtm*, transport agents and the ultimate recipients, the workmen. Furthermore, this in turn suggests that the documentation was accurate enough to suffice for the needs of the villagers, and mistakes did not matter as long as the physical product was handed over when it was required. There is no suggestion in the textual record of a workman fraudulently claiming he had not received his rations, and thus no indication of what happened in the likelihood of this event. The ostraca in particular served as receipts for the workmen in so far that they were reminders to the administration as to the amount of grain to be delivered rather than records to be stored by the village administration.

10 Janssen (2005).

CHAPTER 8

THE SUPPLY OF RATIONS

Exceptionally well documented at Deir el-Medina, the rations were brought to the *ḫtm* and distributed to the workmen from there, and as such formed the core of the structure of what could be called economics within the village. One often forgotten area of study relates to the supply and transportation of grain rations before it reached the village enclosure. Despite the evidence not being vast, it should be noted where the rations originated from, how far along the chain of supply of rations we can go in order to identify these sources, if this is possible, and whether for each part of the supply chain there is any documentary evidence for accounting practices. However, the subject of grain supply and transportation involves a considerable amount of components, such as land ownership and leasing, taxation, and the organisation of granaries, all of which form research questions in their own right. The following chapter will therefore attempt to take what evidence there is available, highlight the areas where the facts are there as well as those where there are gaps in our knowledge, and then to suggest feasible assumptions based on the evidence.

Ideally, the administration system documented the collection and distribution procedure from start to finish[1], but in reality it is highly improbable that this was done. The reasons for this related to differential literacy levels of individuals involved at varying stages of the procedure, and also that the requirements of the administration were not constant at each location, be it threshing floor, granary or village Enclosure. The rations were recorded when the workmen received them, so what was important for the workmen was that they received their rations; problems would occur if this did not happen, as indicated by the strikes in Year 29 of the reign of Ramesses III. Short-term reductions in grain supplies or production in the fields were hardly ever recorded[2]; while this was not an issue if there were no crops, more serious matters such as famine were not mentioned.

Since the initial growing and harvesting of crops was done by illiterate members of society,

1 Janssen (1975b: 167).

2 Häggman (2002: 17). This is either due to non-survival of the material or a lack of necessity as to its recording.

who were not close to administrative centres, apart from land surveys and land registers[3], the survival of records from the first stage of the supply chain is minimal. If accounts were kept, then they would not have survived. The Turin Taxation Papyrus is an exception and provides valuable insights into the organisation of the transportation of grain, and P. Valençay I[4] states that a scribe had arrived in order to collect taxes. In addition, it serves as a valuable aid in one of the hazy areas in the model of ration delivery proposed in Chapter 9, but it must still not be taken as standard practice. Who was responsible for the rations at each stage of the supply chain was not so important to the workmen in the recording procedure of rations, although the role of the *smdt* and their scribes formed a vital cog in the functioning of the village.

§8.1 Original source of the rations

There are only a few instances of a document indicating where the rations originated from. Certainly towards the end of the 20th Dynasty - earlier evidence is not forthcoming - the grain was sometimes grown in the *ḫ3-t3* (usually referred to as khato) fields, which were at least in some instances affiliated to a temple and belonged to the state[5], but were a fiscal category of land described as being "of Pharaoh"[6]. The agricultural land surrounding Thebes would not have been able to support the population of the settlements on both sides of the river[7], so grain was brought in from elsewhere by boat. As well as the fields, the fishing boats which transported rations were often attached to temples[8] so a number of different entities provided grain for the granaries of Thebes; the granaries which belonged to several different institutions such as the state Treasury and the mortuary temples.

The grain came from sources south of Thebes, with the harbour of Edfu (*ḏbw*) being clearly specified on one occasion[9] and "the south" on another[10]. P. Turin 2013+2050+2061 and P. Turin PN 109 are both dated to Ramesses IX, but no distribution details or accounts are recorded in either of these documents. Therefore, there is a complete absence of accounting within the first part of the supply chain, with one significant exception, P. Turin 1895+2006. This document,

3 One land survey is P. Wilbour, which indicates that land was often held and worked by private individuals (Haring 1998: 78).

4 See Gardiner (1948a: 72-73) for the text, and Gardiner (1948b: 205-206) for a translation.

5 Janssen (1975b: 182). P. Valençay I (Gardiner 1948b: 205-206), states that the fields were cultivated by freemen (*nmḥw*) and taxation was paid to the treasury from their produce. P. Turin 2013+2050+2061, vs. I:8 and P. Turin 2018, vs. 19, both mention these fields being associated with temples.

6 Stated on Text B of P. Wilbour, which is concerned specifically with this type of land (Haring 1998: 79). See Gardiner (1948b: 161-190) for a discussion on the administration, the owning institutions and areas of *ḫ3-t3* fields relating to the Wilbour Papyrus, and Haring (2009) for a more recent and condensed treatment based on institutional and private agrarian interests.

7 The geography of the Nile Valley is one obvious factor restricting available land. Strudwick (1995) has considered the possible population of Thebes, suggesting a figure of around 20,000 on the east bank (based on being slightly less than the estimated population size of Amarna and a rural area of 20km^2) and about 6,400 on the west bank (based on a rural area of 15km^2).

8 P. Turin 2013+2050+2061, rt. 2:13; unfortunately the name of the temple is lost.

9 P. Turin 2013+2050+2061, rt. x+4-5.

10 P. Turin PN 109, rt. 2, records *dni* being "brought up from fishing boats from the south".

better known as the Turin Taxation Papyrus[11], was an oddity. Written by the Deir el-Medina scribe Dhutmose, the content is not the same as the other papyri as there are no ration lists, there is a clear link with the village and it has therefore been included as documentary evidence for this part of the supply chain. The accounting procedure within this document is discussed in §8.4.

The recto of the Turin Taxation Papyrus records receipts of emmer and barley originating in the *ḫꜣ-tꜣ* fields of Imiotru (Gebelein), Agni and Esna, all south of Thebes, supervised by (*m-ḏrt*) a number of high officials. The belief that this grain was probably *diw* is based on Gardiner's observation that the individual responsible for the collection of the grain, Dhutmose, was himself a scribe of the Necropolis[12], and his two assistants were doorkeepers (*iry-ꜥꜣ*) who were once sent to get grain before people became hungry and work was stopped[13]. The Turin Indictment Papyrus[14] records that over a ten year period, the boat captain Khnumnakht had taken a large part of taxation grain due to the granary of Khnum at Elephantine. Here, the temple had a fixed revenue, and each year's "remainder due" was recorded. Since both these documents record taxation grain revenues, it highlights one way to attempt to ensure that grain did not go missing, which was to assume accountability on the part of the boat skipper, who got a payment for his services, in order to alleviate the control problem encountered by the state administration[15].

Written records were made at the threshing floors, but unfortunately few have survived. According to Gardiner's translation of P. Sallier IV, vs. 10:1, the grain was "winnowed on a platform of high ground at the threshing floor" [16]. The grain was stored at the threshing floors, which were the primary contact point between the cultivator and the tax collectors[17], where every farmer's grain had to pass through. The recto of P. Amiens-Baldwin[18] has many instances where the grain seems to have been loaded onto boats straight from the threshing floors, while P. Louvre 3171, 2:1, 2:9, and 3:1, record instances of the grain being taken by river to the granary of Memphis[19]. Each threshing floor had an overseer who was in charge of its operation, but what institution or individuals had direct ownership remains obscure[20]. P. Sallier I records that the scribe noted the barley cut, arranged for its removal and set out the threshing floor, which suggests that there was no storage on site. It is not clear what the storage facilities were near the threshing floors, although the storage of grain in the open was not an issue in a dry climate[21]. Therefore, it is likely that there

11 The transcription can be found in Gardiner (1948a: 36-44); cf. idem, (1941: 22-37).

12 Gardiner (1941: 23).

13 See Černý (1939b: 69-70).

14 P. Turin 1887, vs. 1:13-2:11. The details of the case of Khnumnakht are taken from Vernus (2003: 102-104).

15 Suggested by Ezzamel (2002: 29) as part of the tax collection procedure.

16 Gardiner (1941: 63). By the Coptic words preserved, the threshing floor (*ḏnw*) consisted of several platforms (*ḫtiw*).

17 Eyre (1999: 44).

18 Janssen (2004: 12-24). Contrast the first four sections of the recto with the verso, where the grain is usually given "on the riverbank" or "in Takesbu", or another non-specific place.

19 Gardiner (1941: 57). It is likely that the granary of Memphis was similar to the temple organisation at Thebes mentioned in the Turin Taxation Papyrus (*ibid.*, 63).

20 Ownership and known individuals from P. Amiens-Baldwin who managed the threshing floors are discussed by Janssen (2004: 34-37).

21 James (1985: 127). Grain stored in this manner was not for local consumption, but included taxation

were some kind of short-term storage facilities at the threshing floors provided both for convenient short term storage, and also for ease of collection of taxation by the authorities.

§8.2 Provider institutions for grain

Once the grain was brought into Thebes, it was stored in the granaries of a number of state entities[22] before being transported to the *ḫtm* at Deir el-Medina. Three general institutions provided a wide variety of consumables and goods for the village workmen, each responsible for the supply of a selection of commodities, and these are as follows. Firstly, the Treasury of Pharaoh (*pr-ḥḏ n pr-ꜥꜣ*) provided copper, cloth, oil and the like, items which were used not as daily essentials, but in the course of the official work on the royal tomb. Secondly, the Stockyard of Pharaoh (*ꜣḫyt n pr-ꜥꜣ*) supplied baskets and animal fat; and thirdly, the Granary of Pharaoh (*šnwt n pr-ꜥꜣ*) provided the grain. It is not clear where the latter structure was, since there were structures recorded with the same name in both Deir el-Medina and the city of Thebes[23], and any assumption that grain was stored in a building with this title raises the question of whether the granary was an institution or a physical building. At the *ḫtm*, the storage was short rather than long term, since any significant volumes of grain were held at temple granaries. It is likely that any substantial settlement had a "Granary of Pharaoh" amongst its buildings, all part of the same institution encompassing the whole of Egypt, but the extent to which it is a bookkeeping exercise is unclear, and equally the degree by which the accounting procedure maps onto the physical procedure in handling the grain is very unclear.

The records from the late Ramesside period show that the Granary of Pharaoh[24] was not the only granary which supplied grain, although this term may have encompassed all the individual granaries which were documented in the records. Several granaries are named; almost certainly all were in Thebes but exactly where is not known. The best attested is the Granary of the House of Maꜥat, which was linked to the vizier[25], with other named provider institutions being the Granary of the House of Mut[26], the Granary of the House of Amun[27], the Granary of Hapy[28] and the

payments.

22 Grain was also distributed from temples, such as that of Usermaatre-Meryamun recorded on P. Turin 1885, vs. III:7-8, which dates to Ramesses IV, but the relationship between this and the grain distribution previously in the same text (lines 3-4) is unclear.

23 P. Turin 1930+2050+2013, vs. I:2, and P. Turin 2081+2095, rt. I:2, mention a "Granary of Pharaoh in the City". Based on P. Turin 2081+2095, rt. I:7, Janssen (1997: 5) suggests that this structure in Deir el-Medina was situated within the *ḫtm*, where it is recorded as the "Granary of the Enclosure of the Tomb". This assumes that there was a granary in or around the village, but the evidence does not confirm this.

24 Two examples are P. Turin 2013+2050+2061, rt. x+5, and P. Turin 2081+2095, rt. I:12.

25 Häggman (2002: 121). The functions of the vizier resulted in associations with the goddess Maꜥat throughout the Ramesside period. The House of Maꜥat was almost certainly located at Karnak, but a separate entity may have existed outside Karnak (*ibid.*, 122). The Granary of the House of Maꜥat is recorded in P. Turin 1881, rt. II:4-5 and 12; P. Turin 1884 II:4, rt. 2:4 and rt.2:9-12; P. Turin 1906+1939+2047, IV:7; P. Turin 2002, vs. 3.

26 P. Turin 1932 + 1939, II, 2:6; P. Turin 2097/161 + 2105, vs. 6.

27 P. Turin 2097/161 + 2105, vs. 13. The House of Amun was almost certainly not tied to any specific location, but was rather an administrative entity. See Haring (1997: 30-34.)

28 O. Ashmol. 131, vs. 13 (probably dating to Ramesses IV)

Granary of the House of Usermaatre-Meryamun in the City[29]. Documentation on papyri tends to take the form of a statement of rations being brought *m-drt* an individual, or that they were "distributed" or "received" from the granary, such as recorded in P. Turin 2097+2105, vs. 6. In many cases, a total rations amount follows[30]. There are instances where this information is in turn followed by a distribution list to individuals or groups of workmen from one or both sides.

It seems apparent that the importance behind the recording at this stage of the rations chain is not as great as it perhaps should have been. This is reflected in the low number of examples where grain was deposited into or removed from a granary, but even so it is unlikely to be due to chance survival[31]. There is no example of what we would call in modern business a stock take; if this was carried out, the granary was one place to do this. Neither is there anything resembling a goods in notice. The presence of the occasional distribution list proves that the scribes did record grain leaving the granary, and perhaps only when the grain arrived at the Enclosure did the process of distribution become important enough to warrant recording, and furthermore, important not to the scribes and the central administration, but to the workmen themselves. At least up to this point, the accounting of grain can be classified as minimal at best.

One reason for the lack of evidence for granary accounts may be inferred from the presence of Hori, the Scribe of the Mat of the Granary of the House of Usermaatre-Meryamun in the City, who represented the state in many issues involving Deir el-Medina[32], so this particular granary was almost certainly under the ultimate jurisdiction of the vizier. According to the Duties of the Vizier, a text reflecting a system current at the beginning of the 18th Dynasty or even earlier, the scribe of the mat was part of the town district (*sp3t*), the local level element of central administration.[33] Any accounts were, therefore, never associated with the village but stored in Thebes itself and have not survived. It is not known whether the granary at the Ramesseum was used to store rations for the village.

If there is scant evidence for grain arriving in the granaries of Thebes, there is similarly scant evidence for grain rations arriving at Deir el-Medina, consisting of only a very occasional simple statement as part of a Journal entry, and even these are almost always notices of distribution within the village. There certainly was a granary in Deir el-Medina, as recorded on O.Berlin 12654 (vs. 4), whilst P. Bib. Nat. 237 mentions workmen painting cartouches of Ramesses VI on its walls. Apart from a small number of small grain silos[34], there is no indication specifically where any storage facility at Deir el-Medina was. There is the contrast between long and short term storage

29 P. Turin 1906+1939+2047, IV, 5. Given the association of the Scribe of the Mat Hori with the delivery here and also in P. Turin 2013+2050+2061, rt. 2, and 6-9, this building is likely to have been a state institution and not a religious one.

30 A detailed analysis of distribution lists of all ration texts, including recipients and the manner in which the amounts were written, has been provided in §4.3.

31 One notable example discussed and analysed in detail by Megally (1977) is P. Louvre 3226, which dates to the later years of Thutmose III, and is a series of grain accounts relating to a state granary.

32 Scribes of the mat in Deir el-Medina are discussed by Haring (2000: 146-149). The genitive *n* was not written, perhaps implying this to be the source of deliveries recorded (Haring 1997: 272 n. 2).

33 The organisation of the two central levels of civil administration, namely the vizier's office and town district, is conveniently summarised by van den Boorn (1988: 327).

34 See §9.1 for a discussion of silos, including their size and location.

which affected what buildings were needed, therefore at the *ḫtm*, there were facilities for brief holding periods between delivery and distribution not designed for actual storage. We can only speculate how far the nearest granary was from the village, and how much grain it could hold. Although there are many texts which record grain as being distributed from the *ḫtm*, there is an absence of evidence relating to this important part of the supply chain. It is unlikely that these deliveries into the village were omitted completely; partial recording is likely, as was often the case in Egyptian administration, but more likely is that the records of grain arriving at the village from the granaries of Thebes were not kept at the village proper, but at the administration centres in Thebes itself, and they are now lost. It is still surprising that records of grain ration receipts have not been found at Deir el-Medina; it would be expected that the scribes there would have provided at least some surviving records if they accounted for deliveries at the point of arrival as well as that of departure.

§8.3 Accountability within the supply chain

Certainly not as important as the payments of rations, some mention must be made concerning accountability, bearing in mind the increasing importance placed upon the concept at all levels in the state and business affairs of today's developed society. The cycle started out where the managers of the threshing floors were accountable for the grain at its origins, where it was taxed by the state. Even if there were individuals who were tied up with estates; these estates may or may not have been part of state ownership[35]. There was state involvement in the grain cycle from the field to the granaries of Thebes, but there are very few surviving records from which we can say with confidence that an accounting system existed as such, despite Ezzamel's attempts to do just this[36], at least within the sphere of grain rations.

The Turin Strike Papyrus[37] specifically states that the workmen appealed directly to the vizier when their ration payments were not forthcoming, which indicates that the vizier was ultimately responsible for the grain. The presence of scribes such as Hori in necropolis matters indicates that the vizier had scribes to perform administrative tasks and it follows that such individuals managed comings and goings at the granaries. Recto 3:4-5 of this papyrus records Hori speaking with the workmen directly, stating that "he will distribute a half ration to the workmen himself". Other references to Hori seem to be as a result of exceptional circumstances such as workmen travelling to Thebes demanding rations, and as in the Strike Papyrus there are examples where it is Hori who pays them[38]. In P. Turin 1906+1939+2047, rt. 4:4-10, there are three instances of Hori

35 The evidence provided in P. Amiens-Baldwin and discussed by Janssen (2004: 31-36) does not remove the uncertainty of who owned the threshing floors. The grain belonged to one or more institutions, but whether the threshing floors did also is not clear.

36 Discussed by Ezzamel (1994: 237-241) with reference to the Old Kingdom, Papyrus Harris and in particular a baking account from the reign of Seti I. The latter account is discussed more fully by Carmona & Ezzamel (2007: 193-195). These examples show that accounting did exist and the techniques were known, and also how the administration at least on these occasions dealt with it, but they do not serve as proof that a standard system existed, since there are too few examples.

37 P. Turin 1880. rt. 2:20-3:1.

38 There are at least two examples of unusual circumstances involving Hori. On O. Cairo 25305, the crew wrote to Hori about rations and Hori met them the following day, whilst in *Giornale* 17, rt. 2:29, Hori

handing out rations with either the mayor or a granary overseer from the granaries in Thebes. Whether the scribes of the mat got involved in more mundane transactions is possible. In P. Turin 2013+2050+2061, rt. 2:1 and 2:7, the rations are distributed by (*in*) Hori himself.

With accountability and the recording procedure, the link between Thebes and Deir el-Medina is the weakest one, as we have little information to draw upon. Even the donkey-train is unaccounted for in the textual record. There is nothing that mentions the individual who was in charge of the transportation of rations, but even so we do know that on occasions water-carriers delivered rations. O. DeM 34, rt. 11, a Journal document, records *diw* being distributed *m-drt* the water-carrier Panebdemit, and since this individual was a member of the *smdt*, he was almost certainly illiterate. In this instance he was not recording the delivery but actually delivering the grain[39]. Only when the grain reaches the local vicinity of the *ḫtm* at the village, do we have an abundance of material. Even at this point it is easy to assert that a given scribe was responsible for ration deliveries, but in many instances his name was not recorded either upon the arrival of the grain or its subsequent distribution amongst the crew.

As a result, we have no idea how the accounting was carried out at the *ḫtm*, nor do we know physically exactly how the grain was received and subsequently distributed to the workforce. The scribe may have issued the grain and recorded the distribution at fixed times to workmen[40], or less likely the scribe or another member of the village community, or a member of the support staff such as a water-carrier[41] took the grain to the workmen's houses and delivered it in person. The ration texts do not record this additional information so unfortunately, in the absence of any further evidence, these suggestions are merely speculative.

§8.4 P. Turin 1895+2006 (Turin Taxation Papyrus)

The grain was collected from *ḫ3-t3* fields as income. This included the payment of rations of grain to the workmen employed on tasks such as building the royal tombs in the Valley of the Kings. Dated to Year 12 of Ramesses XI, the Turin Taxation Papyrus is set out in short sections: firstly, where grain was collected from its place of origin; secondly, where it was transported by boat; and finally, where it gets delivered to Thebes. In each case, the total amount of grain was noted down as part of the narrative body of text when the grain was put into the boats, and also when it was removed. Perhaps the system here could be regarded as a simplified form of double entry bookkeeping, but there are examples of where the figures do not match. A more organised format would have certainly prevented the need to "correct" the irregularities which will be discussed in the following paragraphs.

It is the methods of recording which are of interest in this lengthy example. The grain was not always accounted for in the same manner, and neither was there always a balance at each stage of

hears the complaints of the workmen. On P. Turin 1884, rt. 2:3, the workmen demanded rations to be paid, subsequently issued by a scribe of the mat in Thebes from the granary of the temple of Maꜥat.

39 Similarly Ashakhet on O. DeM 34, vs. 4, was probably a water-carrier, if it is the same individual whose name is half lost on O. Ashmol. 374.

40 It has been shown in §4.1 that although issue was at the *ḫtm*, workmen were given their rations on days of work as well as days of inactivity.

41 These individuals were involved with distribution of rations in addition to the delivery from outside. O. DeM 381, vs. 1, records Eferikh, a known water-carrier whilst rt. 2 has Pa(nebdemit).

the process. The grain collected from Agni (lines 2:9 and 2:11) was distinctly split into emmer (*bdt*) and barley (*it m it*) using the favoured marking of red writing for emmer and black for barley, although the total is left blank (2:11). When it was collected, the grain came from two areas within the locality of Iumitru and it was written down as two quantities, in red, (2:3, 2:4) with the total also written in red[42]. Upon delivery to the granary in Thebes (2:7), 5 *khar* was specified as barley, the rest being emmer. Summarizing the initial delivery and disposal information (lines 2:1-15) in a modern accounting format gives the following, with units in *khar*:

	Goods in (receipts)			**Goods out (deliveries)**	
II *ꜣḫt* **16**	*ḫꜣ-tꜣ* land	54½	**II** *ꜣḫt* **16**	Grain	131½
	tꜣ ꜥmꜥmt mḥt	80		Barley	5
	Unexplained	2			
		136½			136½
III *ꜣḫt* **19**	Agni: emmer	33½	**III** *ꜣḫt* **23**	Emmer	33
	Agni: barley	3½		Barley	3¼+3⁄32 (*ipt*)
				Paid to fisherman	⅜ (*ipt*)
				Paid to fisherman (*blank*)	–
		37			37
III *ꜣḫt* **28**	Grain from Pkhal	10	**III** *ꜣḫt* **29**	Grain from Pkhal	10
		183½			183½

The difference in the writing of the two varieties of grain may have led to a discrepancy in the balances, albeit a simple one of 2 *khar* more being delivered than collected, but one which seems to be unexplained by anything except carelessness on the part of the scribe and probably not, as Gardiner believes, due to falsifying the account[43]. It is unlikely that 2 *khar* of grain was left on the boat, it may have been a payment to the skipper but this was made three days later. In addition, the small *oipe* fractions in line 2.11 may have confused the scribe to the extent that the final payment to the second fisherman was omitted, thereby creating the required balance of 37 *khar*.

Perhaps a more deliberate attempt to fudge the figures is the recording of the grain transported by two boats. These boats belonged to a skipper (*nfw*) and a fisherman (*wḥꜥ*), and the grain was received at a number of specific places, these being the storehouse (*pꜣ šmyt*) of Thebes (2:5-6)[44], the House of Montu in Thebes (3:1, 3:8), and the Portable Shrine of Usermaatre Meryamun (3:4, 3:7)[45]. Following the text can be confusing, so a breakdown of the details in lines 3:9 to 3:16

42 Although emmer and barley are identifiable in the records by the colour of the writing, when they are counted together the writing is also red, denoting a more generic *šs* "corn". See Gardiner (1941: 24 n. 3).

43 Gardiner (1941: 26).

44 Gardiner (1941: 24 and n. 2) treats this as a granary, or more specifically a "garner". Traditionally, *šmyt* indicates the storehouse, but in this instance a "corridor" may be referred to, which may have been part of the granary itself (Haring, 1997: 366). Grain recorded as being kept in the storehouse was unusual.

45 *ḳniw* may be taken to indicate a portable shrine, throne or chapel; Gardiner (1941: 29).

(receipts) and lines 4:1 to 4:11 (deliveries) is provided as follows, in the same manner as before, with all values being in *khar*.

IV *3ḫt* 20			**IV *3ḫt* 24**		
Goods in (receipts)			**Goods out (deliveries)**		
Boat of the skipper Dhutweshbi			Grain of Dhutweshbi	203¾	
Sahtnufe, harvest-tax	120		Expenses	20	
Butehamun/Nakhtamun	80				223¾
"From their hands"	6½				
"From their hands"	13½				
		220			
Boat of the fisherman Kadore			Grain of Kadore	110¼	
"Put upon the boat"	98¾		Yetnufe, rations	1	
"Put upon the boat"	24½	123¼	Khonsumose, Nesamope,		
Total		343¼	& Kadore	1⅞	
less: Given for expenses		(6¼)	*unexplained difference*	⅛	113⅛
Given to Pharaoh		**337**			**336⅞**
unexplained difference		¼	*unexplained difference*		⅛

The final unexplained difference is incidental, perhaps Dhutmose assumed there would be no problem if the same figure of 6¼ *khar* in line 3:13 was taken off as expenses. In modern accounting even this would have to be broken down. Where the accounts appear to have been falsified is in the following section of the text (the right side of the extract below, lines 4:3-5) where the details of the 337 *khar* are recorded. The total delivered from Esna is given and details follow. This is the reverse of the order in which the balances were recorded in the first part of the grain's journey north.

Brought from Esna[4:3]:	337			
Details of it:				
Grain of the fisherman Kadore	110¼			
Given as rations to the fisherman Yetnufe	1			
Total[4:4]	111¼			
Deficit	*2*	≈	Khonsumose	1¼
			Nesamenope	⁵⁄₁₆ (*ipt*)
			Kadore	¼
			(*Unexplained*)	*1⁵⁄₁₆* (*ipt*)
Grain of the skipper Dhutwebshi	203¾			
Given for expenses of the skipper	20			
Total[4:5]	225			

Although the final balance is only 1⁵⁄₁₆ *oipe* out, the grain delivered from both boats is incorrectly recorded. With Kadore, the difference is 10 *khar*, itself no small amount and close to what a foreman would have been paid as rations for two months. The deficit appearing earlier in the text (Section 2) has reappeared and is explicitly stated as such. Where the difference of 10 *khar* is can only be explained by the scribe's creativity. The balance of the grain from Dhutwebshi is also out. 220 *khar* was put onto the boat, but 203¾ was removed, after taking expenses of 20 *khar* into account. The total is incorrectly stated as 225. The methodology of loading, transportation and unloading the boats, when followed though carefully, is sound, but the figures are not correct.

This laborious example serves only to prove that the scribes made mistakes, which could be accidental or deliberate, and is in accordance with the view in the previous chapter that small errors and numerical inconsistencies did not matter, and did not render a document worthless. Even so, there is still the question concerning the nature of the errors in this specific document. On one hand, such mistakes were due to the use of the small *oipe* fractions, and such errors were considered by the scribe to be immaterial and subsequently overlooked. On the other hand, there is also the possibility that the amounts were significant enough amounts to suggest deliberate tampering. Either way, this exercise does show that a procedure was in place as an aid to the central administration to try and control the flow of their resources at least in a taxation context. Whether these techniques were used in all such scenarios is of course unknown.

Extracting the details from a more narrative styled document and rewriting it in a manner more familiar to modern day accounting shows that the information is in essence the same as what we would expect to find today. The date, places of delivery and origin of the grain, and the names of those responsible for its collection were all recorded[46], the expenses incurred as part of the transport process are clearly stated. All these details would be expected in business today so the monitoring of state resources such as grain was carried out, despite the evidence being scarce. The scribe clearly knew what he was writing down, and based on the frequent use of *m-drt*, overseeing the deliveries in and out was part of his job. What would not be acceptable today is the number of unexplained differences. This did not matter to the administration, and the Turin Taxation Papyrus was one example where no attempt was made to account for them.

§8.5 Conclusion

Aspects of grain supply and transport have been dealt with, such as the transport of grain detailed on P. Amiens-Baldwin, the physical methods of ration distribution for which the evidence is lacking, accounting behind the small number of boats transporting rations recorded on P. Turin 1895+2006, and matters of accountability. This provides the opportunity to attempt to try and link these aspects together, but with the self-imposed restriction of record keeping issues relevant to Deir el-Medina. This in turn limits us to one area and one relatively short time period, so the findings discussed can be used in comparison with other periods or localities. Sources from other areas such as the Turin Indictment Papyrus and P. Valençay can be used to indicate that certain events did take place, even if there is no direct evidence at Deir el-Medina. These documents can

46 An observation made by Ezzamel (2002: 18), based on taxation examples. The examples discussed above, which record deliveries within part of a larger body of text, tend not to exhibit all these characteristics.

augment existing knowledge and develop areas where there are several gaps in the available evidence to necessitate assumptions being made. As a result, the conclusions can both be enhanced and challenged with knowledge from other areas, but it could be argued that the appropriateness of such opposition would have the same limitations.

There are many aspects of grain supply which would ideally warrant further discussion, whilst subjects such as tax collection and the organisation of *ḫ3-t3* fields, storage at threshing floors, and the relationship between the granary as a building and as an accounting institution, are all research areas in their own right. The inclusion of the different components of the ration supply chain has been examined due to its interest and relevance to Deir el-Medina, but also with the aim of producing a model of the complete procedure of ration delivery and distribution, based on the evidence we have. This model will lay the gaps out and include suggestions which may fill in some of the gaps. This model will form part of the conclusion to the present study. The evidence from the fields is unsurprisingly absent, but with sources such as the Turin Taxation Papyrus we have some idea of what took place, if not directly from the Theban area.

Granaries present a problem as the details on their locations, organisation and accounting are still unclear, and the overlap between the "Granary of Pharaoh" as a building and an accounting institution is extremely difficult to ascertain and is outside the scope of the present study. The evidence is not forthcoming since, for example, we know the names of the institutions, but not how the rations were recorded at state granaries. The final link in the complete supply chain is the strongest. It is only when the grain arrives at the village that we have any idea how records were kept, but even then the physical procedure of ration payment is not clear. The names of some of the storage facilities are known even if their locations are not. The rations became far more important to those who received them when they entered the workmen's village, and this is reflected in the abundance of material concerning distributions at our disposal.

CHAPTER 9

A MODEL FOR RATION DELIVERY & DISTRIBUTION SYSTEMS

The collation and examination of the documentary evidence on wage rations have encouraged the discussion of a wide number of issues centred on accounting, the ration distribution process, patterns of delivery, responsibility and the supply of grain rations. The evidence for ration delivery and distribution examined so far is extensive enough to allow us to propose a theoretical model of the complete procedure of ration movement, accountability and recording from field to house. Naturally, there will be many areas of uncertainty and speculation concerning those areas where there is scant evidence at best, but even so light may be shed on exactly where the rations went and how they were or were not accounted for at each stage of the process. The evidence has been presented in the previous chapters and many gaps remain, so here we have to suggest some assumptions based on supposition and attempt to specify what we would need to include in order to make the system work more efficiently.

The idea of proposing a theoretical structure should not be treated as a conclusion on ration accounting, but rather as bringing together many of the ideas explored and suggesting possibilities as to what procedures were carried out. The model can be split into two parts; the first part relates to the movement and accounting for rations from the fields to the *ḫtm* of Deir el-Medina, and the second from the *ḫtm* to the workmen's houses. The latter is the larger component and the more important of the two since it has direct impact in the village and the accounting system. In order to construct the second part, one significant factor that needs to be examined is the presence and likely capacity of silos, and any evidence for smaller areas set aside for the storage of grain. This includes silos situated inside and outside the village with examination for any significant variations in their forms and functions.

§9.1 The evidence for silos

Returning in more detail to the presence in the archaeological record of silos within the village, close examination of the evidence will enable aid for the proposition of a model by which the process of ration delivery and distribution took place. Unfortunately, the recording of silos within the village by Bruyère is limited to a handful of short and patchy references[1] without any measurements or estimates of capacities being supplied, although there is mention of two being square and two rectangular; there is no correlation between shape and size. Fifteen silos[2] have been found outside the village, the largest group of rectangular silos were also situated outside the main entrance to the north in house P1312, summarised by McDowell as having a rough capacity of over 470 *khar*[3], whereas the actual figure is more like 450 *khar*. Other groups of silos were also situated in P1283 (a partitioned group of nine), five in P1258, four in P1276, three in P1297, two each in P1240 and P1262, and a single silo in P1282, P1288, P1330 and P1405[4]. Some silos do not appear to have direct connections with associated tombs, such as a group of four north of P1258, the two west of P1286 and the two between P1251 and Tomb 215. Lastly, two silos in between P1262 and P1282 have direct access from the street, perhaps indicating a facility shared between several chapels and tombs in the immediate vicinity.

The placement of these silos and their partitioning, within a necropolis, would suggest that the grain brought here was not part of the workmen's rations but was intended to be used in offerings for the associated mortuary and divine cults. The dispersal of clusters of silos may indicate that each group was used to provide for several cults. One group of silos, that in house P1312, contained a feature common in domestic architecture, namely a divan[5], so perhaps the link between the domestic and funerary contexts is stronger than expected. It is also perfectly feasible that silos within the village were organised in a similar manner, given the lack of evidence within a domestic context, but a household having their neighbours frequently coming in for grain seems unrealistic. What seems more likely is that the grain here was given to the workmen as part of their rations, and the supervisors or "priests" of each chapel took the grain to their families. Without any knowledge of the requirements for cult provision, or of who made use of them, this is all mere speculation.

Inside the village, the silos recorded by Bruyère are those in Houses NE III, NE VIII[6], SE IV and SW VI (belonging to Sennedjem). The latter two were larger than the others and appear to have taken the space of a whole room. A further silo is situated outside the entrance to SW VI, but it is unclear whether this enabled continual access to the inhabitants in the southernmost part of the village. The only estimates of their storage potential are those made by McDowell. While she correctly states that estimating their capacity to any degree of reliability is impossible,

1 Bruyère (1939: 246, 252-253, 269, 330-331).

2 These are all included in the plan of the western cemetery by Bruyère (1934: Plate X) but the details are absent from the excavation reports.

3 Following McDowell (1992: 204), dimensions quoted are calculated using the scale on the area plans of Bruyère (1937: Plates I and II) in the original excavation reports. The difference in capacity estimate for this cluster of four silos is due to a 1.25m by 1.75m portion being stairs and not silo space. The smallest silo is that in P1288; this had an estimated capacity of about 64 *khar*. The calculations all assume a 2.2m depth, as specified by Bruyère (1937: 26).

4 These houses are included on the area plans by Bruyère (1937: Plates I and II), but unfortunately not mentioned in the text.

5 Bruyère (1937: 24).

6 One of the largest houses in the village (Bruyère 1939: 252); it would follow that it would have had a larger sized silo, but this was not the case.

she still provides a very rough estimate of 13 *khar* for the smallest and 50 *khar* for the largest on the assumption they were one metre deep[7]. These are significantly smaller on average than those in the western necropolis. If a foreman or scribe received 5½ *khar* of emmer and 2 *khar* of barley and the standard ration for a workman was 4 *khar* and 1½ *khar* respectively, then the silo could hold between two and nine times a workman's monthly ration, with many silos being partitioned to facilitate the storage of different types of ration. Despite no mention by Bruyère of any residual deposits of either emmer or barley in the excavation reports, it can safely be assumed that the grain types were either stored separately in partitioned silos or perhaps barley was stored in smaller and more portable containers, so it is unlikely that partitioned sections were allocated to individual houses.

Out of some seventy houses in the village, silos have only been found in four of them, which raises the questions of whether there were any more, and if not, then why not. The statement put forward by the excavators that each house contained silos, which were pits with a depth of between one and three metres[8], is one which is not justified since the archaeological evidence is not forthcoming. However, this does not account for any inaccuracies or omissions in the excavation reports. It may well be that the absence of evidence in this case reflects the significantly low number of silos in the living quarters, in which case evidence for the majority of the grain storage was on a smaller scale than silos for which there is little which survives. It may also be the case that the low frequency of silos within the village is a result of the Ramesseum being the nearest storage point for rations[9]. But since there is no mention of the Ramesseum in the delivery records, this can probably be discounted as normal practice, even though on occasions when village stores got low grain may have been taken from the temple granary. The ration texts often show the distribution of small amounts which supports the possibility that grain for rations was stored in amphorae and other similar containers.

A detailed map of the village and the areas north and east is shown in Figure 7[10] and this shows the distribution of silos within the village and in the buildings to the north-west. The distribution across the whole area is significant, with the concentration of silos in selected areas north-west of the village, single structures to the north and in the village, and a complete absence in the southern parts of the western necropolis. The importance of silos can not be understated in the understanding of how rations were treated both physically and in the accounting, and even allowing for a lack of details there is enough evidence to enable their inclusion into a theoretical model of the entire process.

7 McDowell (1992: 204). Whereas there is no evidence to back these figures up, any calculations will be based upon these estimates as there is no other information available.

8 Bruyère (1934: 84).

9 Bruyère (1952: 35). The Ramesseum may also have been the source of ration payments during the times of the strikes in Year 29 of Ramesses III.

10 After Tosi & Roccati (1972: 28-29) with some minor adjustments.

Figure 7: Location of silos in Deir el-Medina

§9.2 Part 1: From Field to Village Enclosure

Proposing a model for the first part of the ration chain is fraught with danger since there are a number of unknown components for which we can only make suggestions. As a result, what follows is *not what did* take place, but one possibility of what *may have occurred* with the transport, delivery, accountability and recording of the grain, with adjustments and additions provided which may make the system perform more efficiently. The central node here is Thebes, where grain was both received and dispatched, but for both events, there is a scarcity of evidence.

After harvesting, the grain yield was winnowed and measured at the threshing floor near the fields, then loaded onto boats from either a short term storage unit or directly the threshing floor. If the Turin Taxation Papyrus is an example of standard practice, amounts were recorded by the scribe as they were loaded onto the boat, after which the boat's owner was accountable for the grain. However, for deliveries of ration grain which was not from *ḫ3-t3* fields, for grain that was not taken from state owned land any such recording is more unlikely. The population of the city of Thebes and the settlements and temples on the west bank were at least in part fed by produce grown locally[11] on both sides of the river which may be an indication of a reduced need for accounting. Landholdings varied considerably between villages and within individual villages[12], and therefore the need for both accounting and accountability varied. Even so, taxation was important to the state, and was precisely recorded.

The grain was removed from the boats and deposited in the granaries of the Theban temple, the scribes noted the amounts of grain transferred, and the boat owner got paid in grain from the supply on his boat. In order to make the system work properly at this point, stock movement checks would have to be done once when the grain left the boat and once at the granaries thereby ensuring no loss during transportation as well as acting as an additional stock control. The granaries had their own records of receipts and disposals, which they kept for short periods of time before discarding them in locations which have been built over in modern times; if this was done then this may well be the reason for the lack of evidence for granary accounts.

The scribe again compiled a movement list of the grain which left the granaries, and the produce which was not intended for the workmen was transported to the granaries of the Ramesseum and other mortuary temples. Ration grain was transported from the Theban granaries across the Nile. Once on the west side, it was loaded onto donkeys and taken to the village enclosure, that is, the *ḫtm*. There is no evidence of the composition of the human component of donkey convoys so there is no indication of who was in charge, even if we know that water-carriers hired donkeys on a frequent basis and *diw* were distributed by (*m-drt*) a water-carrier[13], such as recorded on O. DeM 34, rt. 11. If a scribe was accountable for the grain at either end of the transportation, there is no indication of who was accountable during the journey.

Since rations were measured in *khar* it is a worthwhile exercise to attempt to test the accuracy of this measure in relation to modern equivalents of what could be carried comfortably by one

11 On the basis of a lack of evidence, McDowell (1992: 205-206) has suggested that the inhabitants of Deir el-Medina itself did not engage in agricultural activity on a significant scale, but see §8.2 above.

12 Eyre (1999: 41).

13 This was a distribution from the Enclosure to the workmen.

donkey or one man, given the extremely high daily temperatures in Egypt. It has been suggested[14] that donkeys could realistically carry either four storage vessels weighing about 15 kg empty or two goat skins which held about 30 litres each, making the capacity of one donkey of about 60 litres, so if we accept the classical measurement of 1 *khar* equalling 76.88 litres, a donkey-load would be ¾ to 1 *khar*. Even if we can make a more precise estimate as to the carrying capacity of a donkey by experimenting in the field we have no way of ascertaining how many donkeys were in a donkey train, so no indication is possible as to what a standard ration delivery to the village was, although this varied according to the availability of grain. Similarly, we could expect either a convoy of donkeys or a steady trickle throughout the day; either is possible and would have depended on the availability of donkeys to a large extent. Despite these limitations, the notion of one man getting multiple donkey-loads of grain per month implies that there was a considerable level of activity between the Theban granaries and Deir el-Medina.

§9.3 Part 2: From Village Enclosure to the Workmen's Houses

The first part of the model requires a number of assumptions in order to fill in the many gaps in the procedure where the evidence is poorly attested. We do not know where the enclosure was[15], its size, the location of any granary or more likely a short term holding facility for grain, or how many men worked at the enclosure; all of which are obstacles in our understanding of the distribution procedure. Despite being at the business end of the complete system, the second part is hindered by the absence of documentation for how the rations were distributed and the uncertainty as to what a complete ration distribution list actually consisted of. Even so, there is considerably more material to draw upon and recommendations can be made as to how the recording could be improved to make the complete procedure more efficient.

The grain arrived at the village from the north side where it was unloaded and deposited into storage in the granary of the *ḫtm*, and the delivery was recorded as part of the Journal by the Scribe of the Necropolis. The Journal recorded the date, but the amount of grain was very rarely specified, only that it had arrived on that day. Based on the Journal documents we have, in reality this was only done very occasionally, so the patterns of ration delivery appear very irregular, even occasional, if we take the Journal as it is. Perhaps many deliveries were recorded on ostraca independent from the Journal or more likely the arrival of grain was not always deemed important enough to warrant inclusion in the Journal. Fuller and regular recording of all grain deliveries would ensure that the Journal was complete in this respect and that the administration had the necessary records. This would make life easier for modern scholars, but the scribes could argue that additional records were not needed as the administration centre knew the grain had arrived and their efforts could be concentrated elsewhere. Irregular and incomplete information are both problems with the system, as grain could go missing or be stolen and nobody would be able to account for the shortage of rations, which was undoubtedly the most important commodity to the

14 This is briefly discussed by Förster (2007: 5) in his study on water supply depots near Abu Ballas, but there is nothing in the study to back up these figures. Even though this study relates to the Old Kingdom and the 1st Intermediate Period, there is no reason to expect any changes in the period at least up to the end of the New Kingdom.

15 See Chapter 2, note 66, for references to the debate on the *ḫtm*.

workmen. In order to make the system work properly, every delivery would have to be recorded as it arrived at the *ḫtm* along with the amounts split up into emmer and barley.

With the rations in storage in the granary of the *ḫtm*, it is not known how long it remained there for. A solution would be to keep a detailed ledger, with dates, of grain delivered and also when it left the *ḫtm* to be given to the workmen, similar to a stock register today. While this would certainly make our life much easier, the administration had to take care of storage, and more importantly, the need to raise such documents and record entries. Since the documents were not audited, creating extra work when nobody was going to use it was not a viable option. Similarly, creating an extra level of bureaucracy by matching deliveries brought in with that given to the workmen was deemed unnecessary even if it would make the system more efficient. In the absence of stock control and stock valuation, there is no indication of the amount of grain lost due to wastage[16], theft or creative accounting.

Most of the surviving material relates to the distribution of the rations from the granary of the *ḫtm* to the workmen, but we do not know how or for certain where this was done. It is possible that an individual delivered rations directly to the houses but this does not seem plausible as it would need two individuals to perform the task; one man carrying the grain around in one or more containers and the other recording names and amounts on an ostracon. It is certainly possible, however, that in times of strikes when rations were not paid on time, additional rations were taken to individual houses and such an event could explain records such as O. DeM 737, which is a continuous list of workmen from both sides receiving rations. There is no evidence for check marks on ration lists consisting of names and designations of workmen, and certainly there was no guarantee that the recipient or his family would be present upon delivery.

The more likely scenario is that rations were handed out to the workmen at the *ḫtm*, and the evidence suggests that this tended to be done one side at a time. One possibility is that the workmen queued up at the *ḫtm*, once a month for their *diw*, and that *dni* was paid upon request which may account for many of the smaller lists relating to both individuals and smaller amounts. The payments were given out slowly and the names and amounts were dictated to allow the scribe to record the details legibly without the need for relying on his memory or a fast and messier hand. Analysis on the days of delivery does not reveal any significant patterns so a regular day of queuing seems unlikely. Instead, it can be proposed, albeit with no supporting evidence, that when rations arrived at the *ḫtm*, the workmen were informed, perhaps a day in advance, and they could collect their rations at the next convenient moment. This would support the view that the grain remained in storage for a short period of time and also a more ad hoc distribution system took place where rations were given out when they became available.

One aspect of the distribution procedure for which there is no evidence is the measuring of rations prior to payment, though the *oipe* scoop as a real object is well attested[17]. Measuring con-

16 The storage facilities would need periodic cleaning to alleviate grain sitting in the bottom of the storage area for months on end. Since no building has survived, there is no way of establishing whether grain removed from the top or from the bottom.

17 One example is Hekanakhte Letter III, 5-6 (Allen 2002: 144). The word for *oipe* scoop was *ipt*, and has the wood determinative, so the measure seems to be deliberate and precise. In addition, O. Leipzig 2 mentions problems about the *oipe*-measure which was being used.

tainers are one possibility, but a portable box, pot or scoop holding 1 *oipe* could seem unrealistic since if this is equivalent to 19.22 litres it could be regarded as too heavy and cumbersome. If this was the case, a ¼ *oipe* measuring container seems a possible alternative. This seems to conflict with the suggestion that small and precise amounts of 1⁄16 *oipe* (or 1⁄64 *khar*) being recorded on several occasions should be treated as "a bit more" and that such measures were actually a more realistic indication of what actually happened. Despite this, as was demonstrated above (§7.5), these extra measures were often used. A related question is that had the foreman received his full payment of emmer in one instalment, namely 5½ *khar* (422.84 litres), he would have been unable to transport it in one journey without the use of more than one donkey. Furthermore, this does not include his barley payment. It is much easier to imagine the carrying of grain in the smaller amounts such as ½ and 1 *khar*. All this is nothing but speculation, since there are no texts or representations from tombs that depict the measuring or transport of rations within the village.

The ultimate part of the model involves the deposit of rations at the houses of the workmen. The record trail ceases once the rations left the *ḫtm*, then it was no longer state property and had passed into the private domain. The issue of how the workmen got their grain from the *ḫtm* to their houses brings up the question of donkeys once again, and if the *ḫtm* was situated nearer to the Ramesseum this would become a real issue, as donkeys would add congestion to an already busy village. If 1 *khar* is taken to be the equivalent of one sack (76.44 litres), then the manual transport of grain sacks by the workmen or their family members would explain the high number of records indicating distribution of smaller amounts, but on the other hand this would point to a larger number of journeys and increased activity between the *ḫtm* and workmens' houses.

The final step in the recording process was that for which we have the most evidence, the ration distribution lists. These suggest that the ostraca were written not for the administration but for the workmen, and were used indirectly as receipts which were effectively reminders to the administration as to the amount of grain to be delivered rather than records to be stored by the village administration. This raises the question as to whom the ostracon was given, and why no ostraca were found in the houses of the workmen. One explanation is that the workmen got their rations and a receipt for the rations, and discarded the receipt as we would do today in a designated area within the *ḫtm*. While an alternative and certainly a more likely reason, based on the documents being used as reminders, is that they were kept at the *ḫtm* and not taken away by the workmen, who could not make demands on arrears for any short payment. The administrators then periodically tidied up their working quarters and deposited the ostraca, which ended up in the Great Pit although probably not directly from the *ḫtm*. The sheer number of ostraca found there suggests that they were stored in a group and discarded in bulk in antiquity[18] but where they were prior to being dumped in the Great Pit and how often this happened are both unknown.

There are only five silos within the village which held a roughly estimated range of between 13 and 50 *khar*, equating to between three and twelve times the monthly ration of a standard workman. Two of these, those in houses SE IV and NE VIII, are located in the cellars so there may be some crossover between the use of cellars as silos, indicating that grain was normally stored in the

18 A group of ostraca written by the same scribe and found together is used by Donker van Heel (2003: 14 and n. 9) as part of the evidence supporting the presence of a central archive, but they are from the Journal and are not ration receipts.

cellars of individual houses and may explain the absence of silos in the village. If the excavators were correct in not recording the presence of more than this, it seems certain that rations were stored in less permanent containers than silos. Amphorae and large pottery vessels could store the grain in the cooler cellars of houses, and the presence of these smaller storage containers is inferred by the number of records which show distribution of smaller amounts of grain.

§9.4 Conclusion

The idea behind producing a framework of ration distribution developed due to two main factors. Firstly, the lack of knowledge of the physical procedure of ration payments is plainly evident, there are too many areas of uncertainty primarily in the recording and transportation mechanisms at various stages in the distribution procedure, which starts in the fields and ends in the houses of the workmen. Secondly, the nature of the existing literature is such that works on rations have approached specific aspects of the subject for which the evidence is more forthcoming. The best example of this is the ration amounts, but nowhere is there any study which has attempted to bring the various branches of the subject together to produce a single theoretical model, so there is a definite space and need for a framework upon which future studies on the subject can add and modify when necessary.

There are many omissions in the knowledge base and the evidence is simply not there to allow many of these gaps to be filled. As a result many suggestions have had to be made about specific aspects of the model. These suggestions are sometimes based on logic and supposition as to what may have happened relating to ration delivery, transportation, recording and accountability. Templates of any given process which include a significant amount of theory or assumptions are always going to be open to criticism, and the model presented above is intended to encourage scholars to add their constructive criticism and suggest modifications and additions.

CHAPTER 10

CONCLUSION

This research has shown that wage accounting was not a minor issue with very little possibility of extracting valuable knowledge on scribal procedures at Deir el-Medina. The documentation of rations was a process which highlighted a number of recording techniques, provided an indication of the level of accountability and revealed some insights into the physical processes involved in the transport and receipt of grain rations. By taking primary evidence in the form of ration distribution lists and utilising existing literature on aspects of the subject, this study has not only brought together what has largely been a somewhat fragmented topic, but has also contributed much to the existing knowledge base both on existing themes and new material not previously researched. In addition, it enables the possibility of comparative studies with other areas of administration or fields, such as the comparison of terminology with that used in the judicial sphere, the delivery and accounting methods of numerous other commodities, and accounting for state property such as copper tools.

The surviving material is almost exclusively from three distinct time periods; the late 19th Dynasty; the period covering the last few years of Ramesses III to the middle of Ramesses IV; and the years encompassing the last three kings of the Ramesside period. For the years in between these distinct periods, there is little surviving evidence. While this is advantageous in many respects, since it allows direct comparisons between a known and specified range of years, the opposite holds when trying to follow and explain changes over time. Unfortunately, this drawback can only be overcome in the event that substantial additional material is found pertaining to these undocumented periods, such as the texts found recently by the Basle expedition in the Valley of the Kings[1].

In §1.1 it was established that the overall aim was to provide a full, detailed and as complete as possible analysis of ration payments in one study. Whilst this has been achieved, there is still enough scope for future additions to the current ration database if additional material is discovered. Within this generalisation, it follows that one important aspect in concluding a detailed study such as this is to assess to what extent the initial aims and objectives have been achieved.

1 Dorn (2011).

These other intentions have been targeted which can now be reviewed, whilst at the same time noting where the evidence is either missing or unclear in relation to date or content. A related matter is the added complication of areas within the distribution procedure for which logical suppositions have to be made to fill in gaps in our knowledge; in many instances possibilities can be eliminated rather than confirmed.

It seemed natural to start the research proper with a catalogue of terminology used in the ration lists, and split them into two parts: words and phrases used as headings and within the documents, and those used strictly in an accounting context. The objective behind Chapter 3 was to determine exact meanings of words, and where possible, look for any changes in frequency of use over the course of the late Ramesside period. The pattern of discussion followed that of Haring, and there were no surprises in the meanings of words taken solely in a rations context in the first category. The only real matter of debate was the exact meaning of *ỉw*, which either translated as "delivered" or "entered". The former was a physical procedure, and the latter an accounting procedure; despite this, even when context was examined, the two may still be interchangeable. The possibility of further research is there to examine the uses of *rdỉ, šsp* and *ỉw* and how they may be interchangeable in non-ration contexts.

Examination of the accounting terminology in §3.2 revealed that some words had a straightforward meaning, while the exact meanings of others were more difficult to determine. The words regularly used throughout the Ramesside period were *wꜥ nb* "each", *ỉr.n* "making" often together with *dmḏ* "total", *wḏꜣt* "balance", and *ꜥḥꜥ* "amount". The range of meanings in a rations context of a single word, *dmḏ*, to indicate several levels of total emphasises the differences between ancient and modern concepts, as well providing an avenue for future research as to whether its meaning was more precise in documents which dealt with accounting for other commodities. On a similar note, although the frequency of use of *ꜥḥꜥ* was low, it is a good example of the differential use of an individual word. It seems it was primarily used in the 20th Dynasty in a non-rations context, but on the occasions it was used in ration lists these are from the 19th Dynasty. On the basis of modern translations, *dmḏ* and *wp st* "details of it" appear to have slightly different meanings, even if this was not intended at the time of writing. Where we would have different levels of total in accounts today, *dmḏ* was used to indicate any total except the running total indicated by *ỉr.n*, but occasionally a different expression, *dmḏ ḥꜣw nb*, was used.

The aims of exploring words used in wage accounting have been achieved in part, with a comprehensive identification of vocabulary and its meanings, but the differential nature of scribal recording techniques over time is much more difficult to assess, because of the periods for which there is no surviving evidence. Comparisons can be made, the presence or absence of terminology and the increased use of any given phrase can be identified, but unfortunately not explained. The contribution to existing knowledge is nevertheless clear; the existing framework used by Haring has been adhered to, although terminology used as headings was only briefly examined in solely a rations context, the majority of the section concentrates on accounting terminology. Despite any possible changes in word use being impossible to explain, the framework is definitely there to allow for intra field comparisons, even if these other disciplines will undoubtedly suffer from the same restrictions, in that the overall pool of documents is the same as that used with ration payments.

Document dates were analysed in considerable detail over two chapters to answer questions about patterns of ration distribution and their variances, the amounts delivered and the recipients of the rations. It is clear from Appendix 1 that rations being recorded was more of an exception than the rule, since the Journal did not usually record ration deliveries, and the instances of clustering proves that deliveries were for the most part frequent, albeit irregular, events. The relationship between *diw* and *dni* was such that the latter followed the former, but the results do not appear to justify this, since on a broad level *diw* payments tended to be in the middle decade of a given month and *dni* during the first decade. This was further complicated by the absence of any indication of a due date or accepted date of payment of basic rations. What this highlighted was that it is a good example of the pitfalls of taking results at face value. Being aware of these issues validated the performing of statistical analysis on delivery dates despite there being so much material absent from key periods. Undoubtedly the importance of tests can be overstated, given the sample sizes, but they can serve to endorse the findings presented graphically, and this is certainly the best that can be achieved.

With these doubts in mind, apart from proving conclusively that scribes did not record everything on a daily basis, how far have the aims of Chapters 4 and 5 been achieved? Ascertaining what proportion of deliveries was late is difficult, since there is no concept of what was classed by the workmen as late. The analysis on the dates of the documents and their related deliveries in Chapter 4 indicated that rations were paid mostly in arrears of one or two months, or else in the same month, and there were consequences if the state got too far behind in supplying grain, as is demonstrated by the workmen's strikes. Contrary to what would be expected, advance payments did exist, and although impossible to prove, these advance payments may well have been a consequence of the strikes[2]. A comparison of delivery days between different periods revealed little variation in delivery patterns of *diw* up to the middle of the 20th Dynasty, but the contrast with the later papyri was striking. Despite the lack of surviving material, the records from the late 20th Dynasty showed considerably less fluctuation; but a higher proportion of rations was given out during the last few days of the month. The reasons are unclear, but it may well have resulted from the deterioration in the social and economic situation at the time. The seasons appear to have had no effect on ration distributions, primarily due to the use of granaries.

After checking the validity of the existing literature in ascertaining what the standard payments were for each category of workman, the foremost objective behind the examination of the amounts paid and the workmen's designation in Chapter 5 was to ascertain how complete the ration lists were, and then to attempt to identify and explain any differences in content over the course of the Ramesside period. Assumptions had to be made as to the number of categories of workmen and a delivery based on the standard ration for each designation of workman and the size of the workforce, or else the exercise would not be possible. Overall, these aims have been achieved, but this research has also revealed some insights into the methods of recording used in the ration delivery process.

The research presented in Chapter 5 is for the most part new, and provided analysis of the data and visual representation of the results for comparison between periods. The difference of

2 It is possible that once the delivery system had "caught up" on itself and the workmen appeased, one or two months' advance payment would be followed by a return to normal timing.

0.32 in the mean number of different category of workmen recorded on the ration lists in the two earlier periods appeared high, but statistically this was not significant. The explanations no doubt returned to matters such as the inclusion of captains and doorkeepers, not so much the guardsmen, and in particular the tendency to record named individuals far more frequently earlier on[3].

The recipients of rations were recorded in a strict order with the occasional exception towards the end, consisting of the foreman, scribe, men, guardsmen, youths, women servants, doorkeepers, and old men, but there were some minor variations in positions between the last groups. These lower ranked groups were included more frequently during the 20th Dynasty, while named individuals were not. Less appropriate to the 19th Dynasty, captains were often designated in the ration lists instead of the foremen and less so the scribes, leading to the suggestion that the position was more important towards the end of the 20th Dynasty, where nearly three quarters of ration lists included one or more captains. A similar proportion of documents included doorkeepers as ration recipients. It may be that these men were given more importance in the light of the tomb robberies towards the end of the 20th Dynasty. At this time, the support personnel were often included in the ration lists, perhaps indicating that in terms of wage accounting they were now treated the same as the workmen. Throughout the Ramesside period, there was a regular inclusion of a number of uncategorised men receiving different ration payments; these were usually written down after the scribe but before the guardsmen in the records. Some men had additional functions such as the doctor or scorpion charmer, others did not work a full month due to one or more of a multitude of excuses, and others were building tombs for individuals other than the king so were not always exclusively on the royal payroll.

The individual payments given to the workmen have been examined before; ration amounts were taken one step further by examining the total amounts on any given ration list and attempting to extract statistics from them as a group, and providing explanations for the resulting observations. This involved the creation of an ideal list which assumed that every workman was on the list and that he got his full allowance. One underlying influence on the results was the size of the workforce, but delivery patterns and therefore grain availability also affected the amounts recorded. Grain was delivered when it was available, but in variable amounts at various times and this would account for smaller ad hoc ration lists. What was much more complex is why the mean ration totals recorded in the 19th Dynasty were considerably lower than those later, but the reasons for this is one area which remains unclear. Consequently, the specific focus of research can establish several hitherto undisclosed elements of ration allocation, but unfortunately the explanations are often not forthcoming, and there is no early 20th Dynasty material available to trace any changes and the development of the recording system.

One completely new area of research was that of examining the writing itself, and Chapter 6 attempted to answer the question of whether scribes prepared their documents, at least in part, prior to the physical handing out of rations taking place. Some would argue that the number of ostraca examined, at a dozen, is too small, so a further twenty-four high resolution images were included to supplement the originals, thereby alleviating the problem to at least some degree. The research is still valuable as it contributes new information as well as providing a framework for

3 Named individuals are not included in the data forming the tables in Chapter 4 simply because there is no indication of their formal designation.

future examination of ostraca and papyri for which access is not so readily available. In particular, it opens up many possibilities in comparative studies by taking the practices used at Deir el-Medina and contrasting them with those used both within Egypt at different periods and in other ancient societies such as Mesopotamia and Classical Greece.

Examination of the pen dips and the position of the writing, and close scrutiny of the relative positions of the red and black ink on the surface of the ostracon, revealed little evidence that forms were written up in advance. Whereas this may seem disappointing and considered to be a negative result, it allowed speculation as to where the scribe was when the grain was handed out; whether he recorded names, designations and amounts after the grain was given out, or recorded so that everything happened at the same time. The high number of low magnitude mistakes in the records and neatness of the writing suggested that the former method took place; perhaps the amounts were called out slowly enough to allow a full and neat set of records to be made. Given the size of the writing and the amount of unused space on the ostraca selected for physical examination, one firm assertion that could be made is that the scribes gained the ability with experience, to choose appropriate pieces of stone or pot to write on, and the documents were to some extent, pre-planned in their minds.

The absence of accounting procedures used in business today did not detract from the efficiency of the ancient Egyptian administration, which centred on need and what was required. The absence of double-entry bookkeeping and auditing did not detract from the accounting system, but even so, some methods used at Deir el-Medina were the same as those used today, even if they were taken in non-profit making situations. Ration delivery lists were much the same as goods received notes today, and what was important was that the workmen received the grain, so once it was delivered at the *ḫtm* it was no longer in the state domain and therefore accountability was relatively unimportant to the administration. In contrast to the quota system used in deliveries of fish and wood, closing off a period in the rations documentation was treated not in terms of time, but once a delivery was complete.

Chapter 7 followed on from, and expanded upon, Janssen's analysis of errors in the ration lists in order to create a full and complete list of ration documents containing what appeared to be mathematical errors and word omissions. The possibility of the use of small and precise fractions to record an unmeasured element of reality was raised, and the scribes' attempt to avoid the use of complicated fractions. The benefit to modern scholars is not so much in the expansion of previously available data itself, but in the extrapolation of possible attitudes of the administration in relation to the motives behind recording the distribution lists, and to a lesser degree comparisons with delivery records for other commodities. The underlying conclusion followed on directly from that of the previous chapter, in that due to the absence of both business entities and auditing within the administration, the degree and magnitude of errors did not matter, despite just under a third of non-ration documents contained one or more errors. This view is substantiated by the lack of visible corrections, smudging and erasing of signs in the ostraca viewed, and indicates strongly that the accuracy was sufficient for what was required. The ration documents can therefore be seen to have been used as reminders to the administration as to what they had to deliver or what they had delivered; and they could double up as receipts in the event of a query by the workmen relating to an incorrect ration payment. The relatively high proportion of documents containing an "error" and low degree of numerical inconsistencies did not affect the overall authenticity and use of the documents, as the requirements of the administration were satisfied.

The provision of rations from the start of the supply cycle formed the basis of Chapter 8. The value of tracing the rations from their source in the field to the houses of the workmen served in stressing just how much evidence is absent from the records as well as how the final delivery, for which there is the most evidence, fits into the complete cycle. Documentary evidence from outside the Theban area had to be incorporated into the analysis to fill in some of the gaps in, for example, the tax collecting process. In addition, the content provides avenues for further research such as land ownership and the organisation of the granary as an institution; while beyond the scope of this study these topics will certainly reward any future research. One line of research could be to examine the uncertainty as to what was meant by the "Granary of Pharaoh", given the frequent references to the term, but the degree of overlap between a physical building and an accounting institution is currently unclear. There were numerous granaries attached to the temples in Thebes, but at Deir el-Medina storage was probably relatively short term with evidence of one granary. Together with the inclusion of the locations and likely capacities of silos within and around the village, it is possible to theorise a possible logistical system which would bring factors such as rations, content and frequency of donkey trains from Thebes, accountability, the recording and handing out of rations at the *ḫtm* and internal storage facilities into the equation. This forms the model that was presented in Chapter 9.

For any research which relies on empirical evidence for accurate results, in particular when statistical techniques are included, the more material that is available the better, and consequently the more reliable the results will be. Perhaps the main criticism of the present study would be that the corpus of 178 documents is not wide enough to obtain accurate results. It is a major limiting factor, but not insurmountable as similarities and differences can be examined, even if a complete analysis of variable accounting techniques over time can not. Much has been achieved with the evidence available, both in producing a detailed study on the techniques employed in accounting for ration wages, and proposing possible suggestions towards fleshing out the physical process of ration delivery. The hope is that the resulting work can be used as an aid for accounting and administrative procedures at Deir el-Medina, whilst providing ample scope for future comparative research to be carried out in areas such as the different commodity types received by the workmen, other periods of ancient Egyptian history and other ancient civilisations.

APPENDIX 1: Daily Calendar Showing Rations and Annual Festivals

Ramesses III, Year 25

	šmw				*ꜣḫt*				*prt*				*šmw*
	I	II	III	IV	I	II	III	IV	I	II	III	IV	I
1		F		F	F			F	F	F		F	F
2				F	F			F	F	F			F
3					F					F			
4													
5								F					
6													
7													
8													
9													
10													
11							F						
12		F	F				*diw*						
13			F										
14													
15		F											
16													
17					F								
18													
19					F / *diw*	F							
20													
21				*diw*								*diw*	
22													
23						*dni*							
24			F										
25		F						F					
26	F							F					
27			F										
28													
29		F			F						F		
30				F	F				F		F		
Ep1				F									
Ep2				F									
Ep3				F									
Ep4				F									
Ep5				F									

F Known Festival

Journal

Non-Journal

Ramesses III, Year 26

	šmw				*ꜣḫt*				*prt*				*šmw*
	I	II	III	IV	I	II	III	IV	I	II	III	IV	I
1				F	F			F	F	F	F	F	F
2				F	F			F	F	F	F		F
3					F					F			
4											F		
5								F			F		
6													
7													
8													
9													
10													
11							F						
12		F	F										
13			F										
14													
15		F											
16													
17					F								
18													
19					F	F							
20													
21													
22													
23													
24			F										
25		F						F					
26	F							F					
27			F										
28													
29		F									F		
30				F					F		F		
Ep1				F									
Ep2				F									
Ep3				F									
Ep4				F									
Ep5				F									

F Known Festival
Journal
Non-Journal

Ramesses III, Year 27

	šmw				*3ḫt*				*prt*				*šmw*
	I	II	III	IV	I	II	III	IV	I	II	III	IV	I
1		F		F	F			F	F	F	F	F	F
2				F	F			F	F	F	F		F
3					F					F			
4											F		
5								F			F		
6													
7													
8													
9													
10													
11							F						
12		F	F										
13			F									*diw*	
14													
15		F											
16													
17					F								
18													
19					F	F					*diw*		
20													
21													
22													
23													
24			F										
25		F						F					
26	F							F					
27			F										
28													
29		F			F						F		
30				F	F				F		F		
Ep1				F									
Ep2				F									
Ep3				F									
Ep4				F									
Ep5				F									

F Known Festival

Journal

Non-Journal

Ramesses III, Year 28

	šmw				*ꜣḫt*				*prt*				*šmw*
	I	II	III	IV	I	II	III	IV	I	II	III	IV	I
1		F		F	F			F	F	F	F	F	F
2				F	F / *diw*			F	F	F	F		F
3					F					F	F		
4											F		
5				*diw*				F			F		
6													
7													
8													
9													
10													
11							F						
12		F	F										
13			F										
14													
15		F											
16													
17					F								
18													
19					F	F							
20													
21													
22													
23													
24			F										
25		F						F					
26	F							F					
27			F										
28													
29		F			F								
30				F	F/ *diw*	*diw*			F				
Ep1				F									
Ep2				F									
Ep3				F									
Ep4				F									
Ep5				F									

F Known Festival
Journal
Non-Journal

Ramesses III, Year 29

	šmw				*ꜣḫt*				*prt*				*šmw*
	I	II	III	IV	I	II	III	IV	I	II	III	IV	I
1		F		F	F			F	F	F	F	F	F
2				F	F		*dni*	F	F	F	F		F
3					F					F			
4			*diw*								F		
5			*diw*					F			F		
6													
7													
8													
9													
10										Strike			
11					*diw*		F						
12		F	F										
13			F										
14													
15		F											
16													
17					F					*diw*			
18													
19					F	F							
20													
21													
22													
23													
24			F										
25		F						F					
26	F							F					
27			F										
28													
29		F			F						F		
30				F	F				F		F		
Ep1													
Ep2													
Ep3													
Ep4													
Ep5													

F Known Festival

Journal

Non-Journal

Ramesses III, Year 30

	šmw				*ꜣḫt*				*prt*				*šmw*
	I	II	III	IV	I	II	III	IV	I	II	III	IV	I
1		F		F	F			F	F	F	F	F	F
2				F	F			F	F	F	F		F
3					F / *dni*					F			
4											F		
5								F			F		
6													
7													
8													
9													
10													
11							F						
12		F	F										
13			F										
14													
15		F											
16													
17					F								
18													
19					F	F							
20													
21													
22													
23													
24			F										
25		F						F					
26	F							F					
27			F										
28													
29		F			F						F		
30				F	F				F		F		
Ep1				F									
Ep2				F									
Ep3				F									
Ep4				F									
Ep5				F									

F Known Festival
Journal
Non-Journal

Ramesses III, Year 31

	šmw				*ꜣḫt*				*prt*				*šmw*
	I	II	III	IV	I	II	III	IV	I	II	III	IV	I
1		F		F				F	F	F	F	F	F
2				F				F	F	F	F		F
3										F			
4											F		
5								F			F		*diw*
6									*diw*				
7													
8													
9													
10													
11							F						
12		F	F										
13			F										
14													
15		F											
16													
17					F								
18													
19					F	F							
20													
21													
22													
23													
24			F										
25		F						F					
26	F							F			*diw*		
27			F										
28													
29		F			F						F		
30				F	F				F		F		
Ep1				F									
Ep2				F									
Ep3				F									
Ep4				F									
Ep5				F									

F Known Festival

Journal

Non-Journal

Ramesses III, Year 32

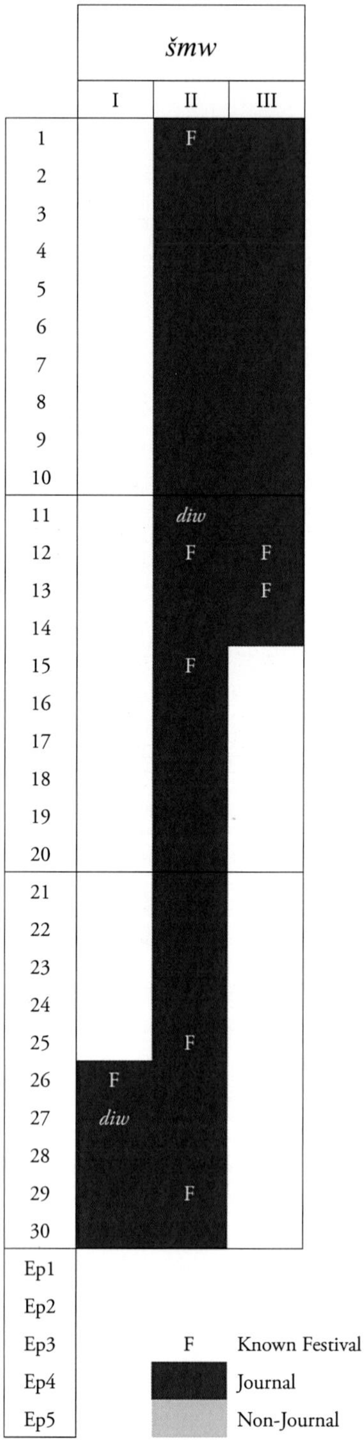
šmw
I
II
III
1
2
3
4
5
6
7
8
9
10
11
12
13
14
15
16
17
18
19
20
21
22
23
24
25
26
27
28
29
30
Ep1
Ep2
Ep3
Ep4
Ep5
F
diw
F
F
F
F
F
F
F
diw
F
F Known Festival
Journal
Non-Journal

Ramesses IV, Year 1

	šmw		*3ḫt*				*prt*				*šmw*		
	III	IV	I	II	III	IV	I	II	III	IV	I	II	III
1		F	F			F	F	F	F	F	F	F	
2		F	F			F	F	F	F		F		
3			F					F					
4									F				
5						F			F				
6													
7													
8													
9													
10													
11		*diw*			F								
12												F	F
13							*diw*						F
14													
15					*diw*							F	
16													
17			F										
18													
19			F	F									
20													
21													
22													
23													
24	F												
25						F						F	
26						F					F		
27	F												
28													
29			F						F			F	
30		F	F				F		F				
Ep1		F											
Ep2		F											
Ep3		F											
Ep4		F											
Ep5		F											

F Known Festival

Journal

Non-Journal

Ramesses IV, Year 2

	šmw		*3ḫt*				*prt*				*šmw*		
	III	IV	I	II	III	IV	I	II	III	IV	I	II	III
1		F				F	F	F	F	F	F	F	
2		F	F			F	F	F	F		F		
3			F					F					
4									F				
5						F			F				
6													
7													
8													
9													
10													
11					F								
12												F	F
13													F
14													
15												F	
16													
17			F										
18													
19			F	F/*diw*									
20													
21													
22													
23													
24	F												
25						F						F	
26						F					F		
27	F	*diw*											
28	*diw*												
29			F						F			F	
30		F	F				F		F				
Ep1		F											
Ep2		F											
Ep3		F											
Ep4		F											
Ep5		F											

F Known Festival

Journal

Non-Journal

APPENDIX 2: Categories of Ration Recipients

	Date	Group	Side	F	S	M	M	M	M	M	G	Y	W	D	O	Other
O. Ashmol. 21	-	-	L	*/*	*/*	30/20							*/*	*/-		SC/SC
O. Ashmol. 48	-	-	R	*		26										
O. Ashmol. 72	-	-											*			N
O. Ashmol. 107	R IV	III		*	*	40							*			N
O. Ashmol. 111	Seti II/Sip	II				6/8/-										N
O. Ashmol. 184	Sip/Taus	II		*	*	17					*	*	*	*		
O. Ashmol. 257	-	-		*		14	4					*				N
O. Ashmol. 262	-	-		?/*	?/*	6/16							*/*			
O. Ashmol. 1139	-	-		*	*	20									*	N
O. Berlin 11249	20th	III											*/*			SC/SC
O. Berlin 12294	R II	II	L	*	*	23					*					
O. Berlin 14210	R III	III		3C		40										
O. Berlin 14219	20th	III		3C		40	11						*			
O. Berlin 14264	20th	III		*/*	*/*	32/32							-/*	*/-		N/*smdt*, N
O. Berlin 14302 vs.	R IV	III		3C	*	44	16						*			N
O. Berlin 14842 vs.	Late 19th	II	L	*	*	22							*			N
O. Berlin 14842 rt.	Late 19th	II		*		20										
O. BM EA 50726	20th	III	R/L	*/*	*/*	31/32	8/8	4/5	7/5	5/5			?/?			
O. BM EA 50739	Late 19th	II		*/*	*/*	?/-										

APPENDIX 2: Categories of Ration Recipients

	Date	Group	Side	F	S	M	M	M	M	M	G	Y	W	D	O	Other
O. Cairo 25517γ	Siptah	II														N
O. Cairo 25592	R III	III		*	*	7	5				*		*			
O. Cairo 25608 rt.	Mid 20th	III		*	*	17					*	2	*	*		DR
O. Cairo 25620	20th	III	L		*	23							*		*	
O. Cairo 25685 rt.	Late 20th	III				32	8									
O. Cairo 25689	20th	III		*	*	31	1	1	1	1						
O. Cairo 25698	20th	III		*	?	32	18	2	4				*			
O. Cairo 25809	R II	II		*	*	64										
O. Cairo JE 72455	-	-		-/*	-/*	1/21	21/-					2/2	*/*	*/*		
O. Cairo JE 72457	-	-		*/*/*	*/-/*	21/22/21							*/*/*	*/-/-	*	
O. DeM 141	20th	III		3C		39							*			
O. DeM 149	R III	III		3C		62	50							*		DR
O. DeM 177	Amenmes	II		*/*	*/*	*/6	-/5	-/12					*/-	*/-	-/*	N
O. DeM 179 rt.	Merenp	II	R	-/*	-/*	1/-	38/-						*/-			
O. DeM 179 vs.	Merenp	II	L	*	*	19										
O. DeM 180 vs.	R IV	III		2	2	43										
O. DeM 181	R III	III		?/3C		61/53										
O. DeM 182	Late 20th	III		-/*	/*	17/16							*/-			
O. DeM 184 rt.	20th	III		*/*	*/?	-/17							*/-	*/-	*/-	
O. DeM 184 vs.	20th	III		*/?		9/23	-/5	-/17								

APPENDIX 2: Categories of Ration Recipients

	Date	Group	Side	F	S	M	M	M	M	M	G	Y	W	D	O	Other
O. DeM 186	20th	III		-/?	-/*	18/18	-/18					-/*			*/-	
O. DeM 188 + 373	Sip/Taus	II	R	*												N
O. DeM 189	R II	II?		*									2		*	N
O. DeM 252	20th	III		*/*	-/*	31/-								*/-		
O. DeM 272	20th	III		*	*	40										
O. DeM 276	R III	III		2/2		40/40							*/*			
O. DeM 301	20th	III														N
O. DeM 329	-	-		*	*	17	4									N
O. DeM 345	20th	III		3C		40/40	?/12	39/-					*/*			
O. DeM 370	R II	II?														N
O. DeM 374	19th	II?		?/*	*/?	-/6										N
O. DeM 375	Siptah	II		*/*	*/*								*/?			
O. DeM 376	Siptah	II		*/*	*/*	17/17					*/*	2/2	*/*	*/*		-/DR
O. DeM 377 rt.	20th	III		*	*	9	8					3	*	*		N
O. DeM 377 vs.	20th	III		*	*	7	10					3		*		N
O. DeM 378	20th	III		3C		56	6									
O. DeM 379	20th	III	R											*		
O. DeM 380	R IV	III		*	*	30	1									
O. DeM 381 rt.	R IV	III		4C		62							*	*		N
O. DeM 381 vs.	R IV	III		3C	*	2	60						*	2		N

APPENDIX 2: Categories of Ration Recipients

	Date	Group	Side	F	S	M	M	M	M	M	G	Y	W	D	O	Other
O. DeM 382	R III	III		*	*	15										
O. DeM 383	20th	III		*	*	17						3	*			
O. DeM 384	R III	III		*	*	15										
O. DeM 385	20th	III														
O. DeM 386	20th	III	R	*	*	?							*			
O. DeM 387	20th	III										7,3,2	*	*		
O. DeM 388	20th	III				21	?									SC
O. DeM 577 rt.	R III	III	L	*/*		4/11	11/4				*/-		*/-			
O. DeM 577 vs.	R III	III		*		11					*					
O. DeM 591	Sip/Taus	II		2?	*	12									*	
O. DeM 611	Siptah	II														N
O. DeM 621 cont.	R II	II?	L	-/*/*		16/6/7	-/-/8						*/-/*			
O. DeM 621 rt.	R II	II?	R	*/*/*	*/*/*	15/8/13							-/-/*			
O. DeM 638 rt.	-	-		*/*/*	*/*/*	?/?/20							-/*/-	-/*/-	-/-/*	
O. DeM 638 vs.	-	-	R	*	*	20							*	*	5	
O. DeM 640	-	-														N
O. DeM 661	R II	II?											*			N
O. DeM 662	R III	III													*	DR
O. DeM 698	R II	II?														N
O. DeM 707	R IV/VI	III											6			

APPENDIX 2: Categories of Ration Recipients

	Date	Group	Side	F	S	M	M	M	M	M	G	Y	W	D	O	Other
O. DeM 712	-	-														
O. DeM 734	-	-				4	15									
O. DeM 735	-	-											*	*		
O. DeM 736	-	-				?										
O. DeM 737	-	-	R/L	*/*	*/*	20/20							*/*	*/*		
O. DeM 738	R III	III		?												
O. DeM 739	-	-	R/L	*/*		5/-							-/*			
O. DeM 742	R III	III														N
O. DeM 743	20th	III	R			16										N
O. DeM 744	Late 19th	II														N
O. DeM 745	Late 19th	II														N
O. DeM 746 rt.	-	-	R	?C/3C												
O. DeM 747	-	-														
O. DeM 837	R II	II?		*												
O. DeM 838	R III	III														
O. DeM 839	-	-		*												
O. DeM 840	-	-	R		*							*	*			
O. DeM 841	-	-		*	*	22							*			
O. DeM 842	R III	III		*	*											
O. DeM 843	R II	II?				13										N

APPENDIX 2: Categories of Ration Recipients

	Date	Group	Side	F	S	M	M	M	M	M	G	Y	W	D	O	Other
O. DeM 844	R II	II?														
O. DeM 845	-	-				15										
O. DeM 846	Late 19th	II														N
O. DeM 847	-	-														
O. DeM 848	-	-														
O. DeM 849 rt.	-	-	R	*/*	*/*							*/-	*/-			
O. DeM 850	R IV	III														N
O. DeM 10031	Late 19th	II		*/*	-/*	23/-	6/-					-/6				N
O. DeM 10032	R III	III		*	*	21							*			
O. DeM 10033	R III	III		*	*	2	17				*	*				
O. DeM 10036	-	-	L	*		2	2									
O. DeM 10039	-	-			*								*			N
O. DeM 10040	-	-										6				
O. DeM 10161 rt.	R III	III		*												WC
O. DeM 10161 vs.	R III	III														N
O. DeM 10162	-	-										*	*			N
O. DeM 10163	R II	II														N
O. DeM 10164	Siptah	II		*	*											
O. Michaelides 34	R II	II?														N
O. Michaelides 65 rt.	Late 19th	II														N

APPENDIX 2: Categories of Ration Recipients

	Date	Group	Side	F	S	M	M	M	M	M	G	Y	W	D	O	Other
O. Munich ÄS 397	R III	III		*/*/*	*/*/*	20/20/20							-/*/*			
O. Qurna 656/4	20th	III														N
O. Qurna 659/4	Mid 19th	II		*	*	53										
O. Strasbourg H110 rt	Late 19th	II		*/*	*/*	19/19										
O. Strasbourg H110 vs	Late 19th	II		*/*	*/*	17/20	3/-						*/*			
O. Turin 57072	R III	III	R/L	3C/-		18/19										
O. Turin 57429	R II	II?		*		4	48									
O. UC 39626 vs.	R III	III		*	*	17					*		*			
P. Turin 1880	Mid 20th	III	-/L	*/*	*/*	8/8								-/2		
P. Turin 1884	R IX	IV	R/L	*/*	*/CD	-/47						-/12		-/*		-/DR
P. Turin 1906	R IX	IV		4C		65										
P. Turin 1932	R IX	IV	-/L	2C/2C		?/16						6/7		*/*		
P. Turin 1960	R IX	IV	-/L	*/*	*/CD	40/39	30/30							*/-		N/-
P. Turin 2002	R IX	IV		4C/4C		69/69								2/2		*Smdt*
P. Turin 2013	R IX	IV	R	3C/-	CD/-	64/25										
P. Turin 2013 cont.	R IX	IV		2/2	*/*, CD	62/63										
P. Turin 2015	Late 20th	IV		4C/3C?		-/62								-/2		
P. Turin 2081 rt.I	R V	III		*/-/?	*/*/*	?/31/30							*/-/-			N/N/N
P. Turin 2081 rt.I	R V	III		*/-/*	?/*/*	?/32/*								-/*/-		-/DR/-
P. Turin 2081 rt.II	R V	III	L													

APPENDIX 2: Categories of Ration Recipients

	Date	Group	Side	F	S	M	M	M	M	M	G	Y	W	D	O	Other
P. Turin 2081 rt.II	R V	III	-/-/R	-/*/-	-/*/-	31/32/32							-/*/-			N/N/N
P. Turin 2081 vs.	R V	III														
P. Turin PN 109	R IX	IV		4C		?	?						*	*		

Key

C	Captain	W	Women servants	WC	Water-carrier
F	Foreman	D	Doorkeeper	*	Category present on ration list
S	Scribe	O	Old men	-	Category not recorded on ration list
M	Men (uncategorised)	N	Named individuals	?	Presence of category uncertain
G	Guardsman	DR	Doctor		
Y	Youth	SC	Scorpion charmer		

Notes

1. Numbers separated by strokes indicates the presence of more than one ration list on the same document.
2. Dates in italics are uncertain or assigned a broad period.
3. The broken condition of many documents renders the reading of some lists impossible; such lists are omitted.
4. O. Berlin 14264 has two lists; at the end of the first are deliveries to "the god", Amenmose and the "Lord of the Two Lands"; at the end of the second are deliveries to the *smdt*, the doctor, the "Lord of the Two Lands" and "The Boat" (*p3 wi3*).
5. The second list on O. DeM 621 records a sculptor at the end.
6. O. DeM 847 records recipients as draughtsmen (recto) and sculptors (verso).

BIBLIOGRAPHY

Allen, J.P.

2002 *The Heqanakht Papyri*, New York.

Anthes, R.

1943 "Die Deutschen Grabungen auf der Westseite von theben in den Jahren 1911 und 1913", *MDAIK* 12, 1-68.

Antoine, J.-C.

2006 "Fluctuations of fish deliveries at Deir el-Medina in the Twentieth Dynasty. A statistical analysis", *SAK* 35, 25-41.

2009 "The Delay of the Grain Ration and its Social Consequences at Deir el-Medîna in the Twentieth Dynasty: A Statistical Analysis", *JEA* 95, 223-234.

Assmann, J., Dziobek, D., Guksch, H. & Kampp, F. (eds.)

1995 *Thebanische Beamtennekropolen: neue Perspektiven archäologischer Forschung*, Heidelberg.

Bagnall, R.S.

1995 *Reading Papyri, Writing Ancient History*, London and New York.

Baines, J. & Eyre, C.J.

1983 "Four notes on literacy", *GM* 61, 65-96.

Boorn, G.P.F. van den

1988 *The Duties of the Vizier*, London and New York.

Botti, G. & Peet, T.E.

1928 *Il Giornale della Necropoli di Tebe*, Torino.

Bowman, A.K. & Rogan, E. (eds.)

1999 *Agriculture in Egypt from Pharaonic to Modern Times,* Oxford.

Bruyère, B.

1928 *Rapport sur les Fouilles de Deir el Medinéh 1927*, Cairo.

1929 *Rapport sur les Fouilles de Deir el Medinéh 1928*, Cairo.

1930 *Rapport sur les Fouilles de Deir el Medinéh 1929*, Cairo.

1933 *Rapport sur les Fouilles de Deir el Medinéh 1930*, Cairo.

1934 *Rapport sur les Fouilles de Deir el Medinéh 1931-1932*, Cairo.

1937 *Rapport sur les Fouilles de Deir el Medinéh 1933-1934*, Cairo.

1939 *Rapport sur les Fouilles de Deir el Medinéh 1934-1935*, Cairo.

1952 *Rapport sur les Fouilles de Deir el Medinéh 1945-1947*, Cairo.

1953 *Rapport sur les Fouilles de Deir el Medinéh 1948-1951*, Cairo.

Burkard, G.

2006 "Das ḫtm n pꜣ ḫr von Deir el-Medine" in Dorn, A. & Hofmann, T. (eds.), *Living and Writing in Deir el-Medine: Socio-historical Embodiment of Deir el-Medine Texts*, Basel, 31-42.

Carmona, S. & Ezzamel, M.

2007 "Accounting and accountability in ancient civilisations: Mesopotamia and ancient Egypt", *Accounting, Auditing and Accountability* 20, 2, Emerald Group, 177-209.

Černý, J.

1931 "Les Ostraca Hiératiques, leur Intérêt et la Nécessité de leur Étude", *CdE* 6, 212-224.

1934 "Fluctuations in Grain Prices during the Twentieth Egyptian Dynasty", *ArOr* VI, 172-178.

1935 *Catalogue des ostraca hiératiques non littéraires de Deir el Médineh* I (Nos. 1 à 113), Documents de fouilles 3, Cairo.

1937a *Catalogue des ostraca hiératiques non littéraires de Deir el Médineh* II (Nos. 114 à 189), Documents de fouilles 4, Cairo.

1937b *Catalogue des ostraca hiératiques non littéraires de Deir el Médineh* III (Nos. 190 à 241), Documents de fouilles 5, Cairo.

1939a *Catalogue des ostraca hiératiques non littéraires de Deir el Médineh* IV (Nos. 242 à 339), Documents de fouilles 6, Cairo.

1939b *Late Ramesside Letters*, Bibliotheca Aegyptiaca 9, Brussels.

1951 *Catalogue des ostraca hiératiques non littéraires de Deir el Médineh* V (Nos. 340 à 456), Documents de fouilles 7, Cairo.

1954 "Prices and Wages in Egypt in the Ramesside Period", in *Cahiers d'Histoire Mondiale*, Vol. I/4, Paris, 903-921.

1970 *Catalogue des ostraca hiératiques non littéraires de Deir el Médineh* VII (Nos. 624 à 705), Documents de fouilles 14, Cairo.

1973 *A Community of Workmen at Thebes in the Ramesside Period*, Cairo.

Černý, J. & Gardiner, A.H.

1957 *Hieratic Ostraca,* Vol I, Oxford.

Collier, M.A.

2004 *Dating Late XIXth Dynasty Ostraca*, Egyptologische Uitgaven XVIII, Leiden.

Conover, W.J.

1980 *Practical Nonparametric Statistics* (2nd ed.), New York.

Cooney, K.M.

2007 *The Cost of Death. The Social and Economic Value of Ancient Egyptian Funerary Art in the Ramesside Period*, Egyptologische Uitgaven 22, Leiden.

Davies, B.G.

1999 *Who's Who at Deir el-Medina: A Prosopographic Study of the Royal Workmen's Community*, Egyptologische Uitgaven XIII, Leiden.

Demarée, R.J.

2002a "O. Heidelberg Inv. Nr. 567: A fragment of a necropolis journal", *ZÄS* 129, 109-114.

2002b *Ramesside Ostraca*, London.

Demarée, R.J. & Egberts, A. (eds.)

2000 *Deir el-Medina in the Third Millennium AD. A Tribute to Jac. J. Janssen*, Egyptologische Uitgaven XIV, Leiden.

Demarée, R.J & Janssen, J.J. (eds.)

1982 *Gleanings from Deir el-Medina*, Egyptologische Uitgaven I, Leiden.

Donker van Heel, K.

2003 "Duplication", in Donker van Heel, K. & Haring, B.J.J., *Writing in a Workmen's Village: Scribal Practice in Ramesside Deir el-Medina*, Egyptologische Uitgaven XVI, Leiden, 1-82.

Donker van Heel, K. & Haring, B.J.J.

2003 *Writing in a Workmen's Village: Scribal Practice in Ramesside Deir el-Medina*, Egyptologische Uitgaven XVI, Leiden.

Donker van Heel, K., Haring, B.J.J., Demarée, R.J. & Toivari-Viitala, J.

2003 *The Deir el-Medina Database,* Leiden. [http://www.leidenuniv.nl/nino/dmd/dmd.html].

Dorn, A.

2011 *Arbeiterhütten im Tal der Könige: Ein Beitrag zur altägyptischen Sozialgeschichte aufgrund von neuem Quellenmaterial aus der Mitte der 20. Dynastie (ca. 1150 v. Chr.)* I-III, Aegyptiaca Helvetica 23, Basel.

Dorn, A. & Hofmann, T. (eds.)

2006 *Living and Writing in Deir el-Medine: Socio-historical Embodiment of Deir el-Medine Texts*, Basel.

Eyre, C.J.

1980 *Employment and Labour Relations in the Theban Necropolis in the Ramesside Period*, Ph.D. Diss. (Oxford University).

1987a "Work and the Organisation of Work in the New Kingdom", in Powell, M.A. (ed.), *Labor in the Ancient Near East*, American Oriental Series, Vol. 68, New Haven, 167-221.

1987b "The Use of Data from Deir el-Medina", *BiOr* 44, cols. 21-34.

1999 "The Village Economy in Pharaonic Egypt", in Bowman, A.K. & Rogan, E. (eds.), *Agriculture in Egypt from Pharaonic to Modern Times,* Oxford, 33-60.

2009 "Again the *ẖtm* of the Tomb: Public Space and Social Access", in Kessler, D., Verbovsek, A., & Wimmer, S. (eds.), *Texte-Theben-Tonfragmente: Festschrift für Günter Burkard*, Wiesbaden, 107-117.

2010 "The Economy: Pharaonic", in Lloyd, A.B. (ed.), *A Companion to Ancient Egypt,* London and New York, 291-308.

Ezzamel, M.

1994 "The emergence of the "accountant" in the institutions of Ancient Egypt" in *Management Accounting Research* 5, 221-246.

2002 "Accounting working for the state: tax assessment and collection during the New Kingdom, ancient Egypt", *Accounting and Business Research* 32/1, 17-39.

Faulkner, R.O.

1962 *A Concise Dictionary of Middle Egyptian*, Oxford.

Förster, F.

2007 "With donkeys, jars and water bags into the Libyan Desert: the Abu Ballas Trail in the late Old Kingdom/First Intermediate Period", *BMSAES* 7, 1-36.

Gardiner, A.H.

1941 "Ramesside Texts Relating to the Taxation and Transport of Corn", *JEA* 27, 19-73.

1948a *Ramesside Administrative Documents,* Oxford.

1948b *The Wilbour Papyrus: Volume II, Commentary*, Oxford.

1957 *Egyptian Grammar*³, Oxford.

Gordon, C.

1956 "The First English Books on Book-keeping" in Littleton, A.C. & Yamey B.S. (eds.), *Studies in the History of Accounting*, Homewood, 202-205.

Grandet, P.

2000 *Catalogue des ostraca hiératiques non littéraires de Deîr el-Médînéh* VIII (Nos. 706-830), DFIFAO 39, Cairo.

2003 *Catalogue des ostraca hiératiques non littéraires de Deîr el-Médînéh* IX (Nos. 831-1000), DFIFAO 41, Cairo.

2006 *Catalogue des ostraca hiératiques non littéraires de Deîr el-Médînéh* X (Nos. 10001-10123),

DFIFAO 46, Cairo.
2011 *Catalogue des ostraca hiératiques non littéraires de Deîr el-Médînéh* XI (Nos. 10124-10275), DFIFAO 48, Cairo.

Häggman, S.
2002 *Directing Deir el-Medina: The External Administration of the Necropolis*, Uppsala.

Haring, B.J.J.
1997 *Divine Households: Administrative and Economic Aspects of the New Kingdom Royal Memorial Temples in Western Thebes*, Egyptologische Uitgaven XII, Leiden.
1998 "Access to land by Institutions and Individuals in Ramesside Egypt", in Haring, B.J.J. & de Maaijer, R. (eds.), *Landless and Hungry*, Leiden, 74-89.
2000 "The Scribe of the Mat: From Agrarian Administration to Local Justice", in Demarée, R.J. & Egberts, A. (eds.), *Deir el-Medina in the Third Millennium AD. A Tribute to Jac. J. Janssen*, Egyptologische Uitgaven XIV, Leiden, 129-158.
2003a "From Oral Practice to Written Record in Ramesside Deir el-Medina", *JESHO* 46/3, 249-272.
2003b "Classification", in Donker van Heel, K. & Haring, B.J.J., *Writing in a Workmen's Village: Scribal Practice in Ramesside Deir el-Medina*, Egyptologische Uitgaven XVI, Leiden, 85-182.
2009 *Economy*, UC Los Angeles, [http:/scholarship.org/uc/item/2t01s4qj].

Haring, B.J.J. & de Maaijer, R. (eds.)
1998 *Landless and Hungry*, Leiden.

Helck, W.
1955 "Zur Geschichte der 19. und 20. Dynastie", *ZDMG* 105, 27-52.
1958 *Zur Verwaltung des Mittleren und Neuen Reiches*, Probleme der Ägyptologie III, Leiden and Cologne.
1964a "Feiertage und Arbeitstage in der Ramessidenzeit", *JESHO* 7/2, 133-166.
1964b *Materialen zur Wirtschaftgeschichte des Neuen Reiches* IV, Wiesbaden, 541-640.
1974 *Altägyptische Aktenkunde des 3. und 2. Jahrtausends v. Chr.* (Münchner Ägyptologische Studien 31), Munich & Berlin.
2002 *Die datierten und datierbaren Ostraka, Papyri und Graffiti von Deir el-Medineh,* Wiesbaden.

Hofmann, T.
2006 "Arbeitseinsätze und Löhne der sogenannten Sklavinnen von Deir el-Medine", in Dorn, A. & Hofmann, T. (eds.), *Living and Writing in Deir el-Medine: Socio-historical Embodiment of Deir el-Medine Texts*, Basel, 113-118.

Hollander, M. & Wolfe, D.A.
1976 *Nonparametric Statistical Methods*, New York.

James, T.G.H.
1985 *Pharaoh's People*, Oxford.

Janssen, J.J.
1966 "A Twentieth-Dynasty Account Papyrus", *JEA* 52, 81-94.
1975a *Commodity Prices from the Ramessid Period*, Leiden.
1975b "Prolegomena to the study of Egypt's economic history during the New Kingdom", *SAK* 3, 27-185.
1979 "Background Information on the Strikes of Year 29 of Ramesses III", *OrAnt* XVIII, 301-308.
1980 "Absence from Work by the Necropolis Workmen of Thebes", *SAK* 8, 127-150.
1991 "Rations with Riddles", *GM* 124, 91-97.
1992 "Literacy and Letters at Deir el-Medina", in Demarée, R.J. & Egberts, A. (eds.) (1992),

Village Voices. Proceedings of the Symposium 'Texts from Deir el-Medîna and their Interpretation', Leiden May 31–June 1, 1991, Leiden.
1994 Debts and Credit in the New Kingdom", *JEA* 80,129-136.
1997 *Village Varia: Ten Studies on the History and Administration of Deir el-Medina*, Egyptologische Uitgaven XI, Leiden.
2004 *Grain Transport in the Ramesside Period*, London.
2005 "Accountancy at Deir el-Medina: How accurate are the administrative ostraca?" *SAK* 33, 147-157.

JANSSEN, J.J., FROOD, E. & GOECKE-BAUER, M.
2003 *Woodcutters, Potters and Doorkeepers*, Egyptologische Uitgaven XVII, Leiden.

JAUHIAINEN, H.
2009 *Do not Celebrate your Feast without your Neighbours*, Ph.D. Diss. (Helsinki University).

KEMP, B.J.
1989 *Ancient Egypt: Anatomy of a Civilization*, London & New York.

KITCHEN, K.A.
1980 *Ramesside Inscriptions: Historical and Biographical* III, Oxford.
1982 *Ramesside Inscriptions: Historical and Biographical* IV, Oxford.
1983a *Ramesside Inscriptions: Historical and Biographical* V, Oxford.
1983b *Ramesside Inscriptions: Historical and Biographical* VI, Oxford.
1989 *Ramesside Inscriptions: Historical and Biographical* VII, Oxford.

KESSLER, D., VERBOVSEK, A., & WIMMER, S. (EDS.)
2009 *Texte-Theben-Tonfragmente: Festschrift für Günter Burkard*, Wiesbaden.

KOENIG, Y.
1997 *Les Ostraca Hièratiques Inédits de la Bibliothèque Nationale et Universitaire de Strasbourg*, Cairo.

KOH, A.J.
2006 "Locating the *ḫtm n pꜣ ḫr* of the Workmen's Village at Deir el-Medina", *JARCE* 42 (2005–2006), 95-101.

LESKO, L.H. (ED.)
2002 *A Dictionary of Late Egyptian* (2nd ed.), Providence.

LITTLETON, A.C. & YAMEY B.S. (EDS.)
1956 *Studies in the History of Accounting*, Homewood.

LLOYD, A.B. (ED.)
2010 *A Companion to Ancient Egypt*, London and New York.

LÓPEZ, J.
1978 *Ostraca ieratici N. 57001-57092*, Catalogo del Museo Egizio di Torino. Serie seconda – Collezioni, Volume III, Fascicolo 1, Milano.
1980 *Ostraca ieratici N. 57093-57319*, Catalogo del Museo Egizio di Torino. Serie seconda – Collezioni, Volume III, Fascicolo 2, Milano.
1982 *Ostraca ieratici N. 57320-57499*, Catalogo del Museo Egizio di Torino. Serie seconda – Collezioni, Volume III, Fascicolo 3, Milano.
1984 *Ostraca ieratici N. 57450-57568 - Tabelle lignee N. 58001-58007*, Catalogo del Museo Egizio di Torino. Serie seconda – Collezioni, Volume III Fascicolo 4, Milano.

MANDEVILLE, R.
forthcoming "The Water-carriers of Deir el-Medina".

MCDOWELL, A.G.
1992 "Agricultural Activity by the Workmen of Deir el-Medina", *JEA* 78, 195-206.
1999 *Village Life in Ancient Egypt: Laundry Lists and Love Songs*, Oxford.

Megally, M.
1977 *Notions de comptabilité à propos du papyrus E. 3226 du Musée du Louvre* (Bibliothèque d'Étude 72), Cairo.
Möller, G.
1927 *Hieratische Paläographie, Zweiter Band (von der Zeit Thutmosis III bis zum Ende der einundzwanzigsten Dynastie),* Leipzig.
Ong, W.J.
1982 *Orality and Literacy: the Technologizing of the World,* London.
Piquette, K. & Love, S. (eds.)
2005 *Current Research in Egyptology 2003*, Oxford.
Pleyte, W. & Rossi, F.
1869–76 *Papyrus de Turin*, Leiden.
Powell, M.A. (ed.)
1987 *Labor in the Ancient Near East*, American Oriental Series vol. 68, New Haven.
de Roover, R.
1956 "The Development of Accounting Prior to Luca Pacioli According to the Account-books of medieval Merchants", in Littleton, A.C. and Yamey B.S. (eds.), *Studies in the History of Accounting*, Homewood, 114-174.
Sadek, A.I.
1988 *Popular Religion in Egypt during the New Kingdom*, Hildesheim.
Sauneron, S.
1959 *Catalogue des ostraca hiératiques non littéraires de Deir el Médineh* [VI] (Nos. 550 à 623) = DFIFAO 13, Cairo.
Schiaparelli, E.
1927 *Relazioni sui lavori della missione archeologica italiana in Egitto (anni 1903-1920)*, Torino.
Spalinger, A.J.
1991 "Suggestive Calculations", *GM* 124, 99-111.
1994 *Revolutions in Time: A Study in Ancient Egyptian Calendrics*, San Antonio.
1996 *The Private Feast Lists of Ancient Egypt*, Ägyptologische Abhandlungen 57, Wiesbaden.
Strudwick, N.
1995 "The population of Thebes in the New Kingdom: some preliminary thoughts", in J. Assmann et al., *Thebanische Beamtennekropolen*, Heidelberg, 97-105.
Tosi, M. & Roccati, A.
1972 *Stele e Altre Epigrafi di Deir el Medina n.50001–n.50262,* Torino.
Valbelle, D.
1976 "Remarques sur les textes néo-égyptiens non littéraires (§ 1-5)", *BIFAO* 76, 101-109.
1977 "Remarques sur les textes néo-égyptiens non littéraires (§ 6-10)", *BIFAO* 77, 129-136.
1985 *Les Ouvriers de la Tombe: Deir el-Médineh à l'époque Ramesside*, Cairo.
Vernus, P.
2003 *Affairs and Scandals in Ancient Egypt*, New York.
Vleeming, S.P.
1982 "The Days on which the *ḳnbt* used to Gather", in Demarée, R.J & Janssen, J.J. (eds.), *Gleanings from Deir el-Medina*, Egyptologische Uitgaven I, Leiden, 183-192.
van Walsem, R.
1982 "Month-names and Feasts at Deir el-Medina", in Demarée, R.J & Janssen, J.J. (eds.), *Gleanings from Deir el-Medina*, Egyptologische Uitgaven I, Leiden, 215-244.
Wikgren, H.
2005 "The Festival Calendars at Deir el-Medina", in Piquette, K. & Love, S. (eds.), *Current Research in Egyptology 2003*, Oxford, 179-199.

Wood, F. & Sangster, A.
1967 *Frank Wood's Business Accounting* 1, 9th edition, Harlow.
Žába, Z.
1952 "La date de la première entrée du recto du Papyrus de Turin No 1880", *ArOr* XX, 642-645.

SOURCE REFERENCES

O. Ashmol. 11: Černý-Gardiner, *Hieratic Ostraca* 25, 2; K*RI* VI, 248-249
O. Ashmol. 20: Černý-Gardiner, *Hieratic Ostraca* 27, 1; K*RI* VI, 263
O. Ashmol. 21: Černý Notebook 37.17
O. Ashmol. 48: Černý-Gardiner, *Hieratic Ostraca* 26, 1
O. Ashmol. 72: Černý-Gardiner, *Hieratic Ostraca* 62, 4
O. Ashmol. 107: Černý-Gardiner, *Hieratic Ostraca* 71, 2; K*RI* VI, 171
O. Ashmol. 108: Černý Notebook 45.7 and MSS. 1.619/620
O. Ashmol. 111: K*RI* VII, 239-240
O. Ashmol. 131: K*RI* VII, 331-332
O. Ashmol. 184: Černý, Notebook 45.86 and 107.17
O. Ashmol. 200: K*RI* VII, 174-175
O. Ashmol. 257: Černý, Notebook 31.60
O. Ashmol. 262: Černý, Notebook 31.65
O. Ashmol. 274: Černý, Notebook 31.76
O. Ashmol. 277: Černý, Notebook 81.1
O. Ashmol. 1139: Černý-Gardiner, *Hieratic Ostraca* 31, 3
O. Berlin 10661: Online publication at Deir el Medine online (www.lmu.de/dem-online)
O. Berlin 11249: Online publication at Deir el Medine online (www.lmu.de/dem-online)
O. Berlin 12294: Online publication at Deir el Medine online (www.lmu.de/dem-online)
O. Berlin 12631: Online publication at Deir el Medine online (www.lmu.de/dem-online)
O. Berlin 12633: Online publication at Deir el Medine online (www.lmu.de/dem-online)
O. Berlin 12654: Online publication at Deir el Medine online (www.lmu.de/dem-online)
O. Berlin 14210: Online publication at Deir el Medine online (www.lmu.de/dem-online)
O. Berlin 14219: Online publication at Deir el Medine online (www.lmu.de/dem-online)
O. Berlin 14264: Online publication at Deir el Medine online (www.lmu.de/dem-online)
O. Berlin 14302: Online publication at Deir el Medine online (www.lmu.de/dem-online)
O. Berlin 14842: Online publication at Deir el Medine online (www.lmu.de/dem-online)
O. BM EA 50726: Demaree, *Ramesside Ostraca*, 34, pls. 120-121
O. BM EA 50739: Demaree, *Ramesside Ostraca*, 36, pls. 141-142
O. Cairo 25280: Daressy, *Ostraca Caire*, 71
O. Cairo 25305: Daressy, *Ostraca Caire*, 78
O. Cairo 25512: Černý, *Ostraca Caire*, 9*-10*; K*RI* IV, 313-315

O. Cairo 25517γ: Černý, *Ostraca Caire*, 15*-17*; *KRI* IV, 320-321, 387-389
O. Cairo 25533: Černý, *Ostraca Caire*, 31*; *KRI* VI, 175-177.
O. Cairo 25592: Černý, *Ostraca Caire*, 55*; *KRI* V, 530
O. Cairo 25608: Černý, *Ostraca Caire*, 59*; *KRI* IV, 426
O. Cairo 25620: Černý, *Ostraca Caire*, 62*
O. Cairo 25643: Černý, *Ostraca Caire*, 67*; *KRI* IV, 309-310
O. Cairo 25685: Černý, *Ostraca Caire*, 82*
O. Cairo 25689: Černý, *Ostraca Caire*, 83*
O. Cairo 25698: Černý, *Ostraca Caire*, 84*
O. Cairo 25742: Černý, *Ostraca Caire*, 89*; *KRI* VI, 658
O. Cairo 25755: Černý, *Ostraca Caire*, 91* *KRI* VI, 168
O. Cairo 25809: Černý, *Ostraca Caire*, 116*, *KRI* III, 514
O. Cairo JE 72455: Černý, Notebook 106.7
O. Cairo JE 72457: Černý, Notebook 106.9
O. DeM 32: Černý, *Ostraca Deir el Médineh* I, pls. 9-11; *KRI* V, 497-499
O. DeM 34 + O. Heidelberg Inv. 567: O. DeM 34: Černý, *Ostraca Deir el Médineh* I, pls. 13-14; O.Heidelburg Inv. 567: Demarée (2002a)
O. DeM 38: Černý, *Ostraca Deir el Médineh* I, pls. 18-19; *KRI* V, 551-552
O. DeM 42: Černý, *Ostraca Deir el Médineh* I, pls. 26-27; *KRI* VI, 109-110
O. DeM 43: Černý, *Ostraca Deir el Médineh* I, pls. 28-29; *KRI* VI, 110-111
O. DeM 44: Černý, *Ostraca Deir el Médineh* I, pls. 30-33; *KRI* VI, 116-118
O. DeM 45: Černý, *Ostraca Deir el Médineh* I, pls. 35-35; *KRI* VI, 119-121
O. DeM 141: Černý, *Ostraca Deir el Médineh* II, pl. 14
O. DeM 149: Černý, *Ostraca Deir el Médineh* II, pl. 23; *KRI* V, 600
O. DeM 153: Černý, *Ostraca Deir el Médineh* II, pls. 28, 30; *KRI* V, 549-550
O. DeM 156: Černý, *Ostraca Deir el Médineh* II, pl. 33, *KRI* V, 519 and 520
O. DeM 159: Černý, *Ostraca Deir el Médineh* II, pl. 35; *KRI* V, 547
O. DeM 160: Černý, *Ostraca Deir el Médineh* II, pl. 36; *KRI* VI, 119
O. DeM 161: Černý, *Ostraca Deir el Médineh* II, pls. 37-38; *KRI* VI, 114-115
O. DeM 162: Černý, *Ostraca Deir el Médineh* II, pl. 40; *KRI* V, 489
O. DeM 169: Černý, *Ostraca Deir el Médineh* II, pl. 44; *KRI* V, 500-501
O. DeM 177: Černý, *Ostraca Deir el Médineh* II, pl. 48; *KRI* IV, 216-217
O. DeM 179: Černý, *Ostraca Deir el Médineh* II, pl. 49; *KRI* IV, 166
O. DeM 180: Černý, *Ostraca Deir el Médineh* II, pl. 50; *KRI* VI, 174
O. DeM 181: Černý, *Ostraca Deir el Médineh* II, pl. 50
O. DeM 182: Černý, *Ostraca Deir el Médineh* II, pl. 50
O. DeM 184: Černý, *Ostraca Deir el Médineh* II, pl. 51
O. DeM 186: Černý, *Ostraca Deir el Médineh* II, pl. 52
O. DeM 188 + O. DeM 373: Černý, *Ostraca Deir el Médineh* II, pl. 53; Černý, *Ostraca Deir El Médineh* V, pl. 8; *KRI* IV, 422-423
O. DeM 189: Černý, *Ostraca Deir el Médineh* II, pl. 53; *KRI* III, 564
O. DeM 252: Černý, *Ostraca Deir el Médineh* IV, pl. 3
O. DeM 272: Černý, *Ostraca Deir el Médineh* IV, pl. 8
O. DeM 276: Černý, *Ostraca Deir el Médineh* IV, pl. 10; *KRI* V, 622- 623
O. DeM 288: Černý, *Ostraca Deir el Médineh* IV, pl. 13
O. DeM 301: Černý, *Ostraca Deir el Médineh* IV, pl. 17
O. DeM 312: Černý, *Ostraca Deir el Médineh* IV, pl. 20
O. DeM 329: Černý, *Ostraca Deir el Médineh* IV, pl. 29
O. DeM 345: Černý, *Ostraca Deir el Médineh* V, pl. 2

O. DeM 369: Černý, *Ostraca Deir el Médineh* V, pl. 7; *KRI* VI, 141
O. DeM 370: Černý, *Ostraca Deir el Médineh* V, pl. 7; *KRI* III, 564
O. DeM 371: Černý, *Ostraca Deir el Médineh* V, pl. 7; *KRI* V, 600-601
O. DeM 374: Černý, *Ostraca Deir el Médineh* V, pl. 8
O. DeM 375: Černý, *Ostraca Deir el Médineh* V, pl. 9; *KRI* IV, 423
O. DeM 376: Černý, *Ostraca Deir el Médineh* V, pl. 9; *KRI* IV, 423-424
O. DeM 377: Černý, *Ostraca Deir el Médineh* V, pl. 10
O. DeM 378: Černý, *Ostraca Deir el Médineh* V, pl. 10
O. DeM 379: Černý, *Ostraca Deir el Médineh* V, pl. 10
O. DeM 380: Černý, *Ostraca Deir el Médineh* V, pl. 11; *KRI* VI, 127-128
O. DeM 381: Černý, *Ostraca Deir el Médineh* V, pl. 11; *KRI* VI, 140-141
O. DeM 382: Černý, *Ostraca Deir el Médineh* V, pl. 12; *KRI* V, 601
O. DeM 383: Černý, *Ostraca Deir el Médineh* V, pl. 12
O. DeM 384: Černý, *Ostraca Deir el Médineh* V, pl. 12
O. DeM 385: Černý, *Ostraca Deir el Médineh* V, pl. 12
O. DeM 386: Černý, *Ostraca Deir el Médineh* V, pl. 12
O. DeM 387: Černý, *Ostraca Deir el Médineh* V, pl. 13
O. DeM 388: Černý, *Ostraca Deir el Médineh* V, pl. 13
O. DeM 427: Černý, *Ostraca Deir el Médineh* V, pl. 22; *KRI* V, 521-523
O. DeM 571: Sauneron, *Ostraca Deir el Médineh* VI, pl. 11
O. DeM 577: Sauneron, *Ostraca Deir el Médineh* VI, pl. 13; *KRI* V, 601- 602
O. DeM 591: Sauneron, *Ostraca Deir el Médineh* VI, pl. 21; *KRI* IV, 424
O. DeM 611: Sauneron, *Ostraca Deir el Médineh* VI, pl. 28; *KRI* IV, 395
O. DeM 621: Sauneron, *Ostraca Deir el Médineh* VI, pls. 31-32; *KRI* III, 528-529; *KRI* IV, 152
O. DeM 638: Černý *Ostraca Deir el Médineh* VII, pl. 7
O. DeM 640: Černý, *Ostraca Deir el Médineh* VII, pl. 8
O. DeM 654: Černý, *Ostraca Deir el Médineh* VII, pl. 14; *KRI* V, 616
O. DeM 661: Černý, *Ostraca Deir el Médineh* VII, pl. 16; *KRI* IV, 232-233
O. DeM 662: Černý, *Ostraca Deir el Médineh* VII, pl. 16
O. DeM 698: Černý, *Ostraca Deir el Médineh* VII, pl. 26; *KRI* III, 565
O. DeM 707: Grandet, *Ostraca Deîr el-Médînéh* VIII, 107
O. DeM 712: Grandet, *Ostraca Deîr el-Médînéh* VIII, 111
O. DeM 734: Grandet, *Ostraca Deîr el-Médînéh* VIII, 136
O. DeM 735: Grandet, *Ostraca Deîr el-Médînéh* VIII, 137
O. DeM 736: Grandet, *Ostraca Deîr el-Médînéh* VIII, 137
O. DeM 737: Grandet, *Ostraca Deîr el-Médînéh* VIII, 138-139
O. DeM 738: Grandet, *Ostraca Deîr el-Médînéh* VIII, 140
O. DeM 739: Grandet, *Ostraca Deîr el-Médînéh* VIII, 141
O. DeM 740: Grandet, *Ostraca Deîr el-Médînéh* VIII, 142
O. DeM 741: Grandet, *Ostraca Deîr el-Médînéh* VIII, 143
O. DeM 742: Grandet, *Ostraca Deîr el-Médînéh* VIII, 144
O. DeM 743: Grandet, *Ostraca Deîr el-Médînéh* VIII, 145
O. DeM 744: Grandet, *Ostraca Deîr el-Médînéh* VIII, 145
O. DeM 745: Grandet, *Ostraca Deîr el-Médînéh* VIII, 146
O. DeM 746: Grandet, *Ostraca Deîr el-Médînéh* VIII, 147-148
O. DeM 747: Grandet, *Ostraca Deîr el-Médînéh* VIII, 149
O. DeM 837: Grandet, *Ostraca Deîr el-Médînéh* IX, 204
O. DeM 838: Grandet, *Ostraca Deîr el-Médînéh* IX, 205-207
O. DeM 839: Grandet, *Ostraca Deîr el-Médînéh* IX, 208

O. DeM 840: Grandet, *Ostraca Deîr el-Médînéh* IX, 209
O. DeM 841: Grandet, *Ostraca Deîr el-Médînéh* IX, 210-211
O. DeM 842: Grandet, *Ostraca Deîr el-Médînéh* IX, 211
O. DeM 843: Grandet, *Ostraca Deir el Médineh* IX, 212-214
O. DeM 844: Grandet, *Ostraca Deîr el-Médînéh* IX, 216-220
O. DeM 845: Grandet, *Ostraca Deîr el-Médînéh* IX, 221
O. DeM 846: Grandet, *Ostraca Deîr el-Médînéh* IX, 222
O. DeM 847: Grandet, *Ostraca Deîr el-Médînéh* IX, 223
O. DeM 848: Grandet, *Ostraca Deîr el-Médînéh* IX, 224
O. DeM 849: Grandet, *Ostraca Deîr el-Médînéh* IX, 225-226
O. DeM 850: Grandet, *Ostraca Deîr el-Médînéh* IX, 227
O. DeM 852: Grandet, *Ostraca Deîr el-Médînéh* IX, 228-231
O. DeM 853: Grandet, *Ostraca Deîr el-Médînéh* IX, 232-233
O. DeM 10007: Grandet, *Ostraca Deîr el-Médînéh* X, 191
O. DeM 10031: Grandet, *Ostraca Deîr el-Médînéh* X, 223
O. DeM 10032: Grandet, *Ostraca Deîr el-Médînéh* X, 223
O. DeM 10033: Grandet, *Ostraca Deîr el-Médînéh* X, 224
O. DeM 10034: Grandet, *Ostraca Deîr el-Médînéh* X, 225
O. DeM 10036: Grandet, *Ostraca Deîr el-Médînéh* X, 227
O. DeM 10039: Grandet, *Ostraca Deîr el-Médînéh* X, 229
O. DeM 10040: Grandet, *Ostraca Deîr el-Médînéh* X, 230
O. DeM 10161: Grandet, *Ostraca Deîr el-Médînéh* XI, 270
O. DeM 10162: Grandet, *Ostraca Deîr el-Médînéh* XI, 271
O. DeM 10163: Grandet, *Ostraca Deîr el-Médînéh* XI, 273
O. DeM 10164: Grandet, *Ostraca Deîr el-Médînéh* XI, 274
O. DeM 10165: Grandet, *Ostraca Deîr el-Médînéh* XI, 278
O. Gardiner AG102: K*RI* VII, 296
O. IFAO 265: Černý, Notebook 103.116
O. IFAO 300: Černý, Notebook 103.125
O. Leipzig 2: Černý-Gardiner, *Hieratic Ostraca*, 34, 4; K*RI* V, 499-500
O. Michaelides 34: Goedicke-Wente, *Ostraka Michaelides*, pl. LXXIII; K*RI* III, 565
O. Michaelides 65: Goedicke-Wente, *Ostraka Michaelides*, pl. LXXVI
O. Michaelides 73: Goedicke-Wente, *Ostraka Michaelides*, pl. LXV; K*RI* V, 556
O. Munich ÄS397: K*RI* VII, 297
O. Prague H14: K*RI* VII, 302-303
O. Qurna 656/4: Online publication at Deir el Medine online (www.lmu.de/dem-online)
O. Qurna 659/4: Online publication at Deir el Medine online (www.lmu.de/dem-online)
O. Strasbourg H110: Koenig, *Ostraca Strasbourg*, pls. 39, 41; K*RI* VII, 234-235
O. Strasbourg H117: Koenig, *Ostraca Strasbourg*, pl. 55
O. Turin 57043: López, *Ostraca ieratici* 1, pl. 27; K*RI* V, 603
O. Turin 57072: López, *Ostraca ieratici* 1, pls. 43-44; K*RI* V, 535-536
O. Turin 57429: López, *Ostraca ieratici* 3, pl. 137; K*RI* VII, 172-173
O. Turin 57475: López, *Ostraca ieratici* 4, pl. 162
O. UC 39626: Černý-Gardiner, *Hieratic Ostraca*, 34, 1; K*RI* V, 501-502
O. UC 39648: Černý-Gardiner, *Hieratic Ostraca*, 19, 1; K*RI* V, 499-500
O. UC 39661: Černý-Gardiner, *Hieratic Ostraca*, 66, 3; K*RI* VI, 170
O. Valley of the Queens 6: Koenig, *BIFAO* 88 (1988), 120-121, Document VI
O. Varille 39 (+O. IFAO 1255): K*RI* VII, 300-302
P. Amiens-Baldwin: Janssen, *Grain Transport in the Ramesside Period*, 91-119

P. Bib Nat 237 Cart.1: *KRI* VI, 339-340
P. Louvre 3171: Discussion and translation in Gardiner, *JEA* 27 (1941), 56-58
P. Louvre E3266: Discussion in Megally, *Notions de comptabilité à propos du papyrus E. 3226 du Musée du Louvre*
P. Sallier I: Caminos, *Late Egyptian Miscellanies*, 79-88
P. Sallier IV: Caminos, *Late Egyptian Miscellanies*, 88-99
P. Turin 1880 (Turin Strike Papyrus): Gardiner, *Ramesside Administrative Documents*, 45-58
P. Turin 1884+2067+2071+2105: *KRI* VI, 644-650
P. Turin 1885: *KRI* VI, 58-60, 223, 224, 371 and 424
P. Turin 1887 (Turin Indictment Papyrus): Gardiner, *Ramesside Administrative Documents*, 73-82
P. Turin 1888+2085: Gardiner, *Ramesside Administrative Documents*, 64-68
P. Turin 1895+2006 (Turin Taxation Papyrus): Gardiner, *Ramesside Administrative Documents*, 35-44
P. Turin 1898+1926+1937+2094: *KRI* VI, 687-699, 850 and 851
P. Turin 1906+1939+2047: *KRI* VI, 624-630
P. Turin 1932+1939: *KRI* VI, 685-687
P. Turin 1960+2071: *KRI* VI, 641-644
P. Turin 2002: Pleyte-Rossi, *Papyrus de Turin*, pls. CIX-CX (hieratic, no transcription published)
P. Turin 2004+2007+2057+2106: *KRI* VI, 650-652
P. Turin 2013+2050+2061: *KRI* VI, 599-603
P. Turin 2015: Černý, Notebook 15.47-48; MSS.3.578
P. Turin 2018: *KRI* VI, 851-863
P. Turin 2062: Černý, Notebook 23.59-61
P. Turin 2081+2095: Černý, Notebook 23.49-54
P. Turin 2097+2105: Černý, Notebook 16.69 and 152.12-13
P. Turin PN109: Černý, Notebook 152.19-20
P. Valençay I: Gardiner, *Ramesside Administrative Documents*, 72-73
P. Wilbour: Discussion in Gardiner, *The Wilbour Papyrus: Volume II, Commentary*

INDEX OF SOURCES

O. Ashmol. 11: 14 n. 31, 51
O. Ashmol. 20: 50 n. 6
O. Ashmol. 21: 23 n. 17, 51, 112, 128 n 51, 139
O. Ashmol. 48: 29 n. 34, 31, 54, 112, 134, 139
O. Ashmol. 72: 50 n. 6, 113, 138 n. 8
O. Ashmol. 107: 14 n. 33, 21, 51, 108 n. 58, 111, 113, 137, 139
O. Ashmol. 108: 24 n. 22, 25, 29, 43-44, 51, 113
O. Ashmol. 111: 4, 15 n. 36, 26, 29 n. 34, 30, 37 n. 44, 45-46, 51, 54, 74-76, 103 n. 48, 113, 134, 139
O. Ashmol. 131: 51, 75, 139, 146 n. 28
O. Ashmol. 184: xiv n. 4, 9 n. 12, 21, 33-34, 38, 51, 88, 114, 128 n. 53, 135 n. 3, 138-39
O. Ashmol. 200: 14 nn. 33-34, 24, 51, 54, 114, 139
O. Ashmol. 257: 34, 50 n. 6, 108 n. 58, 114, 135, 139
O. Ashmol. 262: 6, 21 n. 6, 51, 54, 75-76, 114, 139
O. Ashmol. 274: 14 n. 31, 14 n. 33, 21, 23-24, 51, 124, 139
O. Ashmol. 277: 39, 50 n. 6, 115, 139
O. Ashmol. 1139: 51, 85, 115, 127 n. 50, 135, 139
O. Berlin 10661: 21 n. 6, 51, 121
O. Berlin 11249: 51, 121, 139
O. Berlin 12294: 51, 75, 79, 96, 99 n. 33, 121, 139
O. Berlin 12631: 13 n. 30, 21 n. 6, 22, 51, 63 n. 17
O. Berlin 12633: 13 n. 30, 16, 24, 51, 65 n. 24
O. Berlin 14210: 21 n. 6, 51, 96, 122, 135, 139
O. Berlin 14219: 51, 75, 79, 122, 139
O. Berlin 14264: 27 n. 28, 29 n. 34, 51, 57, 102 n. 47, 103, 105, 109, 122, 139
O. Berlin 14302: 51, 74, 77, 102 n. 47, 122, 140
O. Berlin 14842: 51, 96, 99 n. 33, 122, 140
O. BM EA 50726: xiv n. 5, 50 n. 6, 99 n. 33, 101, 115, 140
O. BM EA 50739:
O. Cairo 25280: 21 n. 6, 51, 54, 115, 140
O. Cairo 25305: 148 n. 38
O. Cairo 25517γ: 54, 76-77, 81, 97 n. 31, 108 n. 58, 136, 139
O. Cairo 25533: 14 n. 31, 51

O. Cairo 25592: xiv n. 4, 29, 40 n. 49, 54, 97 n. 31, 127, 140
O. Cairo 25608: xiv n, 4, 15 n. 39, 18, 24, 51, 75, 78 n, 55, 85-91, 96, 102 n. 42, 128, 138-39
O. Cairo 25620: 50 n. 6, 54, 97 n. 31, 136, 139
O. Cairo 25643: 50 n. 6
O. Cairo 25685: 15 nn. 35-36, 21 n. 6, 51, 54, 75-76, 125, 140
O. Cairo 25689: xiv n. 5, 38, 50 n. 6, 101, 128, 136, 139
O. Cairo 25698: 21 n. 9, 37 n. 44, 51, 64 n. 22, 100 n. 36, 101, 128, 140
O. Cairo 25742: 43 n. 55
O. Cairo 25755: 43 n. 55
O. Cairo 25809: 21 n. 6, 41, 51, 128, 140
O. Cairo JE 72455: 25, 50 n. 6, 54, 124, 127 n. 50, 128 n. 53, 134, 139
O. Cairo JE 72457: 43 n. 55, 50 n. 6, 127 n. 50, 128, 140
O. DeM 32: 8 n. 5, 11, 13 n. 30, 24, 51, 59 nn. 10-11, 65
O. DeM 34 + O. Heidelberg Inv. 567: 137
O. DeM 38: 13 n. 30, 21 n. 6, 51, 59 n. 11, 65 nn 24 & 26, 75
O. DeM 42: 13 n. 30, 21 n. 6, 51, 59, 65, 79
O. DeM 43: 13 n. 30, 51, 59, 64 n. 23, 65 n. 24, 75
O. DeM 44: 13 n. 30, 52, 59 n. 11, 65 n. 25, 75, 78 n. 56
O. DeM 45: 13 n. 30, 21, 52, 59 n. 11, 64 n. 22, 75, 78
O. DeM 141: 52, 137, 139
O. DeM 149: 50 n. 6, 102, 105, 137, 139
O. DeM 153: 14, 15 n. 35, 22, 27, 52, 63 n. 17, 64 n. 22, 75
O. DeM 156: 13 n. 30, 21 n. 6, 52, 64 n. 22
O. DeM 159: 13 n. 30, 22 n. 10, 52, 75
O. DeM 160: 16
O. DeM 161: 65 n. 25
O. DeM 162: 13 n. 30, 15 n. 41, 52
O. DeM 169: 16
O. DeM 177: 24, 38-39, 52, 57, 64 n. 23, 75, 77, 78 n. 55, 79, 127 n. 50, 128, 136-37, 139
O. DeM 179: 4, 15 n. 36, 24 n. 22, 25, 52, 54, 99 n. 33, 127 nn. 48 & 50, 140
O. DeM 180: 23, 52, 128 n. 51, 140
O. DeM 181: 29 n. 34, 30, 50 n. 6, 128, 134, 139
O. DeM 182: 50 n. 6, 100 n. 35, 127 n. 48, 134, 139
O. DeM 184: 15 nn. 36 & 40, 24 n. 22, 52, 54, 75-76, 140
O. DeM 186: 33-34, 39, 52, 56, 75, 100 n. 36, 140
O. DeM 188 + O. DeM 373: 29 n. 34, 31, 50 n. 6, 138 n. 7
O. DeM 189: 29 n. 34, 31, 50 n. 6, 108 n. 58, 140
O. DeM 252: 15 n. 36, 21 n. 6, 35, 52, 54, 64 n. 23, 140
O. DeM 272: 52, 140
O. DeM 276: 21 n. 9, 52, 64 n. 22, 127 n. 48, 140
O. DeM 288: 13 n. 30, 52, 56
O. DeM 301: 138 n. 6
O. DeM 312: 27-28, 52, 140
O. DeM 329: xiv n. 4, 38, 52, 140
O. DeM 345: 15 n. 38, 21 n. 9, 22, 52, 58 n. 9, 59-60, 73 n. 49, 75, 134, 139
O. DeM 369:50 n. 6
O. DeM 370: 50 n. 6, 108 n. 58, 140
O. DeM 371: 24, 52, 140
O. DeM 374: 15 n. 36, 25 n. 23, 52, 54, 140

O. DeM 375: xiv n. 4, 52, 140
O. DeM 376: xiv n. 4, 9 n. 12, 18, 24, 29, 52, 85-91, 114, 128 n. 53, 135, 139
O. DeM 377: xiv nn. 4-5, 24 n. 19, 41, 52, 140
O. DeM 378: 52, 135, 139
O. DeM 379: 4-5, 21 n. 9, 34, 52, 75, 86, 140
O. DeM 380: 27, 29 n. 34, 30, 35, 52, 56, 75, 98, 140
O. DeM 381: 15 n. 35, 22, 39, 52, 84-85, 98, 102 n. 47, 103 n. 48, 125, 136, 139, 149 n. 41
O. DeM 382: 15 n. 36, 24 n. 19, 52, 54, 97 n. 31, 140
O. DeM 383: 36, 50 n. 6, 136, 139
O. DeM 384: 21 n. 6, 34-35, 52, 95, 140
O. DeM 385: 54, 140
O. DeM 386: 23, 52, 75, 96, 128 n. 51, 139
O. DeM 387: 139
O. DeM 388: 36, 57, 138 n. 7
O. DeM 427: 3 n. 12, 13 n. 30, 21 n. 6, 23, 52, 63 n. 19, 68
O. DeM 571: 73 n. 51
O. DeM 577: 14 n. 33, 50 n. 6, 128, 139
O. DeM 591: 50 n. 6, 139
O. DeM 611: 21, 23, 53, 75, 77, 103 n. 48, 108 n. 58, 128, 139
O. DeM 621: 15 n. 35, 21, 24-25, 53, 56, 58 n. 9, 60, 73 n. 49, 75, 78 n. 55, 84 n. 2, 99 n. 33, 102 n. 45, 103 n. 48, 124, 127, 136, 139
O. DeM 638: 21 n. 6, 23, 53, 139
O. DeM 640: 38-39, 50 n. 6, 139
O. DeM 654: 16 n. 45
O. DeM 661: 50 n. 6, 108 n. 58, 138 n. 7
O. DeM 662: 43-44, 139
O. DeM 698: 108 n. 58, 139
O. DeM 707: 24, 25 nn. 23-24, 50 n. 6, 53, 139
O. DeM 712: 14, 26-27, 50, 53, 56, 76, 79, 116, 125, 127 n. 48
O. DeM 734: 21 n. 6, 53, 116, 138 n. 7
O. DeM 735: 50 n. 6, 138 n. 7
O. DeM 736: 53
O. DeM 737: 15 n. 36, 21 n. 9, 53, 55, 63 n. 18, 76, 99 n. 33, 116, 136, 139, 160
O. DeM 738: 40 n. 49, 53, 60 n. 43, 116, 139 n. 8
O. DeM 739: 24 n. 22, 53, 69, 76, 99 n. 33, 116, 140
O. DeM 740: 50 n. 6
O. DeM 741: 50 n. 6
O. DeM 742: 138 n. 7
O. DeM 743: 138 n. 7
O. DeM 744: 108 n. 58, 138 n. 7
O. DeM 745: 138 n. 7
O. DeM 746: 138 n. 7
O. DeM 747: 139 n. 8
O. DeM 837: 24 n. 22, 50 n. 6, 138 n. 7
O. DeM 838: 14 n. 32, 50 n. 6, 116, 140
O. DeM 839: 24, 38-39, 45, 53, 140
O. DeM 840: 14 n. 34, 23, 53, 140
O. DeM 841: 5-6, 53, 117, 140
O. DeM 842: 53, 60, 73 n. 49, 117, 140

O. DeM 843: 43-44, 50 n. 6, 108 n. 58, 117, 140
O. DeM 844: 14 n. 32, 97 n. 31, 117
O. DeM 845: 15 n. 36, 53, 55, 118, 140
O. DeM 846: 53, 108 n. 58, 118, 140
O. DeM 847: 100 n. 38, 139 n. 8
O. DeM 848: 23, 53, 118, 140
O. DeM 849: 15 n. 36, 53, 55, 118, 140
O. DeM 850: 50 n. 6, 138 n. 7
O. DeM 852: 21, 29 n. 34, 32, 45, 50 n. 6, 53, 57, 76, 118, 125
O. DeM 853: 119
O. DeM 10007: 43 n. 55
O. DeM 10031: 50 n. 6, 108 n. 58, 119
O. DeM 10032: 23, 40 n. 49, 53, 119, 140
O. DeM 10033: 40 n. 49, 53, 69 n. 43, 96, 119, 135, 139
O. DeM 10034: 23, 39, 53, 119, 138-39
O. DeM 10035: 50 n. 6
O. DeM 10036: 29 n. 34, 32, 53, 120, 140
O. DeM 10039: 24 n. 22, 50, 53, 76-77, 81, 120, 140
O. DeM 10040: 50, 53, 120, 140
O. DeM 10161: 53, 87 n. 10, 105, 120
O. DeM 10162: 55, 97 n. 31, 120
O. DeM 10163: 53, 120
O. DeM 10164: 53, 76, 121
O. DeM 10165: 53, 56, 58 n. 9, 60, 73 n. 49, 76, 121
O. Gardiner AG 102: 45 n. 16
O. IFAO 265: 23, 42, 50 n. 6, 57
O. IFAO 300: 23 n. 17, 53, 125, 140
O. Michaelides 34: 50 n. 6, 108 n. 58, 138 n. 7
O. Michaelides 65: 25, 50 n. 6, 108 n. 58, 140
O. Michaelides 73: 14 n. 34, 23, 53, 76, 140
O. Munich ÄS 397: 15 n. 35, 21 n. 6, 35, 46, 53, 68, 76, 78 n. 55, 125, 140
O. Prague H14: 53
O. Qurna 656/4: 50 n. 6, 138 n. 7
O. Qurna 659/4: 50 n. 6, 138 n. 7
O. Strasbourg H110: 15 n. 36, 24 n. 20, 25 n. 23, 53-55, 76, 78 n. 57, 79, 97 n. 31, 127 n. 48, 137, 140
O. Strasbourg H117: 14, 26, 42, 54, 140
O. Turin 57043: 13 n. 30, 15 n. 41, 16 n. 45
O. Turin 57072: 10 n. 21, 13 n. 30, 39-40, 54, 57, 95, 96 n. 28, 97-98, 99 n. 33, 125, 140-41
O. Turin 57429: 14, 26, 29 n. 34, 31, 43-44, 50 n. 6, 128 n. 53, 140
O. Turin 57475: 54
O. UC 39626: 3 n. 12, 55, 97 n. 31, 127 n. 48, 140
O. UC 39648: 13 n. 30, 15 n. 41, 23, 54, 64 n. 22
O. UC 39661: 14 n. 33, 22 n. 10, 55, 76
O. Valley of the Queens 6: 55
O. Varille 39 (+IFAO1255): 54, 140
P. Amiens-Baldwin: 145, 148 n. 35, 152
P. Bib. Nat. 237 Cart.1: 55, 76, 147
P. Louvre 3171: 145
P. Louvre E3226: 28 n, 32, 38, 147 n. 31

P. Sallier I: 145
P. Sallier IV: 145
P. Turin 1880 (Turin Strike Papyrus): 16 n. 44, 54, 76, 80 n. 60, 128 n. 51, 148 n. 37
P. Turin 1884+2067+2071+2105: 11, 27 n. 30, 36, 42 n. 53, 71 n. 46, 99 n. 33, 102, 103 n. 49, 104, 135, 140
P. Turin 1885: 54, 146 n. 22
P. Turin 1887: 145 n. 14
P. Turin 1888+2085: 10 n. 21
P. Turin 1891: 90 n. 22, 94 n. 25
P. Turin 1895+2006 (Turin Taxation Papyrus): 144, 149, 152
P. Turin 1898+1926+1937+2094: 10 n. 21, 23 n. 18, 55, 71, 103 n. 49, 104
P. Turin 1906+1939+2047: 10 n. 21, 29 n. 34, 33, 35 n. 39, 42, 104, 126, 127 n. 46, 128, 135, 140, 146 n. 25, 147 n. 29, 148
P. Turin 1932+1939: 36, 105, 126-27, 140
P. Turin 1960+2071: 27 n. 30, 71 n. 46, 103 n. 49, 104, 140
P. Turin 2002: xii, 55, 95 n. 26, 105-6, 140, 146 n. 25
P. Turin 2004+2007+2057+2106: 27 n. 30
P. Turin 2013+2050+2061: 11, 22, 23 n. 15, 29 n. 34, 32, 35 n. 39, 37 n. 41, 42, 63 n. 19, 70, 71 n. 46, 95, 103, 126, 127 n. 48, 136-37, 140, 144, 146 n, 24, 147 n. 29, 149
P. Turin 2015: 21, 23, 37 n. 44, 55, 105, 140
P. Turin 2018: 55-56, 104 n. 51, 105, 144 n. 5
P. Turin 2062: 23 n. 14, 24-25, 35 n. 39, 46, 55, 106
P. Turin 2081+2095: 23 n. 16, 29 n. 34, 32, 35 n. 39, 37, 46, 54-55, 76, 84, 99 n. 33, 102 n. 47, 126, 127 n. 46, 135, 140, 146 nn. 23-24
P. Turin 2097+2105: 23 nn. 14, 17-18, 25, 27, 55-56, 71, 105, 126, 146 nn. 26-27, 147
P. Turin PN109: 56, 97 n. 31, 128, 136, 140, 144
P. Valençay I: 144, 152
P. Wilbour: 2 n. 2, 130 n. 60, 144 nn. 3 & 6